D0949818

The Workers

In the same series:

PREPARED FOR RALPH NADER'S
CENTER FOR STUDY
OF RESPONSIVE LAW

Kenneth Lasson

AFTERWORD BY RALPH NADER
GROSSMAN PUBLISHERS, NEW YORK, 1971

The Workers

Portraits of Nine American Jobholders

for my parents

ACKNOWLEDGMENTS

Research Assistants
    Peter Lance (Northeastern University, 1971)
    Julie Portnoy (Mount Holyoke College, 1971)

Besides the considerable legwork contributed by my student research assistants, editorial and technical advice on various chapters was provided by Tom Stewart (Grossman Publishers), Sylvia L. Mehlman and Richard Rubin (independent), Noel Farley and Walter Morris (Goucher College), Stuart Rawlings (National Law Center), and James Sullivan (Center for Science in the Public Interest). Transcribing and typing were done by Linda Christ and Nancy Keller (University of Maryland), Linda Kirk (Goucher College), Leona Son (Northeastern University), and Susan Fagin and Connie Jo Smith (Center for Study of Responsive Law). WGBH-TV (Boston) generously provided tape recording equipment. Perhaps most important, however—both in time shared and in friendships begun—were the contributions by the subjects of this book, the workers themselves.

CONTENTS

THE WORKERS: A Foreword

*The callous palms of the laborer are
conversant with finer tissues of self-respect
and heroism, whose touch thrills the heart,
than are the languid fingers of idleness.*
                    —*Henry David Thoreau*

*Labor is the curse of the world, and nobody
can meddle with it without becoming
proportionately brutified.*
                    —*Nathaniel Hawthorne*

Punching time clocks, swinging lunch pails, still chasing the American Dream, most wage earners find little escape in their frenetic mass exoduses from work every afternoon at four thirty. Although there have been changes over the years—seldom anymore do shrill factory whistles toll the noon-hour break and rarely today do men plumb coal mines with picks and shovels or work sixty-hour weeks for beggars' wages—many other conventions long associated with manual labor are as firmly entrenched and drudgingly monotonous in the 1970's as they were at the turn of the century. For eighty million Americans there is no such thing as an interesting job. They are the blue-collar workers.

Statistical profiles cast them without color or personality and in clinical detachment, parts of a highly specialized labor force—people who earn between five and ten thousand dollars a year, live in semisuburban semighettos, attend church on holidays, have 2.3 children. Whether they lay bricks or bake bread, they usually pay a disproportionate share of taxes. To much of the remaining American public the stereotype goes further, assuming the form of a flag-waving construction worker struggling to preserve his hard-won middle-class citizenship through increasingly strident patriotism. There was a time when the blue-collar worker's less than peaceful demand for unionization gave him a radical hue; to turn-of-the-century capitalists he was merely the rabble roused by occasional crusaders like Upton Sinclair. We are at the point now, however, where management may rue that what it thought was its great simian labor force has swung the ideological jungle vine from liberal to conservative. Unions have become as powerful as the industries they confront. Strikes in critical services can cripple large cities in a matter of hours.

But that same growth of unionism has served to obscure the blue-collar worker's individuality. While he has been studied and explained by anthropologists, economists, sociologists, and political scientists, while he has been computerized beyond recognition, the worker himself has rarely been given a chance to speak his own mind. Few people know about the personal qualities which make him unique, or realize that what he does day in and day out, for decades on end, bears great influence on the quality of everyone's life.

The portraits which follow are drawn largely from the true stories of nine American jobholders, each of whom has spent most of his or her working days in blue-collar labor. They are not meant to be statistically typical, but that does not mean they necessarily deviate from the norm. The subjects (whose names have been changed) were chosen for their sensitivity and willingness to talk about their lives and families, frustrations and satisfactions. They were interviewed in a variety of settings, both on the job and at home. Willie Elma James (The Maid) lives in St. Louis; Elmer Tiso (The Coal Miner, retired without a pension) in Morgantown, West Virginia; Mary Wills (The Waitress) in Washington, D.C.; both Dotty Neal (The Telephone Operator) and John Ragin (The Baker) in Baltimore; Alex Panos (The Cabby) in New York;

and Nick Abbruzzi (The Bricklayer), Terrance Galvin (The Cop), Ray Murdock (The Garbage Man), all in Boston.

There were problems along the way. Mary Wills's husband found it hard to accept the idea of a profit-motiveless book about regular people; he was not about to be exploited, he said, before consenting to a taped interview. Mary herself had to get her company's permission to talk, as did Dotty Neal, even though they have been employees for two decades. Before locating Nick Abbruzzi, Research Assistant Peter Lance waded through a number of construction workers who had difficulty expressing the origins of their discontent, and he got the heave-ho from' the first three refuse removal companies he visited in search of a garbage man. There were satisfactions, too: Julie Portnoy charming her way past an age-old superstition that it's bad luck to let a woman in the coal mines; Alex Panos insisting that it would be his pleasure, if not his obligation, to tell what it's like to be a big-city cabby; Willie Elma James spinning storybook tales that were as true as the day she was born. After working on the bakery line with John Ragin we were given a week's supply of fresh cream puffs. Terrance Galvin has his own way with people who have been to college: a wink, a few words of police-professor wisdom, and an educated tour of his classrooms at "The University of Avery Street."

We soon found that their autobiographical narratives not only yielded fascinating blends of the mundane and the profound, but engendered troubling questions as well. For example, what manner of man is the garbage collector, making daily predawn departures in gray-black solitude to compete with flies and rodents for industrial refuse? Can he (or anyone) sniff beyond the stench of the local dump to fathom what will happen when the capacity of our garbage reservoirs is exhausted? Does the calloused tedium of the bakery-line worker, firmly caught in but just as resigned to the monotony of his routine, portend something significant for us all? Is the happiness of the New York policeman who was overjoyed at having just been transferred from the noise and heat of Manhattan to the open spaces of La Guardia Airport (*"this is like the country to me"*) barely a suggestion of how many environmental insults we all absorb without question? In everything they do and in many attitudes they take, blue-collar workers lend a disturbing credibility to theories of adjustment by necessity. Are they merely the prototypes? Will everyone in time adapt to once intolerable levels of pollution and congestion?

It may be important to note that in writing this book there were no preconceived attempts to validate or destroy existing theories or to depict the alienation of Middle America. If anything there has been a tacit displeasure with abstractions and generalizations. Although the liberal temperament might be shocked by the overt racism of some mild-mannered laborers or surprised at the extent of their unrest, neither economic frustrations nor racial biases are the exclusive province of the blue-collar class. Past the predictable complaints of the working man, however, a striking similarity seemed to wend its way through each subject's story, a theme subliminal yet still hard to ignore: all considered themselves relatively contented, but their lives pasted together show clearly a surrender process at work. It is an insensitivity born less of "what-can-you-do?" resignation than of an apparently unconscious adaptation to increasing levels of pollution and congestion.

Many blue-collar workers have entered that surrender process with no thought whatsoever that they are surrendering anything. Their sensibilities have often been dulled by the dollar: perennial demands for higher wages and pensions, and nary a whimper for less noise, less pollution, less mindless monotony. Few workers realize that while inflation has steadily eaten away most of their dollar increases since 1965, a number of so-called benefits are illusory or nonexistent. According to a recent survey by the University of Michigan, 28 percent of all blue-collar types receive no medical or hospital coverage, 38 percent have no life insurance, 39 percent are not included in a retirement program, and 61 percent do not have available to them employer-sponsored training programs. Meanwhile, industrial accidents account for fourteen thousand deaths each year, over two million disabling injuries, and 245 million man-days lost. Although blatantly oppressive working conditions are occasionally corrected, the more subtle environmental intrusions are rarely if ever protested. (The Department of Labor cites an in-depth study of auto workers which found that mental health varies consistently with the level of jobs held. One-third of factory workers interviewed said they were often worried or upset—compared with 10 percent of white-collar job-holders—and half of those who labored on mass production lines felt unable to make better future lives for themselves.)

For many workers in the lower-middle-income bracket, going home merely means substituting one set of environmental problems for another. Blue-collar workers often live in neighborhoods that have been eroded by freeways and pocked by crime. They are sandwiched somewhere on the economic scale between welfare recipients and junior executives, and caught in a uniquely American *cul-de-sac:* too affluent to receive governmental subsidies for food or medical services or day-care centers, but unable to lower their tax burdens or secure their property by savings and investments. Some 15 percent of lower-middle income men find it *necessary* to supplement their earnings with extra work, although moonlighting is limited by the availability of jobs and by the individual's own stamina, not to mention his willingness to give up leisure time with his family.

Still, the sociologists tell us that the blue-collar worker's essential frustration could well be something else: the utter stagnancy of his status. Wages may continue to increase, but his opportunities for advancement—even the ability to move over instead of up or out—are practically nil. He feels that society does not value his work. It is as if he has been betrayed by the very system he so passionately defends. At best the semiskilled workingman has been taken for granted and forgotten, but more often he has been socially degraded. Neighborhood parks are rarely found in the semisuburban residential areas where he lives. He usually doesn't want his children to follow in his line of work (and indeed he often insists that they go to college), although it is easy for *him* to understand that what he does is important, and that his interests and those of the white-collar worker are ultimately the same.

Forgotten? Certainly not by the government. Political opportunists have fingered the vast blue-collar constituency eminently ripe for the picking. In July of 1970 the White House received a vote-oriented analysis of the dissatisfied working class, prepared by Jerome R. Rosow (Assistant

Secretary of Labor for Policy, Evaluation and Research)
and submitted to the President under a "highly confidential"
covering letter from George P. Schultz (past Secretary of
Labor and now Director of the Office of Management and
Budget). The Rosow-Schultz report sketches the plight of
40 percent of all American families, those which are
"caught on a treadmill, chasing the illusion of higher living standards." Blue-collar workers inevitably reach a
plateau in their capacity to earn, yet their expenses continue to rise as their families mature. "Economic insecurity
is compounded by the fact that blue-collar workers are
the first to feel the effects of an increase in unemployment,
feel most threatened by automation, and are more dependent on sheer physical health for their livelihood than
white-collar workers." In addition, the report continues,
the blue-collar class is less mobile, less organized, and
less capable of using legitimate means to either protect
the *status quo* or secure changes in its favor. The effects
of these pressures and frustrations are reflected in waste-
ful, low-quality and low-quantity production, absenteeism,
high rates of turnover, and excessive wage demands.

To combat such mass discontentment, the Labor Department recommends federal support for job and income
upgrading, educational subsidies, cultural and recreation-
al improvements, and morale boosters such as postage
stamps which depict the nobility of manual labor. The
message to the President is made perfectly clear: blue-
collar workers "are overripe for political response to the
pressing needs they feel so keenly."

The government's analysis and recommendations have
not gone unchallenged. Many sociologists and economists
feel that blue-collar workers have made real income gains
over the last three decades, are relatively satisfied with
their position in society, and on broader issues such as
Vietnam or the poverty program voice opinions similar
to those held by the rest of the American public. They
argue that tax cuts for the Middle-American Family
would serve only to exacerbate present inflationary pressures, and that the laboring class's disenchantment, if it
in fact exists, focuses upon black competitors rather than
on loss of identity or lack of federal attention.

Yet everyone seems to ignore what is perhaps the pri-
mary significance of the blue-collar trap: that the environmental abuse from which the worker now suffers most

keenly, and in which he must participate in order to live, may soon affect us all. Whether or not the wage earner is satisfied with his dead-end labors may indicate only the degree of his numbness to the subtle environmental violence that he swallows over many years on the job. And even wealthy executives are finding it more difficult to avoid repugnant air and water by fleeing to country homes. The question may be whether we will respond with broad frontal attacks on noise and pollution and monotony, or with postage stamps—whether, through the accumulated smog, the powers-that-be can discern the white-collar journeymen who for slightly higher incomes endure endless computer chatter or pencil-pushing tedium.

It would be folly to claim that we can do away with blue-collar jobs. Somebody will always have to do distasteful work. But there is no reason why we cannot make that work a little cleaner and safer, a bit less degrading. Besides raising wages, it should make good business sense to reduce the heat and noise in our factories, to dissolve the massive traffic congestion in our streets, to offer alternatives to boring and fatiguing jobs. These are not pipe dreams—they require little more than imaginative applications of our current technology. It should not be hard to conjure ways by which gargage may be disposed of more efficiently, by which strong safety standards in coal mines can be enforced, by which convenient mass transportation systems may be planned and implemented. It is probably much less realistic to think that the generation about to enter the job market is going to settle for work that is morally and physically degrading.

Whether or not blue-collar workers have indeed been forgotten remains academic, but more than academic questions are at stake. Civilization continues to leap forward blindly, sometimes choking on its poisoned environment, for the seemingly sacrosanct causes of Progress. We have lost perspective. In an American chapter of the human comedy, cosmetic industry profits show a healthy bloom while the stock market struggles to stay alive—but we're going to need a lot more than cosmetics to counteract our burgeoning problems. Is the public consciousness in the least bit sensitive to the subtle though unremitting brutalizations it faces everywhere in the environment? If laborers are on the front line of a great surrender process, how far behind is the rest of society?

To what extent do people realize the similarity between
blue-collar and white-collar workers, not only in the
uniqueness of their personalities but in the quality of
their lives?

Perhaps the stories which follow will strengthen that
awareness.

ONE

The Garbage Man

The necessity of labor is part of the primeval curse; and all the beauty, or glory, or dignity pertaining to it, depends on the ends to which it is the means.

—*Charles Bristed*

– **M**y father didn't work. He's still alive today but he had bad luck all his life—heart condition, pneumonia two and three times a year. He was a house painter, and I guess the painting all fell back on him. During the war he worked at the navy yard and he busted his leg. I was the only boy. So I ended up taking things over as soon as I could work.

When I was young I always had a paper route and a shoeshine box and delivered orders, and most of that money was turned in at home. I only lasted a year in high school, because I had to go to work. Things weren't good then, I mean we were on welfare and all. We lugged milk two miles from where we picked it up at the welfare office. Welfare then wasn't like it is now—they wouldn't send a cab down to pick you up. You walked through the snow with your sled and brought it home. In the wintertime I can remember we used to seal off the apart-

ment around the one room with a stove and space heater.
The other rooms you couldn't live in 'cause they were too
cold. I used to sleep in one of them with about five extra
blankets. In the summer you went down to the welfare
and they gave you two pairs of dungarees and sneakers
and a couple of green tee shirts and that was it for the
summer. But we did it. We lived on the top floor and even
though my mother kept the apartment clean, rats and
roaches and bedbugs would come because people on the
lower floors were dirty. There's a lot of things my kids
don't see today that we lived with. We never had a refrigerator. You know it was a big thing to have a Sunday
dinner with some meat loaf. We never saw steak, but we
survived. I don't regret it. When you had free time you'd
be playing ball all day. I couldn't afford a glove so I
would stuff cotton in a mitten. Or we played street hockey. When I got older, my cousin who worked at the
Boston Garden got me some old Bruins equipment and I
started playing on the ice. When I was a freshman in
high school I made the varsity hockey team. They said
making it the first year was an unusual thing. They said
if I had stayed in school I would have gone on to be
captain. But my father couldn't work, so when I was
fifteen I quit school and started shaking barrels on an in-
town garbage run. It was the only work I could get at
the time. In the winter I froze my ass, but I got the food
on the table and we got by.

Not long after Dick Cavett waves good night to Boston's
television insomniacs and the national anthem ends Chan-
nel Seven's broadcast day, an alarm clock buzzes on the
table next to Ray Murdock's bed. He has lived through
two harsh decades of premature reveilles, but Murdock
still needs the clock to shake him out of slumber. On the
double bed beside him, his wife sleeps through the commotion. She learned a long time ago to ignore the noise
that brings her husband to the bathroom at three o'clock
every morning; a clock radio and four noisy children will
wake her four hours later.

Murdock lets the water run cold, then splashes himself
awake with a face cloth. He is thin, a prematurely gray
Art Carney of a man, with hair flecked white and flapped
into the short beginnings of a wave in front. His heavy

blue eyes are small but expressive. One tooth protrudes from under his top lip, which gives the impression that he's always grinning.

Getting into gray coveralls and grabbing his black baseball hat from the bedpost, Murdock steps downstairs to the kitchen, where he shaves quickly, without a mirror. He is never without his baseball cap. Even indoors he keeps it hanging from a back pocket, like some lanky kid almost forty years old. Soon he is out the door. It's nearly half-past three in the morning, and dark. He pulls yesterday's garbage from one of the barrels in the backyard, slides the bag onto the rear seat of a 1966 maroon Biscayne sedan, and drives off.

Usually his are the only headlights to be seen at this hour coming in on Route 138 through suburban Stoughton. Seven years ago he brought his wife and four kids here, to a small white six-room house, which he got on a twenty-year mortgage with no down payment.

Murdock cuts down the Southeast Expressway. At 3:45 A.M. he reaches the venerable Irish ghetto of South Boston and pulls into an all-night diner for coffee. Ten minutes later he leaves and makes the short drive to the fenced-in yard of Walter A. Digby, Inc., the city's largest refuse contractor. It is a chilly morning for July. Murdock puts on a pitcher's jacket over his overalls, leaves the key under the floor mat in case they have to move his car during the day, grabs the garbage bag from the back seat, and walks across the lot. He tosses the bag into the hopper of a very big truck. There are over two hundred very big garbage trucks in the yard, most of them still half-full from yesterday's collection. Murdock punches his timecard and checks with the dispatcher to see if he'll have to change his route today, to cover any called-in orders for refuse removal. There have been two calls. With his own route engraved in his mind, he figures this will be an above-average day: thirty-three stops.

Out in the yard now, enclosed by barbed wire, he winces at the approaching headlights of Ronny Reardon's car, and checks his watch. Five after four. Reardon is a burly twenty-eight-year veteran trash man and he's late every morning. Murdock waits for him to punch in. Together they walked across the filthy yard. Heavy trucks are serviced and berthed on this acre of maimed land, hidden behind a broken MBTA terminal near the Expressway. The soil beneath the three-foot tires is smothered in oil-soaked ash. Everywhere there are puddles of grease, and around the fences lie rusting bodies of cast-off trucks and service vehicles. It looks as if the garbage collectors may be delinquent when it comes to cleaning up their own countryside, but the Digby mechanics are scavengers—picking apart the wrecks like harpies, salvaging every part that works.

The scene is stale gray. Black-and-white film would be good enough to capture the color of this small fenced-in scar of earth, Murdock's ball park. It's a dreary home field for one of the league's bleaker assignments. Collection, compression, and burial of waste is what the Department of Labor calls it, but to Murdock it's a contest. He's been playing this game—and liking it—every somber morning and sultry afternoon for the past seven years.

—When I started shaking barrels as a kid they made me join the Teamster's. Course they never asked how old you were. In them days it was only "get it up." It wouldn't matter if you were twelve years old. I had a friend in the business and the money was pretty good so I went in. That was around 1947. It wasn't a bad job in them days. You started at six and the longest day we ever had was till noon. You worked hard but the time wasn't bad, even if it was with the barrels. Me and another guy would ride on the back of a truck and jump off when we hit the alleys where the trash was. You were young then and you had the rest of the day to yourself. You could go out and play ball in the afternoons and you weren't tired. I think in those days I must have been making, for five and a half days, sixty or sixty-five bucks a week. It was good pay and my father wasn't working, so that more or less kept the family fed. There was my parents and two sisters and me. I was the only boy. I shook barrels for another company for a while and then I went into the service. It was 1950 and I was eighteen —just young and foolish enough to go gung ho into the Marine Corps. Korea broke out and I enlisted. I wanted to get over there real bad. A little after that they started to draft, but at the time it was tough to get in, so I had to fight my way in. I went to Parris Island and then on to Camp Lejeune in North Carolina, then to advanced infantry, four months at Pendleton. We made a landing on the Korean Gold Coast. I was there thirteen months. I begged for combat duty and got it—I didn't want twenty miles behind the line. That's what I enlisted for, some action. I don't regret it. I'd do it again. I came home a sergeant after three years in the Corps, with two meritorious decorations. I thought I owed the country something.

When I got back I felt like a pretty big shot. I began driving a truck this time, dumping at construction sites. Dumping was still all I wanted to do. Eventually I went to work for Digby. I could have worked for him sooner but in about '62 I had wanted to get out of trash and get into the police force. I was on the waiting list and Mayor Collins was running at the time. They just took say the top ten guys and used them. I was fifteenth at the time, but there was colored on my list and they didn't want to make them policemen so they ripped up the list I was on and I suffered. They just took say the top ten guys. I really wanted the job at the time.

Murdock and Reardon dodge the black spots on the ground as they walk over to their trucks, parked side by side, and step up onto the fenders to unlatch the hoods covering the massive power plants. Then, removing four-foot-long dipsticks and holding them out of the shadows and in the light of big arc lamps above the garage, they read oil levels. Company mechanics maintain and feed the trucks with high-octane gas, but it is up to each driver to see that his vehicle is well oiled. Murdock climbs six feet to get into his cab, which is a small compartment in relation to the entire rig. There is just enough room for a passenger's seat next to the driver's cockpit. When he's not pitching, he's piloting, and he views this rig, less than a few months old, more as an airplane than a garbage truck.

Actually, it's a Brockway Huskey dumper-compressor with a Leach body and two sets of gears. One stick controls the double-H pattern of five forward speeds and a single reverse; an auxiliary transmission moves in phase with the first, for difficult grades, with HI, LO, and INTER-MEDIATE gears. Through the shatterproof windshield Murdock looks out over a four-foot hood fronted with a chrome statuette of the Huskey dog. On Mack trucks, it would be a bulldog. Steel rods, for perspective on difficult steering maneuvers, rise from each fender near the head-lights. On the dash inside there is a series of safety switches, among them a solenoid toggle to power the hydraulic compressing mechanism which squashes waste material into the truck's huge stomach. A two-way radio sits on top of the dashboard, waiting for any last-minute call-in jobs. The seat is springy, upholstered in dark-brown vinyl.

Murdock switches on the ignition. It takes a full minute for the air pressure in the brakes to build up to sixty pounds; Brockway Huskeys don't move until the sixty mark shows on the pressure gauge. Then he turns on his head lamps, releases the hand brake and lets the big gray elephant roll slowly out of its place toward the gate.

Municipal barrel-shakers run greater risks than commercial bin-dumpers, because they may fall off the narrow back running boards of their trucks, or get cut by rusting corrugated garbage cans or be maimed by the powerful rear door press that stuffs refuse into the humpbacked trucks. A well drilled team of shakers can toss cans at back-breaking speed over fifteen yards, in a chain gang of silent heave-ho's, but one miss means a five-minute de-lay to pick up the scattered garbage. The worst part of shaking barrels is the weather. When it's cold the cans feel heavier and harder; when it's hot the stench penetrates the lungs and nostrils, and stays there. Like the barrels themselves, the technique for shaking hasn't changed in fifty years. Most of the men working the big dumpster trucks at one time or another shook barrels for a living.

Ray Murdock drives solo on his daily runs. He has graduated from cans to containers—huge trapezoidal dumpsters rented and filled by large industrial concerns. In addition to a monthly service charge, it costs $1.40 for each cubic yard of trash removed, and the size of each dumpster and the frequency of collection vary ac-cording to the needs of individual firms.

Murdock rolls out of the Digby yard and turns toward the Expressway and his payloads. The massive grass-hopperlike arms behind his cab reach to steel lips above the back fender, which bite the edges of the dumpster container and lift it up with the help of a winch-driven hook and wire. The driver positions his truck and flicks a switch, and then the winch pulls and raises the rear of the container skyward. The garbage is momentarily displayed to the heavens as the dumpster teeters for an instant on the rear lip of the truck, but the precarious balance is soon disturbed inward, and a mass of sticky garbage spills out into the hopper. All the while during the dumpster's rise, the driver must work the controls that set off the hydraulic compressor, so that his truck can eat up the rubbish as the container is feeding it. The job is simple, and dangerous.

—Dumpsters have become moneymakers for the refuse collectors because it only takes one man to run a route and you can pick up more yardage than if you were messing around with barrels. On a barrel setup the driver carries his lumpers with him, usually young guys who ride the back of the truck and dump the barrels by hand into the hopper. That's the way I started. Even though lumpers get paid the same hourly rate as I do, they hardly ever get overtime, and overtime is what makes this job for me. The lumpers are out by six in the morning and they're home by say noon or a little after. Lumping's all right for a young guy. You don't mind riding outside in the cold or rain. You don't mind the danger of maybe falling off. But when you get older you like to be able to ride inside.

With these jobs you can lose a finger if you're not watching and the lid of the container slams down. But if you're careful the danger part of it doesn't scare you. The tough part is working the containers in cold weather. These trucks can be a bitch to handle. You have to back up to the container just right, and in the winter, with the snow, you're uneven. Sometimes you dump and you miss the hopper with some of the shit, which you have to pick up by hand. And you can never get warm. You're in the cab three minutes, then you're out again. If you think it's cold at noon in the winter, try driving at four in the morning. Then you have to watch out for the frozen container tops. I feel it in the ears first, the cold. Then, after seven or eight hours, I get the pain in the groin. Thank God I don't smoke because it's easy to get short of breath on the very cold days.

At 4:15 in the morning Ray Murdock, alone and riding

high in the Brockway rig, feels like a king of the road. The noise in the cab while his truck moves is deafening —if Murdock could talk to someone he'd have to shout. The gear ratio permits a maximum speed of fifty-seven miles per hour, and the resulting differential between horsepower and speed seems to be drained off in noise. Murdock pilots the big rig out over the Expressway that cuts off South Boston from the city proper. Howard Johnson's restaurant in Dorchester is his first stop. Two containers. Murdock dumps one on Tuesdays and the other on his heavy days—Mondays, Thursdays, and Fridays. He checks to see if the other dumpster might not have filled up on him, which happens sometimes on an off day. Only half-full. He fits his truck around the lip of the second container. Riding the curves of the Expressway, changing speeds on and off the ramps, passing through the causeway tunnels and over the bridges requires one kind of ability. Murdock's skill must be applied just as carefully to negotiate the parking lots, back alleys, and construction sites of industry, or to maneuver his ten-ton loader into the cloisters where men hide their garbage.

While the engine idles he reaches next to the seat for a pair of soiled gloves and engages the solenoid. Murdock climbs out. The hook latches onto the rear of the container, which jolts and lifts until its lip balances on the hopper. At a forty-five-degree angle off the ground, the refuse begins stickspilling into the truck. With his gloved right hand, standing to the rear, Murdock starts the hydraulic press which stuffs the garbage into the bowels of the truck, while he pushes the trash from the container with his left hand. The engine roars and heaves with each gulp of trash until the entire load has been swallowed. Then the compressor moves far into the elephant's belly, crushing every carton and can in the load. Murdock lowers the dumpster slowly, until it rests flat and its cable grows limp, and makes a mental note of how many yards he has crammed into the truck. Since Digby charges by the garbage yard, drivers have to record not only the total number of yards taken but the portion removed from each customer. After seven years of daily tabulation, Murdock can quote from memory the refuse volume of each customer by cubic yardage. By two o'clock, when he has punched in and listed his breakdown, he will not have to refer to notes. Now he takes off his gloves, climbs back into the cab, releases the brake, and moves away from Howard Johnson's toward Dorchester.

Murdock removes his black baseball cap to wipe his forehead. He has begun to sweat and the sun isn't yet in the sky. He is of medium build, solid and slender, weighing maybe one hundred-eighty pounds for his six feet. Years of moving barrels have given him a weight-lifter's arms. The job requires that he have a half-dozen pairs of green coveralls, each of which his wife must launder after one wearing or the smell of stale perspiration will stay in the material. On his black cap there's an orange Teamster's pin.

—The unions have helped a lot. When I first came on, the pension was only $150 a month for retirement. Now it's up to $330, if you went out with full time in service. We've got the dental benefits now. That just started. They pay for every dentist's bill say over ten dollars. If you went to the dentist and he said you got about three-hundred-dollars' worth of work there, I think it would only cost you ten dollars. I've got Blue Cross, too. A lot of these benefits came through our negotiations. Instead of giving us a one-dollar raise, they would give us fifty cents on benefits and fifty cents on the check.

When I started shaking barrels there were no benefits and the union dues were three bucks a month. Now with all we've got the dues are only six dollars, so actually for what the dues have gone up, we've gone a long way. When I was young I couldn't see the benefits, I just wanted the money. Now I can see the importance. Hell, I retire at forty-eight. I'll still be young enough to work at something else and I'll have a thirty-years' pension. When my first kid came, we had nothing. Now with the union benefits, we get help on that kind of thing.

The Howard Johnson's job is close to the Digby camp, a few minutes away. But during the day Murdock's route will take him on an odyssey of shopping centers, factories, and industrial parks, more than sixty miles through metropolitan Boston, and as far as twenty miles out and back again, passing through commercial and residential

areas which reflect every social and economic stratum
and every shade of color.

When he rolls into the rear parking lot of Carney Hospital in Dorchester, at 4:40 in the morning, the July sky
is still half dark. He brakes carefully to let the big rig rumble slowly down the earth road, around the new hospital
wing under construction, to the dumpster in the rear.

—The air pollution stuff has increased my work. When
they used to burn here, I would dump a five-yard container twice a week. Now that the state has come down
on them about burning trash, I dump a ten-yarder twice
a day. I'm not complaining though. This pollution shit
is real bad.

On the loading platform near the container there are
three dozen large corrugated medicine boxes, which
Murdock pitches into the hopper. He leaves Carney and
heads out through Dorchester onto Route 138 extended,
the same road he came in on this morning. At 4:50 A.M.
he enters the Howard Johnson's in suburban Milton, with
its six-yard dumpster. The load is light today. On other
mornings, the container overflows with half-chewed chicken
bones and fly-infested fish fry bags.

4:55. The sky is lightening to a pale orange-gray as
Murdock pulls into the driveway of Nimstron Electronics,
one of the sixty or so government-contract plants that
have sprung up in the industrial settlements sprawling
along Route 138. He dumps one of the company's two
containers, half-full. Murdock thinks to himself how bad
business must be. He used to empty two full dumpsters
daily. Electronics is supposed to be a big thing these days,
he thinks. When a place like this slows down, things must
be hurting. Murdock the Garbage Collector ponders the
state of the economy just as much as Thompson the Shoe-
maker or Jacobs the Tailor. His measuring stick is the
volume of industrial trash, a primal test for fiscal heart-
beat: the amount of a company's garbage is directly
proportional to its corporate good health. He spills out
the half-full container and scribbles a mental note not to
charge the plant for a full load. Charity for the corporate
poor.

Out onto the beltway again. Murdock floors the gas

pedal but the rig won't go any faster than fifty-seven miles an hour. He takes the exit toward Interstate Route 95, switching headlights on and off in silent greeting to the freight trucks passing opposite. By the time he lumbers off the Wrenthem exit, fifteen miles from Boston, the sky has gray-oranged to the point where he can tell it will be a good day. The truck pulls into the driveway of a chain pancake house which, with the Foxboro Raceway open, has been busy enough for Murdock to check three times a week. Its container is in the rear, hidden by a grove of evergreens. For the first time today the stench of rotten garbage makes Murdock breathe through his mouth.

—I been working around garbage all my life and it still makes me puke. If I have too much of it on a hot day, with the bouncing in the truck, I puke my guts out sure as hell by noontime.

He clips on the dumpster and spoiled food slides slowly into his truck. The loose mass is dotted with throw-away colors: banana-peel yellow, watermelon-rind green, and red, apple-core brown. Garbage here has not been packed in plastic bags and some of it sticks to the bottom of the container. As it is squeezed into the truck, a vomit-colored puddle spills out of the loading section and forms on the ground. The big vehicle is not watertight and excess liquid squishes onto the fenders and drips alongside the capless hubs. Murdock grabs the hose from the side of the truck and switches on the compressor to flush wet paper and peels out of the container. He knows that if he leaves any offal sticking, it will be swarming with flies on his next trip. Jobs like the pancake house he can do without. Rubbish and trash are one thing, but now the sickening stench of spoiled food will be with his truck for the rest of the day. He knows it's going to be hot, and as long as he's been dumping, he knows that, later on, there's a good chance the smell will get to him.

—The younger fellas today, I've found, shy away from our kind of work. I guess they figure why should I do that stuff when I can work in a factory for the same pay? Course somebody's got to do it—it's vital for the people.

What would happen if nobody picked up the barrels? This country would stop sure as hell. I'm glad to be working containers. You've got your low points, like winter and dumping garbage on hot days, but if we didn't do it, who would? It's crucial.

Now the sun is visible through the haze. Murdock heads back down Route 95 to the beltway, taking the Walpole exit to the Spring Valley Country Club, and rolls in past the dew-covered fairways. The course is deserted. Many mornings here, Ray Murdock becomes Walter Mitty. He thinks how life would be if he could afford the time it takes to play a game of golf: pleasant dreams, no bitterness. That's life. Some hot mornings he tells himself he'll strip and take a quick swim in the green oval pool. But he knows there's no time. He has another twenty-six stops to make, and if he wants to beat the commuter traffic he has to keep hustling. He leaves the idle thoughts behind, except for one.

—My kids are going to college all right. I want them to be able to make twice the money I make and do half the work. I don't mind the job, but it's not for my kids. If I send my kids to school and I see them starting up with these radicals, though, I'll kick their butts from one end of the yard to the other. I'm not going out to work to put my kid there to have him get in with radicals. I'm afraid now that they're going to start shutting down some colleges, and that's a tragedy. I was reading someplace where in a school of thirty thousand there was actually only fifteen hundred of them radical, but still the others went along, why I don't know. I think the kids that want to get an education, they should stop these others instead of bringing in the National Guard and all. I mean, after all, we know what's right and wrong.

The way I was brought up, right is right and wrong is wrong. Some got an education and some don't, but the people that have a little common sense can still tell you what's right and what's not right. I can't see this breaking windows and locking the dean in his office—if I didn't like the way they were running the college, I'd just turn in my books and go home and get a job.

You really can't have the police going in and breaking

heads because you have a lot of innocents in there getting hurt. The only way it will be solved is if the students that want the education clean out the other ones, throw those other donkeys out. It wouldn't take much, if they could just get together.

Attached to the side of one of the large buildings Murdock passes, near the Expressway, is a big black square upon which little lights blink the time and the temperature. Now it's 5:45 and seventy-eight degrees. Murdock picks up and dumps a dozen heavy cardboard cartons at a large warehouse twelve miles out of Boston. From there he points the lumbering Brockway toward a long low strip of shopping centers and small plants. In an hour and a half, the rig gorges a six-yard container tucked in back of a supermarket parking lot, an eight-yarder at a construction firm, an unscheduled dumpster at a ball-bearing factory, six more routine loads in toward the Hub, refuse from four gas stations along Route One, two four-yard containers behind a large apartment house, and a dumpster full of light wooden crates at a small rubber-coupling plant. There are two more gas stations on the way into town. By 7:30 Murdock tells himself that, weatherwise, it will be a good day. Moving past the Forest Hills MBTA station, he steers his truck through Roxbury. Here, thirty-eight years before, when the neighborhood was all Irish and English, Ray Murdock was born. Now it's a black ghetto.

—I worked with colored people and the couple we have at Digby are good. They don't go for this militancy. The race thing is bad. People are looking for weapons. I know I'd like to get myself a little something. I mean I hope I never need it, but nobody's gonna walk in my door and take my place over. The thing that's got me mad is that until lately there's been so much work for these people. The papers are full of jobs, but they just won't go out and find anything. It's not like they're gonna have to work for forty bucks a week while the white guy is getting seventy-four. No—they get the same pay. But I'd say a good 50 percent of the colored people just don't want to work.

And this stuff you see, white girls and black guys.

That's where you stop and say right is right and wrong is wrong. Course wherever I see this I say you can't blame the guy that much if she's willing to go out with him. But if my daughter told me she was going to marry one of these guys, I'd say okay, you've made your decision—then I'd buy the tickets to Africa and kiss her goodbye. I just can't see it.

Take the civil rights movement. There's money coming in from somewhere for this. I don't know who's financing it but most of it is communist-inspired. I gotta go with that. I was in the South in the 1950's, in North Carolina. There was a little town near the military base. You went into town and the colored had their own sections. They stayed there. They were happy. They didn't come in with the whites and the whites stayed in their part of town. I never saw any trouble. They walked into a liquor store and bought their jug like everybody else and nobody bothered them. Course I've got no use for them because as a kid I was beat up and robbed a couple times. As far as I'm concerned, with this looting and stuff, the sooner they pass laws that they can shoot you for looting, the sooner they'll stop looting.

The biggest thing needing change is the welfare. It's positively ridiculous, the biggest expense we've got in the state right now. I go through one section of Roxbury and when I pass the welfare place I see the Cadillacs, Buicks, and big black mommas sitting outside. They get their check and go right over to the liquor stores and get a jug of spooty-ooty juice and go into a parking lot and have a good time. I can understand welfare, since I was on it as a kid. I say give people their bread, pay their rent. But when they want to go down to the grocery store and they want a cab to take them down, it gets ridiculous. Face it, if a guy in America wants to make it, he can, I don't care what color he is. I'm not saying he can go out and earn fifty thousand dollars, but he can do okay. We could cut the welfare in half and the money could be spent on other people. This money they say we're spending on weapons and space—even though it costs so many millions, it's like you have to keep up with either the Joneses or the Russians. If they spend, you have to spend, too, to keep your strength. But if they cut the welfare in half, then our taxes would go down and you wouldn't have any freeloaders living high, at the average guy's expense.

Moving past a large suburban shopping center, Murdock drives the truck over to the side of the road, shifts to neutral, pulls the hand brake, and goes into a paper store. He nods hello to the man behind the counter, as he hands him a dime for the Boston *Record American* and a small package. It is a piece of paper folded around some coins. On the inside of the paper there are three numbers. The man behind the counter chaws into his cigar, reads the numbers, and writes them on a small pad. He also jots down Murdock's name and the amount of money inside the paper.

Murdock began playing the numbers as a young man. Now, every morning, he lays out a quarter or a half dollar—depending on his mood that day—and plays a different combination of three digits. He chooses his numbers from everywhere: business addresses, phone listings, the date, his children's birthdays. Last year he played three dollars on his phone number and almost won three thousand dollars. The money would have financed two weeks for his son at a basketball camp and a vacation for the family. Murdock doesn't smoke, drinks sparingly, and turns over his entire pay check to his wife. He considers the numbers game a modest vice.

Murdock really lives for two things: getting food on the table and following ice hockey. He was on skates even before the sport became a populist movement in the Northeast, and if Bobby Orr ever came up for canonization, Ray Murdock would probably become a churchgoer again. He works sixty-six hours a week handling what other people choose to throw away; when he gets home there's little time for anything but forgetting how he earns his money and planning to take in the next hockey game. On Sundays he carts his oldest son around to the hockey clinics.

—Working say sixty-five hours a week I make about $275, but I take home just over two hundred dollars after union dues, taxes, social security, and Blue Cross. I take out fifty dollars for food right away, so that's $150 left. Then I can start figuring other expenses like city taxes. Last year the taxes for the house were about $750. We pay $134 a month for the rent, including the mortgage and the interest and taxes. The life insurance for the kids and me plus the insurance for the house mounts up, close to three hundred a year. Electricity, the phone, water, oil, it all adds up pretty quick. I try to save something every week to pay off the bills like for the two cars and the car insurance. But look at clothes for the kids. It costs my wife like one hundred dollars each just to get the two girls set for high school. The two boys are still in grammar school but they have to wear something decent too. Five years ago on the same job we were a lot better off. We could save like forty dollars a week for the bills. Now things are bad as far as money goes.

Murdock makes no stops between his numbers place and the Boston College High School in Dorchester, across the Expressway. The school cafeteria uses a big eight-yard container, and there's another the same size for general waste. In the summer, with classes out, only a handful of Jesuit priests live on campus. Murdock backs the rig up to the container, slips on the hook, and trips the solenoid switch. Raw garbage is mixed in with the trash; he will have to wash out the dumpster with the hose. When the container is clean, he turns off the engine and goes into the cafeteria. He has been dumping BC High for six years now and has become friendly with the white-shirted cooks. Back in 1965 he started trading ball scores with them, and before long they were serving him breakfast. A free meal each morning. The priests always have plenty of food. Murdock pauses just long enough over his ham and eggs to check the headlines in the *Record American*.

—I'm a Marine Corps veteran. I've been to Korea and I know this Vietnam mess isn't something we're going to get away from by admitting defeat and leaving the country. It's a different war than Korea. You don't know who's the enemy and who's not. You have to go all the way in and get it over with instead of dilly-dallying around and stretching things out. If they'd said to me, "You did your thirteen months, let's do five more and go right up to the Manchurian border and clean them out,"

I'd have said, "Let's go!" Why pitter-patter back to the thirty-eighth parallel? If you're going to lose a hundred thousand men in the long run, let's lose them now and get it over with. Otherwise they'll be right in our backyards. You have it right now, this country is loaded with communists. That's why there's so much trouble going on. You can't just let them go in and take over country after country. I mean, they're vicious people. I've seen the things they did in Korea. They're insane. They're fanatics. They're all doped up. I've seen night attacks where we were set on a hill and they start coming at you in waves, and you go out in the morning and check the bodies—young kids, thirteen, fourteen years old and they don't even have a gun—they're carrying firecrackers. They're nuts, and if we don't stop the reds in Vietnam we're going to be forced to stop them on Cape Cod.

It's 8:20 A.M. Murdock scrapes off his dishes sets them in the stainless steel washer, and says good-bye to the cook. His toughest haul of the day is coming up, and if he wants to stay on schedule he's got to move. He cuts back across the Expressway, makes one wide sweeping turn, and after about two more miles pulls into the rear lot of the Northeast Printing Company. Murdock dumps Northeast twice a week. Each time, in addition to an eight-yard container, he empties fifteen or twenty barrels filled with damaged labels and rolls of paper. Once Murdock empties the dumpster, a routine job, he backs the truck up to the rear of the warehouse, where printing work is done on the second floor. He signals to two men upstairs, and they begin to drop big galvanized aluminum cans from an open loft fifteen feet above ground. After the barrels are turned over and dumped. Murdock must toss them back to the men in the loft. He feels his back wrench when he hurls the cans up. The thought passes through his mind that it's been twenty-three years since he shook his first barrel. He grits his teeth and lets the pain subside. Things could be worse—he's only got to do this twice a week now. It's a living.

8:45. Murdock looks back from the driver's seat and sees that the truck is full, a good hundred yards. He sets yards. He sets out for Quincy Dump.

Quincy is a suburban town filled with old quarries,

which, years after the seams of stone became exhausted, the city fathers in their wisdom decided to use for land-fill refuse dumps. The pits have a natural lining of granite and they fill up slowly with metropolitan waste. Until last year, Quincy let the collectors dump for free. Now the town charges twenty-six dollars to vent the contents of a full one-hundred-yard truck. At 9:00 A.M. he passes through the Dump's black iron gates, hands the guard a credit slip, and takes a receipt of payment.

The burial ground at Quincy greets the eyes and nose with a stomach-turning kind of movable feast. It is a placid enough setting in a natural amphitheater of granite, around whose walls are spray-painted fraternity letters and lovers' initials—remembrances of a time past, when the quarry's clean water basin was a gathering place for teenyboppers. Now it's hard to imagine those days. Squadrons of sea gulls line the rocks, gobbling down scraps of garbage pillaged from the rubble. The dumpster trucks have to back in, slowly, to the area being filled. The drivers trip switches that open rear doors and move the trucks forward to spill the offal onto the ground. Almost immediately bulldozers smooth a thick layer of topsoil over the garbage. Meanwhile other trucks idle their engines, waiting their turn to excrete the waste of Greater Boston.

If Murdock lingers too long at the Quincy Dump, he begins to swallow the dirt. Loose soil clouds up and he catches it in his nose, eyes, and mouth. If he gets out of the truck and stands in one place, he will sink a foot or two in the waste. In or out, the smell evokes the dry heaves. Even after twenty-three years Ray Murdock gags if he spends too much time here. He'd like to take it all in once, but he knows he'll have to come back tomorrow, and the next day. Somebody's got to do the dirty work. It is necessary, this environmental insult enclosed by barbed wire. So Murdock is told, and so he says.

With his hopper empty at 9:15, he still has seven more stops to make. Before 2:00 P.M. when he retires for the day, he will drive another twenty-five miles in and around metropolitan Boston. He works a commercial route; his customers are dispersed along the industrial arteries to the southeast. It takes nearly forty-five minutes to dump at Jordon Marsh, New England's largest department store complex, which has just built a cavernous supply house three stories high and the length of ten football fields. This is to be Jordon's northeastern distribution warehouse, near Boston Harbor in Quincy, and it will produce a small city's share of packing waste. Because of recent antipollution legislation, the enormous incinerator here can be used only under clear skies. The rest of the time the crates and cardboard must be carried away. Murdock stops at the warehouse three times a week and almost half fills his truck each time.

From the Jordan warehouse he moves out, at 10:00 A.M. for his last gas-station run: two large stations, a three-yarder at each. He is once more away from Boston. A pair of electronics firms that weren't ready for dumping earlier in the morning are full now. By 11:30 A.M. he is in Dedham again, at a rubber belt factory. Two eight-yard containers.

Murdock begins to feel the effects of seven hours driving and dumping. After riding in the noisy cab he finds it difficult to talk without shouting, even when he is stopped at a light and the engine is idling. His ears start to throb and his stomach, filled with breakfast and the smell of garbage, feels queasy. Twelve noon. The truck is three-quarters full and he has one more stop.

Carney Hospital, first visited in the dead of morning, has served two more meals. This time Murdock holds his breath while he dumps the leftover food and washes out the container. He has never gotten used to the smell. As he heads out of the parking lot, he turns the truck away from Boston toward Quincy and the second big dumping of the day.

At the iron gate he picks up another receipt and spills out another load. It is 1:25 in the afternoon. So far today the Digby Company has collected $280 worth of refuse on this run, and Quincy's municipal deficit has been reduced by fifty-two dollars. Murdock turns the truck back toward Boston. After he passes through the chain metal fence at the yard and parks his rig, he begins to tally the day's score.

—Thirty-three stops today. I figure I do an average of twenty-six a day. Sometimes I might have thirty, thirty-three, and on Saturday I might be down to seventeen.

You can do a hundred yards in a load and I can get in two loads a day if I go over the average. The company gets $1.40 a yard for collecting the shit. You bring in good money for them. If you figure twenty-six dollars as the cost to dump a load, that's fifty-two dollars a day off the $280 you might bring in. Take off my pay and the cost of the trucks and they're still making good money. And the trucks in town that don't do the driving I do, they might have forty stops in a row within a mile. They can do three or four loads in the time it takes me to do two, so the company's got even more money coming in. I'd say that refuse is one of the big businesses to move into. It's a necessity. You always have a demand for your service. No question, there's big money in it, although I suppose management feels the unions are their enemies.

I don't have any regrets. I'm not complaining. There are better jobs around, and I'm not all that crazy about this one with the grind and the hustling and the smell, but I don't think of it as the lowest of the low. Somebody's got to do it. Can you imagine what it would be like if nobody wanted to pick up garbage? I work hard at it, hustling overtime and stuff, so it gripes me to see these people on welfare who could get jobs if they wanted to. I don't know much about social problems, because I don't have time to think about things like that, but I do know about people on welfare. I think about them a lot.

Two in the afternoon. Murdock returns to his own car after he punches out, and for the first few moments at the smaller wheel he finds the driving difficult. A Biscayne feels like a kiddy car after ten hours in a Brockway Huskey. When he gets home, a half-hour later, he is ready for a beer. The heat has turned into humidity. He takes a king-sized can of Narragansett Lager from the refrigerator and drinks it. Then, slowly, he peels off his clothes and shuffles into the shower. His wife has left reminders about the work around the house. She is out shopping with the kids. Front and rear steps need scraping and painting. There is a broken window in one of the bedrooms, and the oil filter should be changed in the car. After showering, Murdock slips into bermudas and a jersey and flops into the kitchen for another beer. The pace of things is a lot slower at home. The work can wait. Murdock's wife is embarrassed about her husband's job or at least what other people think of it, but she knows how hard he works. She is used to his putting off the household chores.

—The hours I put in take all the free time from me. Yesterday I got home early, I only worked eight hours, so I fixed the steps. But after I put in ten hours I'm kind of punchy so I don't feel like scraping no paint. By the time I take a shower and have a few beers and relax and have supper, I'm beat. By then you've been up fifteen-sixteen hours and worked eleven of them. There's not much time for home life. I don't work Sunday. Maybe I'll take the kid to a basketball game or something. Saturday is a short day, eight or nine hours, and maybe we'll go out Saturday night. Then Sunday you say to yourself you're gonna have to start it all over again tomorrow so you're not gonna go out and whoop it up. The only bad thing is there's not a great amount of time to spend with the kids, not like what a guy with a forty-hour job has.

I'm satisfied. You get up in the morning, go get the week's pay, bring home the bread. If you get a little extra and you can do a little extra, wonderful. If you can't, well just get by with what you've got and hope everything turns out all right with the health and the kids.

Even with the hustling I do, though, it seems that we're still short. We can't save ahead that much for a trip or anything. If any long sickness came we'd be hurting. But we're eating, and sometimes it's sirloin steak. To me we're not that bad off, because I know it could be an awful lot worse. When I go around and see some poor kid that's crippled, that makes up for everything. I say at least my kids aren't crippled. This lets me put up with whatever struggle it is to get what we have. If I can have my roast beef Sunday and the kids are healthy, the sixty hours a week are worth it.

After a meat loaf dinner with the family, Murdock pours himself a shot of rye and sits in front of the TV to watch the news. Halfway through the first situation comedy, his eyes close and he is asleep. He stays on the couch until his wife wakes him. It is 11:00 P.M. He talks briefly with her, mostly about bills and the kids, and checks in with each of them, the two boys and two girls, then goes to bed.

Before falling off to sleep, he reaches over to the table next to the bed and sets the alarm clock that will buzz him awake, four hours later.

TWO

The Maid

There was a very severe winter; Jean had no work, the family no bread. The baker was just going to bed when he heard a violent blow against the barred window of his shop. He got down in time to see an arm thrust through the aperture made by the blow of a fist on the glass. The arm seized a loaf of bread and took it out. The thief used his legs valiantly; Isabeau pursued him and caught him. The thief had thrown away the bread, but his arm was still bleeding.

—*Victor Hugo*

We didn't have any milk and we didn't have any money and my husband said, "I just can't let these children starve." Nobody wanted any steps washed or anything. When he left home, he knew we didn't have any milk. So he took half a gallon of milk off somebody's step and brought it home for the children; that's the first time I'd ever known him to take anything. Later on when he got a job he went out there to try to pay the people, and they told him no. Said they didn't feel bad long as they knew that some hungry child had some milk.

—*Willie Elma James*

Willie Elma James lives on a long, well-traveled, respectable street in an old ghetto of St. Louis, where each row house has a small front yard and the cracked sidewalks pass by an occasional tree or tiny garden. Rusting metal fences set off the cookie-sheet buildings. They are old houses, but on this street, in this neighborhood, they're all well kept.

At 7:30 in the morning, while it is still half-dark, Elma leaves home for work. For the past eighteen of her sixty-two years, she has been a maid, one of two million black women in the country who serve as household domestics. Willie Elma James is too old and mellowed to be bitter about things. She is tall, almost five nine. She carries herself straight, as she has been taught by her religion, and it emphasizes the pride she feels as mother and wife. Her skin is milk chocolate, not black. When she smiles, which is often, her big ivory teeth sparkle around a single gold cap. She has black-silver hair. She is strong for her age, but it is a strength compounded with an essential kindness, or perhaps caused by it.

Early this morning Elma manages a window seat on the bus, where she spends the hour-long ride waking up, as the barred storefronts and muted neon congestion gradually lighten into the broader and greener boulevards of suburbia.

The Petersons, who have employed Elma for the past eighteen years, live at the far end of a carefully manicured *cul-de-sac,* entered through a long, tree-lined driveway. The centrally air-conditioned ranch homes of Colonial Village are concealed by tall shrubs and fronted by large, healthy lawns.

Elma makes a leisurely half-mile hegira from the bus stop. She has the time and, on the cooler summer days at least, she likes the walk. She knows that the work awaiting her is drudgingly unremarkable. She will have a relaxed cup of coffee, exchange some pleasantries with the lady of the house, change into her white uniform, and start in on the routine she has followed for almost twenty years. Among other staggering monotonies, Willie Elma James has made more than forty thousand beds during that time. Somebody else might call it voluntary enslavement. To Elma it's honest work.

—Nothing challenging about it. There's not much thinking I need to do, just cleaning and watching out for things. It's just routine. I can't say I'd really recommend this job to others, especially young people who can get something better. But for people like me, with their age and skills against them, it's good. I enjoy the job 'cause it's easy, the same routine over and over. It's not that tiring. It's just like being at home.

The morning sunshine gleams on the percales. Elma lifts one side of a white cotton sheet and tucks the end beneath the mattress. She secures the fold into a hospital corner and smoothes the rest across the large double bed. She flattens a light-blue summer blanket between the top sheet and the quilted bedspread, fluffs and covers the two feather pillows. The ritual nears completion. Her strong arms stretch to pull the spread between the bedposts and tuck it under the pillows in a horizontal crease. Then she smoothes the spread with gentle slaps. She makes four, beds each day, three minutes per bed. She does not look beyond the next one—to twenty this week, eighty this month, a thousand this year—and she doesn't step back to admire the tight finished product before her. She has made too many beds. She knows how it's done, feels no pride, thinks about other things. (*The only thing I ever thought about beds was when Poppa says to me, "Remember, if you make your bed hard, you just roll over that much more often." He was talking about my marrying Andrew. I didn't know what he meant then, but I realized it later.)*

As she dusts around its top and sides, Elma switches on the color television set in the bedroom and dials through detergent commercials to her first soap opera of the day—a different kind of tedium.

She does not see too much of the family she serves. Mrs. Peterson often leaves before she arrives, leaving notes about the special chores to be done. Except for brief contacts with delivery people, there is no office small talk or factory clatter in Elma's daily six hours on the job. Radio and television become subliminally necessary appliances, the day programmed according to a scheduled talk show or melodrama. For Elma, morning is television, afternoon radio. Plots have not changed much through the years and the actors are as everyday as the people they play. It is not hard for Elma to suspend disbelief. Her identification with the characters is reflexive.

Elma stoops to unwrap the cord that has been wound tightly around the vacuum cleaner. She continues to watch the living color on the other side of the room, but once the vacuum is plugged in and turned on, it reduces the television to a silent electric flicker. Elma reaches under the bed, around the chairs, and across the thick carpet which was practically clean before she began. This is the Thursday vacuuming. She always vacuums on Thursday. When the dirt has been fully sucked from the heavy pile, she pulls the cord. The television returns to normal. Despite Elma's tall, big-boned carriage of nearly a hundred and sixty pounds, she is almost graceful, caught against the sun at the window, as she wraps the wire round the vacuum cleaner. The colors of the room are orange and brown.

—I was always tall and slender and skinny. My dad called me "head and legs." He was an easy-going person, rarely angry, but when he was mad at me he used to say, "Get outta here, legs." That was just like a whipping to me.

I was born in Birmingham and we moved to St. Louis when I was four years old. I remember Dad so well riding back and forth on a bicycle over the bridge across the Mississippi River. Every day he went to work on that bike to Arnold's Packing House over in East St. Louis. That was right after we moved here from Birmingham. There was only three of us then. My oldest sister had had tonsilitis and at the time the doctor didn't know what it was, so she choked to death. My next oldest sister only lived eight or nine months. My brother hadn't been born yet.

The packing house closed down and there wasn't much for Dad to do, so he started a little business of his own. He was an easy-going fella. He just thought everyone was honest, and he let out ice and coal and wood on credit and never got paid.

Things were pretty rough, so Mom opened up a restaurant over on Welston Avenue. She did very well, her business got bigger than she was able to take care of, and she hired people to help. Of course at that time, as always, it was kind of difficult to get competent help. We helped occasionally when we come from school. But soon after that Momma got ill. She had some sort of bone rheumatism and she wasn't able to walk for a whole year. She had to sell the business, and then we just subsisted on what Poppa was able to pick up here and there. He's still in the ice and coal business.

The doorbell rings. Elma stops in the middle of stripping down the big double bed in the master bedroom. She knows who's calling. Every Thursday morning the laundry man brings cleaned and pressed shirts. Elma checks the bathroom hamper, grabs two handfuls of dirty shirts from the laundry room, then opens the front door. The quick conversation is the same each week; both she and the laundry man are usually in a hurry: *Hello, how ya' doing, good-bye*. She takes the pressed shirts and carries them to a dresser in the big bedroom.

—In 1925, I really wanted to go to school. I think I would have loved to be a dietician or a home economics teacher. But my mother took a job with a family in Des Moines. Things were still kind of rough, and that's why she took the job. My dad said, "With things as they are, I'd hate to have you drop out, but I don't see where I'll be able to send both you and your sister to high school." Opportunities weren't really too good for Negro girls. The only thing you could look forward to was probably being a teacher, and there was brilliant girls that couldn't even get teaching jobs. So I said, "Oh well, what is there for me? Maybe I'll just go on and get married. I can't do any worse." So I did.

It was 1926 when I married my first husband. It's a funny story. We were neighbors, but I just thought that he was too old for me. I wasn't too interested in boys anyway, but my girl friend, she was having fits and conniptions over him. She said, "That handsome man living next door to you, and you're not paying any attention!" One day she was over to the house and she said, "Come here, come here quick." She pointed out the window. There he was. He had on his uniform, and he was really handsome. He was with Loew's Theatre, as a porter, and he had a white uniform with epaulets on it, real fancy with gold braid. You'd think he was a captain or something, the way Loew's State dressed up their doormen at that time. Well, just about then his mother gave a party. She was really interested in me 'cause she wanted Andrew to settle down (and she thought, well, that's a nice girl living next door), so she gave a birthday party. His sister and I were close friends. So she said, "Come in and see the party." They had the punch bowls all set up on the tables and everything. I went in to see it, and he was standing in the hallway, and he grabbed me and kissed me. Scared me to death! I guess I was about seventeen and I didn't know him more than two months when we got married. Really I don't know how he knew me out in the hallway— I guess it was his mother talking to him. When he asked Poppa could he marry me, Poppa said, "Elma, that boy over there is a pretty wild guy. I don't know if I want you to marry him, but if you want to, I guess it's all right." That's when he said, "Remember, if you make your bed hard, you just roll over that much more often."

Lingering in the doorway of the first bedroom, Elma watches the TV plot thicken. She says to herself that there will be plenty of time to finish the other two bedrooms before lunch. She often changes the order of her business for the day, but somehow after all the years at the same place she still feels a vague sense of resignation: no matter when she gets to the beds, they'll have to be done sometime today. They'll get done, and so will the bathrooms and the kitchen. Routine.

Elma stares at the television, transfixed by the images but not really thinking about plot or dialogue. At times she follows the serials with a maternal intimacy, but every few months she tires of the same faces. Today she daydreams. Outside, through the big bay window behind the television set, the day is clear, blue, bathed in a rare sunshine. This summer in St. Louis it has been even more hot and hazy and humid than usual, and there have been few mornings so clear and cool. Inside, the air-conditioner makes Elma feel like a flower in a florist's refrigerator. Today she envies Peter, her second husband, who is a full-time gardener. The television, in living color, stares back at her.

—I remember when I was first married and our oldest boy was about three years old. Andrew was one of these staunch kinds—he thought it was just terrible for a man not to be able to support a wife. He had a job at a filling station, and he was kicking a fuss about me working. During that time there was this lady who lived in University City who was going to have a baby, and my next-door neighbor said she wanted someone to come in and help her after she came home, just half a day. I said I thought I could do it but my husband couldn't know about it. She was going to pay $5.75 for the three days, which I thought was good. I went to my mother-in-law, who lived next door, and asked her to keep my two little boys—but she was determined as her son that I shouldn't work, although she wouldn't tell him. So I asked a neighbor who lived on the next block if she would keep my sons for me so I could go and work those half days. She said, "No, I couldn't be bothered with children, I'm too nervous. But if you want to leave them with my oldest girl, it'd be all right with me." Her girl was about fourteen something years old and I thought she'd take care of them all right. But she did terrible. One Saturday she was gonna do the hall steps, and she did a very stupid thing. Instead of diluting the water before she brought it up, she boiled the water downstairs and just set the hot bucket on the steps. The children came in from outside, came in through the kitchen there, and my son didn't know the bucket was on the steps and he stepped in that bucket of scalding water. He had third-degree burns. We didn't really think he'd ever walk again. He laid flat on his back for ninety days.

After he come out of the hospital, the doctor told me to massage his muscles. I did that and he got better, but he still has scars and will have them until he dies. So I quit work then. My husband said he forgave me, but I always felt that it was my fault 'cause I shouldn't have tried to work. I had to quit then and we just made out on what he made.

Elma sweeps through the other two bedrooms according to the same pattern she followed in the first. The bathrooms offer variation. In one, whose walls are papered in washable pink, orange, and red, she sprinkles a pastel-blue powder into the toilet bowl. The water hisses and bubbles a darker blue. Then she sponges the seat and lid, and turns her attention to other fixtures. Soon several newly cleaned sinks and cabinets shine through wet spots.

Kneeling as if in church, Elma bends into the pink bathtub to scrub its bottom and sides. It takes three minutes. As she pulls herself up, slowly, she notices the parquetry has been imprinted on her knees. Then she bends over again, and turns on the tap to rinse the tub clean. She scrubs around the toilet bowl, and flushes its deep-blue water to clear. Her sponge mop and bucket are waiting in the corner.

—I was baptized in 1917 in a pool at the church in Arkansas, and how I remember those big ceremonies! At that time they usually baptized at the river. People from all around would always go down to the baptizing. It was really a big community thing, with everybody from churches from all around, even some white churches, coming down.

The river bank was just loaded with people, it was really

something. They were all dressed in white robes with their heads tied in white towels. A tent was set aside, one for the ladies and one for the men. Then they came down the center aisle to reach the preacher and the minister-helper in the river. Shortly before they finished the baptizing, some lady jumped off in the river and committed suicide. This was just before the Depression. Then through all the commotion, I got lost from the people that had taken me down; they were wondering where I was, and I couldn't find them. But I remembered that the trolley car came in front of our house, and I just followed that trolley car. Walked all the way from the river. It was about 9:30 'fore I got home. Momma had called the police, and everyone was out looking for me. She didn't know where in the world I was. They were happy when I walked in the door.

The mopping is an easy chore. Elma does it in five minutes, pulling her new sponge-on-a-stick across the tile floor of the bathroom. It will not need washing again until next Thursday, according to the carefully established routine of eighteen years. The other bathroom will be ready to scrub clean after lunch. Blue Magic in hand, water hissing and bubbling as she leaves, Elma hurries off for the kitchen. The teakettle is whistling. Ten minutes to twelve. She has to fix dinner, make her own lunch, and listen to *The Noon Hour*. Elma takes the potful of water and pours it into a heart-shaped metal mold filled with Jell-o crystals. She shakes the mixture without spilling any and puts it in the refrigerator. Then she makes her lunch, usually half an egg salad sandwich or a plateful of last night's leftovers. For the first time since coffee early in the morning, she has time to sit. The radio sounds in the background.

—It never bothered me when I worked that I had to eat in a separate place. I just never went in there. I knew they wouldn't serve me, and rather than be humiliated, I just didn't go in. But I remember one job I had, in a dress shop on Washington Avenue, where they had two ladies' rest rooms, and they had them separated—the whites go in on one side and the blacks go around in the back. Well, now the black rest room, they never cleaned that; but the white one, they always had it cleaned. The white women would go in there, and it was clean enough for them to eat their lunch. I was working in the section for pleated garments, and I was determined that I wasn't going in that filthy washroom. But when I went in their white rest room a couple of the white girls gave me this bad look, and then one of 'em went and reported it to the manager. So he spoke to me.

He says, "What's wrong with you, you can't use the washroom that's specified for you?" I said, "I'm not going in nobody's filth!" I said, "I wouldn't send a dog in that place there, and those girls who do go in, they're foolish. I wouldn't work here if I have to go in there, and I'm not going in there." He said, "Well, the girls don't want you using the same washroom with them." So I said, "If that's how it is, I just won't stay on the job—I'll leave." Now the NAACP were just beginning to investigate these different job things, and I think he was reluctant to really fire me because I protested. Anyway, he didn't. And I was the only one. All the other girls, they went around in that filth, but I wouldn't go in there. I went in with the white girls. They were very indignant, but I just ignored them. I figured, well, I'm human same as they are—they're no better than I am.

Mom and Dad always told us, "Never feel inferior because you're black. They said, "You be proud of being black, the same way that the white man is of being white." They said that he's no different, that God created only two people, Adam and Eve, and from them came every natonality of the world. You have no right to feel any inferiority toward anyone. Dad always told us that it's you, it's how you feel and how you act and your character that makes you either inferior or superior, it isn't the color of your skin. And we all just grew up like that.

My brother, he took this aeronautics course from Illinois. He was in the service there. I think there were only three black people in the group, out of sixty-five, and he made the highest average on the aeronautics test. So the Army sent his records to the place where he was supposed to get this job and they interviewed him on the telephone and everything and they accepted him. But when he got there and they discovered that he was black, they told him they had made a mistake. He was fit to be tied. It's a cruel thing. You don't know until you have had to live through it, how you feel to know you're qualified but you have to work doubly hard to get a job, and then someone inferior in ability to you will be elevated to the job which really should come to you. And you're always the first to be fired when there's a cutoff.

—I never wanted but two children, and I just prayed so hard not to have any more. I really wanted a boy and a girl, but I got two boys instead. We were having a hard enough time making ends meet with just the four of us, and I don't know what we would have done if we had more. I was just determined not to have any more. My first husband had at that time a job making six dollars a week, working in a grocery store. We had been living in Gary, Indiana, and then we came back to St. Louis after he couldn't find any work there. It was then that I started working at the walnut factory, picking walnuts. You pick all day long, five days a week, for two dollars and a half the whole week. We were living in this house paying ten dollars a month for two rooms, everyone had to use the same bathroom, and no hot water. So my husband got himself a bucket—paid twenty-five or thirty cents for it—and got him some rags, and went out in the West End to wash steps and windows. I think he was getting a nickel a window. That's how we lived.

One day I never shall forget. We didn't have any milk and we didn't have any money and my husband said, "I just can't let these children starve." Well, those that could afford it had people at the dairy deliver milk to them at their house. Now he was out here in University City and nobody wanted any steps washed or windows washed or anything. When he left home, he knew we didn't have any milk. So he took half a gallon of milk off somebody's steps and brought it home for the children; that's the first time I'd ever known him to take anything. Later on when he got a job he went out there to try to pay the people, and they told him no. Said they didn't feel bad long as they knew that some hungry child had some milk. He really went back to try to give 'em the price of that milk.

Elma lifts herself out of the kitchen to begin her afternoon rounds. One of the small rooms she passes, filled with teddy bears and high school souvenirs and pennants, reminds her of its last full-time occupant. Susan was a girl whom she helped raise, who is now married with a family, and who sometimes borrows her for a day's cleaning. Elma remembers all the big moments in Susan's life as if she were her own daughter.

She spends the afternoon much as she spent the morning, but in other parts of the house. There's not much difference between cleaning a bedroom and cleaning a living room. The pillows are fluffed with the same pomp, the furniture dusted with the same circumstance, the rugs vacuumed with the same diligence, accessories returned to the same corners and shelves and tables. But for Elma, by now wizened and calloused, the repetition is more a certain security than an inexorable boredom.

—In 1952, my job here was only temporary. My second husband was working for Mrs. Peterson in her yard, and the woman that was working for her as a maid was getting married. So she asked Peter if he known of anyone that she could get, and he asked me if I'd like to do it for awhile, and I did—for eighteen years.

I really don't think about much during the day, just whatever is on my mind when I leave the house, a personal problem or something I have to do when I get home. It's not tiring, it's just routine. There isn't one particular job I dislike or like more than another, I just dislike the going and coming.

I've never been on welfare, and I don't want to be. This welfare system makes people lazy. Why, I know this one woman whose husband had up and left her with two little boys, so she applied for welfare. First they inspected everything she had, and after a time she finally started receiving the money. But she encouraged her two boys to work. They got themselves a paper route and brought home something themselves, but when the welfare people found out, they cut her monthly check. So the boys just stopped working.

I don't really like President Nixon, but I do think he had a good idea in wanting to change the present welfare system, to give a man an incentive to work and take care of his family. The only trouble is that when you train this man, you have to be sure he can put what he's learned to practice.

Some opportunities have opened up for black people. When my son first started for Bell Telephone, he was with the company about five years and the only job he could get in there was porter. Then after all the protests, they had him take his tests and he passed them all. They saw that he was qualified to do more than menial jobs, so they elevated him to installer. Since that time they have hired other Negro boys and are training them. But it wasn't all that easy for my son. Mind you, he had to *request* those tests. If he'd never spoken up, I guess he never would have gotten promoted. There were black men in the system years before he was, but they were never anything but porters.

I think that what helped open up these opportunities was Reverend King's preaching nonviolence, and then the white man realizing the potential that the Negro had, and the Negro realizing himself what he can do if given the chance. It was like in Jesus' time. Martin Luther King was the Moses of our day. I don't think anything has opened up as broadly since he died. He was a man that believed in right and justice for all people, he preached that and he downgraded hate and separation. He was wonderful. I think that a lot of white people, knowing his life and how well-qualified he was, began to see where they had been remiss in treating their black brothers, and the cruel things they had done to them.

The way he preached about love to your fellow man opened the eyes of the white people more than anything that ever happened. Reverend King started nonviolent sit-ins, and this protesting helped bring to light what his preaching said.

In the Peterson dining room, knives and spoons lie in a pile on the white linen tablecloth. Elma walks around the table, putting spoon, knife, then fork and spoon, knife, then fork at six place settings. She ties cloth seat covers onto the Hepplewhite chairs, and with another trip to the kitchen produces a half dozen stemmed drinking glasses. Often she remains until nine in the evening to serve dinner and then wash the dishes, but according to Mrs. Peterson's morning note, tonight there will be no guests. Just family.

At 2:00 P.M. Elma enters the den and family area. She

does not wear a wristwatch and rarely looks at a clock: her routine is her sundial and "den time" means there is only about an hour's work to go. Elma, old enough to roll with the monotony, does not need incentives to finish the day. Work, or having to do it, has never tried her soul.

—One of the things that bugs me most is political-type people, the ones who come into your neighborhood and promise you everything. They say I'll do this and I'll do that, and after they are elected and put into office, you go to 'em with some of the same problems that you've already had and nothing is done. My husband says they're mismanaging, squandering the money foolishly, and employing more employees than necessary. Course we all realize that they do that 'cause they're paying back political debts, but I believe that they ought to have a civilian group, one that's disinterested in politics, to see to it that this money's spent right. I don't have any objection to taxes. We want these services, we want street lights and other things, and we just have to pay for them. This is good. But the burden of taxes is on the middle class and poor people. We need to see that justice is done in all cases. We don't always have that.

I remember a while back some women in the community circulated a petition against the increase in taxes. They cited the fact that middle- and lower-income people pay the greatest amount of taxes for their earnings, and they felt that was wrong. I signed that petition. I don't mind paying taxes, but the rich, they got to pay, too. I don't believe in special benefits, not for me *or* for the rich people. I know we're always going to have some people trying to get out of paying their share, but the government must force them to pay, too. It's just unfair if they don't.

Balancing on a chair as she dusts a high bookcase, Elma reaches on tiptoe to wipe the top shelf. She doesn't look at the titles. Monday she will have to wash, wax, and buff the den's large wooden floor, and she won't have time to reclean this room so thoroughly. She is still a conscientious cleaner—Mrs. Peterson is frequent and lavish with compliments—even after all these years.

Working conditions have not changed for household

domestics over the past several decades. Their places of employment are usually more pleasant than their homes. Nobody has ever thought of housework as body-wracking or mind-wearying. The repetition and the tedium are assumed by employers and accepted by employees. Elma gets down from the chair and moves to wipe the windows.

—It used to be busier when the children were growing up. There'd be more rooms to clean and food to prepare, and more looking after to do. But mainly the job's stayed the same. Of course now I work for the children some days, and just like before, I'm helping take care of their kids.

I remember when my children was growing up. There was a time when they used to come home from school and some classmate would say something about my kids being black. Children can be kind of cruel sometimes. Andrew Jr. come on in and he'd cry, "Momma, they told me I was a little ol' black boy." I'd say, "Well, honey, you are black. That's your nationality. You're black. Don't ever feel bad 'cause they call you black." I said, "If they call you nigger, that's when you get mad. But when they call you black, that's what you are. You're black." So the only thing they ever got indignant about was being called a nigger. Nowadays I find that children are proud to be called black.

But the Black Panthers have gone too far. They may be tired of the cover-up that the white man has used, but they're wrong in preaching separatism. The United States is supposed to be united. Preaching hate, whether it's the black man or the white man talking, is just no good— we will never be a democratic country with separatism like that. We're all human beings, whether black, red, yellow, polka dot, or green. We all live, we all breathe the same air, we die, we stink. There shouldn't be any division, because we're all alike. But we'll never be to-gether until man has ·really accepted God and realized that God is the infinite being and that God has the full control of our lives. Until man accepts God in that sense, there won't be any universal love.

The Panthers have done some good things, too. It's the newspapers and television that have played up the bad side. The Panthers have this building over on West-minster where they give boys who couldn't get work some-thing to do. They are out there giving 'em training and things, and the police just harass them to death. That's what makes 'em militant. Instead of the police trying to get along with the black people as long as they're not breaking the law, trying to understand them, they get afraid. Take those Panthers down there on Franklin Avenue, the police just went in there and tore up that place. So how can you have any feeling and any love for the police?

The white man feels that all black people will steal. If you're black, you steal, that's all. But the black man feels the same way toward the white man and the police—in the first place, you're out to do me wrong. You don't mean me any good, see.

I hope the violence has just about spent its course. It isn't helping anyone. I have never seen our community like this. People are afraid because there've been so many break-ins. You have to have steel wire over your windows to protect yourself. I've never seen anything like that before. I think it's terrible. And the government is talking about law and order. Who was the first one to break the law? Men in high office were—President Nixon, for one. They harp more on law and order than about doing some-thing to eliminate the crime that's happening in the cities. If they know that the highest crime rate is among the unemployed and the poor, then why don't they do some-thing to raise the level of employment? Give these people something to do, some work where they can make a living, rather than harping about crime.

I think the thing that's most disturbing was when Nixon said that if he was elected, he was going to try to change the 1954 school desegregation law. The next thing you knew, he was pledging to help the South by not going forth and holding out the law that was passed by the Supreme Court to desegregate the schools. This being the law of all the land, it would seem like he was not being a president of all the people—that he was still causing a division. Why hold out after fifteen years? Why do they still try to placate those that were determined not to go along with the law?

Only the kitchen remains to be cleaned. Elma repeats her tasks for the last time today—here. Her own kitchen at home, her beds and bath, her living room, still have to be done. Gingerly she unfolds the hot foil covering the roast, sinks a fork deep into the meat, and nods with unconscious satisfaction that it is done. She unloads the dishwasher, and rinses the dishes that have been left in the sink from breakfast. Then she sweeps the floor, sprinkles detergent on the cabinet shelves, around the stove, and on the oven door, and sponges them clean. Done.

Without sponge, dustrag, or mop, her hands appear incongruously bare. Elma takes off her white, round-collared uniform, hangs it neatly in the laundry room, and changes into street shoes and a print dress. Taking her time, she walks out to pick up the evening paper. She does not like to leave the house empty. She has waited for Mrs. Peterson before, and it does not bother her.

It's three o'clock. Back in the kitchen, Elma sits down to look at the headlines. She is too tired to be impatient and it's too warm now, even inside, for anything but daydreaming. Ten minutes later the sound of the garage door lifting nudges her out of reverie. Mrs. Peterson calls hello, and Elma scurries to assist with the packages. Inside, she quickly organizes the new groceries and receives instructions for the next day. Mrs. Peterson smiles a compliment on her cooking, after looking at the roast. After a few quick pleasantries, Elma says good-bye.

Her afternoon walk to the bus stop is a bit more hurried than usual. She doesn't want to miss the three-thirty express. Traffic will not peak for another two hours, but to someone who has been alone inside all day, the streets seem crowded. She reaches her corner and finds that the bus is a few minutes late.

Elma is warm from hurrying and from the sun. She fans herself with her hands. A continuous flow of second cars—some sporty, some compact, some air-conditioned— has deposited other maids in a small black congregation at the bus stop. Small white hands wave good-bye to their nanny from the back seat of a blue Pontiac.

The express bus arrives at 3:40. When Elma gets on, it is still half white: fourteen year olds and senior citizens. The other half is mostly housemaids heading downtown.

As the streets narrow, the houses become door-to-door, and the lawns shrink, the population of the bus slowly changes until it is all black.

—We believe in negotiation, let's get together and talk things out. The majority of black people believe in that. If you have a grievance, let's hear it. Even though you've been waiting for a long time, just to say we want this and we want it now is still no way to get it.

But we have been through certain things. You go in and apply for a job, and you're as qualified as the next man, but they tell you, "Sorry, we don't have any openings." At the same time, you hear at the next office they're hiring ten or fifteen people. It's injustice. It seems that the white man won't deal justly with all men, he'll always want to keep his foot on your neck, you're supposed to do what he wants you to do. And that isn't fair. You'd think that people in high office could eliminate this, but look at this housing deal. They tore down all this housing over here and just moved the people from one section to another, but not in the same quality houses they tore down. And the rent was too high for the poor to move in. That's happening all over.

We'll have to get together. It's like the two donkeys that were hitched to the same wagon. One was pulling this way and the other one against him, and they weren't getting anywhere. The story is that they sat down and reasoned everything out and now they're pulling together.

At 4:45 Elma reaches the downtown bus stop she left at 7:30 in the morning. Five other women get off the bus with her and head in several directions along the broken street. The bus is still three-quarters full as it continues downtown. Elma steps into a corner market, a small store built in the 1940's. She picks out several things for supper, some of which she knows cost Mrs. Peterson less at the Colonial Village supermarket. She pays cash; she never uses credit.

Elma's dinner and her housework await. The summer months mean Peter's gardening work will continue until dark, so she has time to clean. She climbs the steps to her own house. It is fronted by a small lawn, Peter's pride, which he keeps tailored like a golf green.

Inside, Elma opens up the living room and kitchen

windows and turns on the fan in the dining room. Then she changes from her street clothes into a loose-fitting summer dress, cooks up the chicken, rice, and vegetables she has bought, and goes to the back bedroom. Almost as if a phonograph needle were caught in a groove, she lifts the top sheet and folds each side into tight hospital corners, then pulls up the blanket and finishes with a light cotton spread. Her work blends into her leisure, morning is like afternoon, afternoon like early evening. Willie Elma James has never heard of Sisyphus. She makes $13.50 a day. Somebody has to clean houses.

—I'm happy. There are some things I want that I don't have, but I'm saving. My job isn't tiring, and really I don't think about it. I think about my church and my grandchildren, and about going to the Holy Land one day.

THREE

The Baker

*And he humbled you and let you hunger
and fed you with manna, which you did
not know, nor did your fathers know;
that he might make you know that man
does not live by bread alone.*

—Deuteronomy 8:3

*O God! that bread should be so dear,
And flesh and blood so cheap!*

—Thomas Hood

—I'll never forget that first morning I went to work. It was 1928, and jobs were a little hard to come by. I got up early in the morning, got a paper, and saw down in the classified ads: *Boy wanted to work in bakery*. I wasn't working or didn't know exactly which way to go, so I answered the ad. I was the first one at the door, I suppose around five in the morning. It was a small place, called Mickey's Electric System Bakery because they had an electric oven, which was something new at the time, and electric doughnut fryers in the window. This was done in full view, the baker pouring the batter into an electric fryer and heating element. All they done was greased it a little bit, but it went over big. What made that first day funny was that while I was working in one end of the building, all of a sudden I saw my brother at the other end. I didn't even know he worked there! Then he saw me, and said, "What the heck *you* doing here?" It was a shock to both of us.

John Ragin has never chewed a piece of straw in his life, though he's always wanted to live on a farm. For him the vast wheat fields of burnished gold, with a single meandering road sewn on the quilted patches of country-side, where everything is calm and quiet except for a few slow-moving men and their machines, all chewing grain and spitting chaff against the powder-blue sky, and the good clean sweat of hard work at harvest time—these are idle pipe dreams. Ragin gets the flour, not the grain.

For the past forty of his fifty-seven years he has lived and worked in and around commercial bakeries, in the fetid congestion of an American city, where there are many people and streets and where the machinery is bolted to the floor.

—The bakery was my first job. I cleaned pans, swept up, and got sick off of whipped cream. Strawberry whipped cream shortcake. That stuff looked so delicious, and it was my first day being in the place. A colored man was cutting the trimmings off, and he was cutting a little wide 'cause I was eating 'em. Maybe he knew what was gonna happen. I just got too much of it.

I was there a month or six weeks when somebody said, "John, I know where you can get a couple more dollars each week." Well, John went there. It was in a picture-frame place and I stayed almost a year. There was quite a crowd of young people right about my own age, girls and fellows. I wasn't paid what you call a great amount, but still everybody enjoyed themselves.

I worked in a couple other places before the Depression struck the following year, and ended up in another bakery. I remember laughing at the foreman when he said, "The way things look, in a few weeks from now you might be working for eight dollars a week instead of twelve." I wasn't aware of what was going on in the financial world or how it would affect me. So I just laughed at him, not realizing what a Depression could be, and sure enough, things crashed. Before long, I *was* working for eight dollars a week.

My father died the year things went bad, in 1929. I was seventeen, but I always managed to find a job. I was never hungry during the Depression. The only time I was hungry was at the orphanage—so much so, in fact, that when I first got out, I overate for three days and got sick for three days. I just couldn't get used to the idea, all that food there out on the farm, compared to what I used to eat.

I kept jobs. I was never out of a job very long, 'cause I'd get up so early in the morning and if there was an ad in the paper, I was there. I must have worked at least fifty places and I'm not exaggerating. Mostly I just changed jobs from one bakery to the next. I just couldn't stay out of bakeries. Every time I went to work someplace else, something would happen. Mostly seasonal jobs, like working at a distillery—after the Christmas rush was over, I got laid off. Three or four summers I worked in a can-making factory, I was laid off. I worked at Martin's as an airplane mechanic. So every time I'd find myself back in a bakery, no matter what I'd done.

The Ragins' small duplex in southwest Baltimore sits among thousands of others, all brick, all with well-kept front lawns, all connected in the rear by concrete alleyways and tiny, fenced-in backyards. In the sweltering Baltimore summer, the citizens inhabiting Edmondson Village and its environs bake in their brick oven homes, in a hodgepodge of heavily traveled avenues, medium-sized shopping centers, and low-priced residential developments. There are trees—some large enough to give shade, but most too young and far between. This is the Southwest ghetto, lower-middle-class, white, one air-conditioner per home.

John Ragin no longer has to leave here in the middle of the night to work the early shift at the bakery. After forty years on and off the job, he doesn't punch in now until nine in the morning. He negotiates the way downtown in his five-year-old compact at the tail end of the rush hour. It takes him fifteen minutes. For some reason traffic patterns flow better in Baltimore than in other cities its size. Things started to get worse about ten years ago, but a new expressway system was squeezed through the political congestion to save the town the massive fiscal pain of building subways. Baltimore, the largest unknown city in the United States. Ragin has lived here all his life.

—I was born in Rosedale, just outside of the city, in 1912. My father had come from overseas, from Hungary, in 1904. The Baltimore fire was still smoking when he got off at Locust Point—they had ships coming in with immigrants at that time, right here to the Port of Baltimore. It was a funny thing that happened. He swore he was in the wrong place because of all these colored people at the pier. He thought he was in Africa.

My father was a very small man, much smaller than I am, and he didn't know what to do at first. Comical, in a way. He must have been forty-one years old, or right about that. In Hungary, he had been a rope- and harness-maker. That was his trade. Years ago all those ropes had to be twisted from hemp fibers by hand. He often told me how it ached the muscles in the arm, twisting that fiber and then twisting them again into a bigger rope. But as small as he was, he had such a grip in his hand that he could grab a big man by the flesh on his chest and twist him down to his knees. He came to this country because it was practically slavery working for anyone over there in Hungary, same as it was here years ago.

I never knew my mother, she died three years after I was born. I was in an orphanage until my father remarried seven years later. He couldn't take care of all of us. There were six at the time. I never did realize that my mother had died until I was around seven years old. Seeing other children's mothers there, I supposed I had a mother, too. When my father came out to visit me on Sundays or so, I'd always ask why.

At the orphanage it was brutal. The first one was St. Vincent's Infant Home. When I got to be about five and a half or six, I was transferred to St. Vincent's Male Orphanage. I had two older brothers there, but life was still rough. At that time orphanages could hardly get a hold of any money to feed the children. It seems incredible now, but I remember so many nights going to bed with just bread, syrup, and coffee for a meal, and maybe in the morning, if we were lucky, we got the same thing.

I remember hearing about how Babe Ruth came out to

the orphanage one time. I guess he was more or less sentimental 'bout those places, being he spent a few years in one. And he threw the ball around or beat a ball around there with some of the kids for a while. I couldn't say I remember him, being seven years old or so.

In an orphanage you'd generally find two or three kids who'd get together. We played out in the sand in the summertime and built castles and roadways. We really didn't have anything to do, there was no play equipment. You had to occupy yourself. There aren't too many children, I imagine, who, if they're by themselves, will take a little bit of mud and know what to do. I don't remember how many nuns there were to take care of us in the orphanage. I think there were about 110 boys altogether.

It never even crossed my mind to wonder why I was there. Quite often now I think I must have been awful stupid. I recall I was happy about hearing that my father had remarried, because this woman who became my stepmother came out sometimes with him to visit us and she was very nice to him. I found her to be a wonderful person. She got just about as much kick about having us, me and my brothers, as I had having her as a stepmother.

I got out of the orphanage when I was about nine and a half. My father didn't work after he remarried. He got a little place out in the country, two and a half acres. He had it all figured out. He didn't want to work, not for anyone else. Being so small, he found it difficult to get a job in his trade. And there was no more handwork. It was all done by machine. But he had this thing that you might call God's five acres, only it was two and a half. He had something to sell almost all year. Starting in early spring, he'd have lilacs for sale, and then plums, and so on.

I missed the first year of school when we moved out there. I didn't have much schooling when I was released out of the orphanage, although I think I was in the second grade. But the following year when I started again, I had to begin in first grade, which knocked me way back. Here I was ten years old and in the first grade. Fortunately, I was only in there a month or two. Some of the things came back to me and I was put in the second, but I was still behind, considering I was ten years old. It was also lucky that I was very small and puny.

In '25 we moved away from our little country place.

My older brothers, who were working, didn't like the idea of having to walk too far from back there, so they picked on my father until he said, "Well, we'll have to move, that's all." I know he didn't like it very much— he didn't want to go. I wasn't crazy about it myself— that being my first real home, I guess I had fallen in love with it too.

I went to a parochial school after that for seven years. I was born Catholic, but we weren't too religious. I don't ever remember my father or stepmother going to church, even on Christmas or Easter, although we celebrated the holidays at home. We weren't a very tight-knit family. Everybody seemed to go about their own way. It's hard for me to understand what a close family is. I didn't finish the seventh grade. From there, I went to work.

At nine o'clock in the morning, fifteen minutes after John Ragin leaves his house, he punches in at Rizer's Bakery. For most of its half-century existence, Rizer's, which makes a large portion of all the rye bread and submarine rolls consumed in Maryland, has operated out of a nondescript two-story processing plant in the heart of black Baltimore. Here there are no high-rise tenements with their window fronts scarred by rusting iron fire escapes; long rows of low, dark buildings, dilapidated brick, line the streets for dozens of square blocks. Black confronts white in the back alleys. The city has its share of racial hostility but it is still hard to stir up a riot, because the ghettos are too self-contained, the ethnic divisions too clear and accepted. North Baltimore has Catholics to the east, Jews to the west; lower- middle-class Poles and Italians live in the southeast and southwest sections, and most of the city's four hundred thousand black people populate the areas around Druid Hill Park and the harbor.

—I've worked here two years. Where I was before, at a fancy bakery I had to mix cookie batches all the time and each one had to be the same as the next. Certain cookies had to be creamed to a certain texture. There was more of a challenge, and always a pride when you were working with a quality material and putting out a quality product. I guess you don't even realize it, but it's there. You feel bad if and when you make a mistake, which I have done. I had to leave there because I wasn't making enough money. Here there's nothing to the work, except you have to turn it out. There's no great amount of thought to it.

My brother and I had our own small bakery for thirteen months and we were going along fine. It's just an entirely different feeling working for yourself than it is working for someone else. Maybe it's pride or you got the feeling you're independent. You don't even get tired, it seems. We were in a very small shop in a very poor neighborhood. We only paid twelve hundred dollars for the business, but even so we got hooked. The guy that sold it to us had had it all set up the day we were there for a lot of customers to come in, so it looked very busy. We heard about it some months later. But that was a common practice at the time, like salting a gold mine. That's the way they done it.

After punching in, Ragin goes to a corner room where he changes into gray-white coveralls and puts on an oversized white hard hat, similar to the yellow ones worn by construction workers. Then he passes through the bread-baking plant to the sweet shop.

Twenty-four hours a day, almost every day of the year, Rizer's Bakery turns out thousands upon thousands of rolls, loaves, and buns. The sweet shop where Ragin works is more a sideline than anything else; Rizer's found out a long time ago that the money is in the bread. A thousand submarine rolls—the dough mixed in vats on the rickety second floor, fed through a chute into a kneading machine on the level below, cut into lumps, passed along a conveyor which presses them into tube-shaped pieces, placed ten on a rack with cornmeal spread as a base, then stacked for baking—is a modest day's production.

The line workers, mostly black women, stand or sit on stools, chattering rapidly as their hands move in a syncopated rhythm, kneading dough and spreading cornmeal or picking a chewing gum wrapper out of the flour. The belts move continuously, and hour after hour the racks are loaded and stacked and the ovens are filled. It's hot and noisy. That is one reason why the rate of attrition for line workers is high, much higher than for the bakers, who are master tradesmen in the system. Most of the bakers are white. They are distinguished by their white hats, which often take years on the job to earn but are coveted as much as an executive's carpeting or title.

Ragin waves to one of his former buddies as he passes in front of the huge hearths filled with loaves of baking pumpernickel. Before he moved over into the sweet shop eighteen months ago, Ragin baked bread for Rizer's. At that time he found out for sure what he had always suspected—that there's a certain monotony to the science of commercial bread baking, although it is spiced with the uncertain headaches of mass production. A year ago Rizer's had to scrap a seventy-thousand dollar kneading machine because the hot dog rolls it made would not hinge right when sliced.

Ragin also found that bread baking is a seasonal business—more bread is eaten in winter than summer, more at the end of the week than during. Rizer's has been in the game long enough to play it well, and its managers are accustomed to the special tedium of balancing supply and demand the year round. They oversee an endless production of rolls (kaiser, blunt, horn, button, plait, split-top, onion, dinner, sesame, hamburger, submarine, foot-long, and finger rolls, English muffins, bagels, and bialeys) and loaves (light and dark rye, Italian, Vienna, French, frame, fish, pullman, raisin, whole wheat, and challah). The company has never competed for the soft white bread market; it has never camouflaged its products with words like "enriched" or "fortified with minimum daily requirements of riboflavin."

In the manager's offices the preoccupations are with the wholesale price of flour and the financial condition of the railroads transporting it, and with perpetually imminent union negotiations. The main reason that a loaf of rye is now thirty-eight cents—ten pennies more than a decade ago—is the rising cost of labor. Without the men to pay, each loaf would cost about a dime. John Ragin does not think about price-wage structures or how much flour costs by the hundredweight or the solvency of the nation's railroads.

—The rich have money and the main thing they worry about is a way to keep it. The poor average people don't expect to accumulate a whole lot, so they don't have a lot to lose. I would say they're less bored, too.

If management paid the employee a fair share, he wouldn't have to support all these unions who take hundreds of millions a year. I've often tried to figure out why management can't see that, but that's business. But the unions, instead of trying to get higher wages for the people and keeping this inflationary cycle going up, should try to knock prices down, even if salaries have to come down with them. I'd be satisfied to take less pay if I knew I had to pay less for things, because I'm gaining nothing this way. The costs come back to me. I don't know whether the workers realize that. Maybe the only reason I do is because I once had my own business. If I get a thousand dollars more, then GM wants so much more for each car, and so forth. I won't be ahead and I don't see where they will be either.

Ragin enters the sweet shop and nods a greeting to Salomon, his bun-making partner. It is a large, old room, where both the red-tiled floors and the people are covered with flour and pieces of dough. Even the salmon-colored walls are filmed with dirt and dough, over and through which have been scrawled anachronistic graffiti: *Lee Loves Jeanie, Ban the bomb*. Several windows in the plant, way up high, appear to have been punctured by bullets. All of them are covered with iron bars. The insulated ceiling holds about ten skylights and several banks of fluorescent lamps. Besides the large ovens in the center of the room and off to one side, the shop contains a number of pieces of semiautomated equipment, including a machine which pumps custard into cream puffs and a strange-looking crust flattener for French pastry.

Although there is plenty of room to walk around in the shop, it's very warm. Each worker seems to labor mostly by himself, but knows that another man's job waits on his own. The bun pans can't be loaded until they are greased. Ragin starts to work as soon as he comes in, nonchalant but serious. While others chatter, he listens and nods, responding more out of habit or politeness than from interest. He is small and stocky, about five feet six and one hundred forty-five pounds, with white, balding close-cropped hair. His eyes are a soft, clear blue, quiet but expressive. A small but uncamouflaged hearing aid is hooked onto his right ear. He wears white pants, a short-sleeved white shirt, and a large white apron. On his head is the oversized white construction hat. When Ragin worked in the bread plant, he used to bump his head, more often than he'd like to remember. There are eight other line workers, four men and four women, in the sweet shop. Five of them are black.

—A lot of college students pity the colored, want to do everything possible for them. I think they feel guilty themselves for having held the colored people down.

In a way, you can't blame the colored for being lazy. The white people brought them over here and took them away from a paradise. Same as the Indians—they had a paradise, and we came and destroyed it. In Africa, all they had to do was wait along some trail for game to come along, kill it with a club, arrow, or a snare. They didn't have to work. They all lived that way. The white man got a hold of them and slaved them. The whites showed them luxury here and there, a little TV, and they worked their poor brains out to get it. But they don't want to work really. Maybe a lot of white people don't want to work either, except for when they really have to. I and maybe every other average white family workingman doesn't know what to do but work in order to live. There are colored people who are good people; you can't hold them down. They're going to go ahead in spite of everything. And there are those who definitely will not work, don't intend to work, but they want to be paid. I've worked with lots of them, and I know that there are some who do not want to work and have no intentions of working.

All that could change with better education, but only if the colored can get their fair share. Separate but equal is fine, but that doesn't work for them. They never get their equal share—poor teachers, poorer buildings. We really don't have integration in the schools. They're practically all white and all black. They've tried it from first grade on, but as it goes up to the higher grades, it seems like they separate. We had many schools right around here, practically all white. The colored moved in and it was all black—the whites just left. You either have to shove the blacks down the whites' throats, or else they're going to have to take the lower step.

The racial situation concerns me a lot, because right

now I might have to move away from this place. You don't see any white people staying when the colored move in. They're breathing down our necks now. I feel it's my right not to want them in the neighborhood. It's not an economic pressure, it's a personal feeling. If I don't want to live with them, I don't have to. Maybe I'm a racist myself at heart, but I've never been able to see integrated housing. Maybe it's a bum argument, but it seems to me that God made black to stay black and white to stay white.

The colored naturally wants everything the white man's got. White moves out ten more miles, the colored man wants that. Eventually he'll get there. I asked one colored man why is it he doesn't like the law. He came right out and says the law is the white man's law. I said, "Yeah, but put there to protect the colored man, too." It's not unusual for a colored man to lay right down on the pavement. Only way to remove him is to put him under arrest, take him away in the wagon. But when they go to take that man away, you'll have a whole bunch of colored people hollering at the policeman. I've seen a group of colored people getting after a policeman, hitting him, scratching, biting him, shouting insults. They'll do anything. The officer had the colored man's hand in the back and held him by the wrist and belt so he couldn't move. It's a common occurrence in the city for a policeman, if he doesn't have a buddy with him, to let a misdemeanor go by.

The colored are linked through hatred more than anything else. He'll git that whitey. The hatred is actually taught to the children right in the family. Because the older colored man, even though he would smile, wait on you and all, be your friend, he still hated your guts down to the last drop of blood.

I have no hatred for them, but I know they have a hatred for me. I wouldn't restrict their rights in any way. I pity them, being robbed and cheated in their food stores. I say give the colored a good place to live, but don't give them money and say "Don't work." Give 'em a good house and a good chance, but don't keep giving them money. I put the majority of the colored people as being the way I was as a teen-ager. I didn't realize what education could do, and they don't realize what it can do. They don't realize they've hit a dead end as soon as they stop their education. I didn't realize it.

The colored man is supposed to be a religious person, but I don't know if all their religion is true or a sham. There's a black man at the shop who's a Catholic, I found out. We have a little draw of togetherness because of that, I guess, and we get along very well. But I don't see religion helping us out of our present troubles. Maybe one of those supersaints of ancient history would know, but we don't have it nowadays. I've had mixed feelings about Martin Luther King. I get suspicious whenever I hear or read of a leader going to Russia and he was there more than once, visiting. I remember that Eleanor Roosevelt was in Russia a few times. In '45 when her husband went over to the Yalta meetings, she's supposed to have told him what to say. That's true. She was the woman behind the man. And look what we've run into with Russia since then. It all looks so fishy.

Ragin picks up a big lump of dough and plops it onto a big table. Salomon is on the other side. Their sweet shop routine varies little from day to day: at 9:30 they begin to manufacture seventy dozen cinnamon buns, assisted by an old bun-cutting machine—a simple conveyer belt passing under a guillotinelike slicer—and a black woman who loads and carries baking pans. Ragin and Salomon take large hunks of raw dough from a refrigerator, knead it at the end of the long table, then feed it through a wringer at the beginning of the belt. Flattened, the puttylike sheet is covered with flour, stretched, spread with a mixture of grease, brown sugar, and cinnamon, rolled, cut by the guillotine into two-ounce pieces, and finally lined up on large cooking pans. Ragin and Salomon repeat the procedure for the next ninety minutes.

At eleven o'clock, they shift to jelly buns, which are just as simple but less tedious. Ragin arranges equal gobs of dough into rows and puts them on large metal pans. With his left thumb he indents their middles, one by one, while his right hand squeezes bright-colored fillings—cherry-red, blackberry-blue, pineapple-yellow—into the depressions. On the other side of the table Salomon mirrors the same process. By noon they are ready to roll twenty dozen jelly buns, an average day's production, into the oven.

Ragin pauses to chat with two students who are touring the plant today. He sometimes misses the old days, the small satisfactions that came with having his own bake shop, talking with customers, getting compliments on a cake, giving free cookies to the children. The monotony of making dozens of buns bothered him less when he could see the little kids whose eyes lit up at the sight of custard doughnuts and fancy cupcakes. John Ragin's own blue eyes sparkle as he looks at the two students, who are fascinated by the multicolored jelly buns and the huge ovens.

Even the executives at Rizer's seldom meet their customers. The truck drivers double as salesmen, and they have most of the contact with the small-store owners, army supply clerks, school nutritionists, supermarket managers, and restaurateurs who buy rye bread in bulk and submarine rolls by the hundreds.

—There's nothing to the work to amount to anything, except that you have to turn it out. There's not a great amount of thought involved. You're liable to think about fishing, crabbing, anything. It's so simple, rolling a piece of dough up, putting it on a belt, getting it the proper size. Then the machine cuts it, it goes to the other end, the girls put it on a pan. I don't mind the work, it doesn't mean much to me. I wouldn't say it's any great challenge.

Spencer, the man in charge of the sweet-shop ovens, comes over to pull away the big wheeled tables upon which rest the pans of prepared buns. Ragin continues to reminisce with himself, as he watches the touring students. He remembers the late 1920's when he had to stay in his shop all day and night, when he baked a solid twelve to fourteen hours daily. Normal work hours didn't come about until there was a general increase in automated baking equipment. Ragin wasn't born into baking like some of his coworkers, but toiling in and out of odd jobs he always came back to it. Maybe he'd have done some things differently if he had had the chance.

—I didn't have anyone push me to stay in school. My father never mentioned a word, never asked why don't you go to school. Many folks were truly ignorant then as far as education goes. The idea was to get out and make money, there was nothing else. That's why I'm so different about my own children, why I tell them they have to go to school. Here's my boy twenty years old and I don't even care if he finds a job this summer or not. He can learn to relax, but he's got to get an education. I'll pay for it.

Ragin moves away from the warm, tight air of the sweet shop into the cold, quiet refrigeration room, cluttered with large tins of fillings. He comes in here several times a day, brief respites from the noise of the rollers and the heat of the ovens, to get the containers he'll need of premixed creams and jellies.

On the hot days, Rizer's linemen find more opportunities to soak up some of the refrigeration room's comfort and color. Ragin usually limits his trips to those times when he needs the jellies for his jelly buns. The noise doesn't bother him, he can turn down his hearing aid. And he does not really mind the heat. The others in fact have also become accustomed to it, although for eight hours every day the immense ovens keep them bathed in perspiration. Subconsciously they learn to think about other things.

—I lost my hearing while working at Martin's, around these jet engines. There were about forty of them testing all over the place. You don't feel a thing. All you hear is the deafening noise. It gets so that you don't even hear that—you don't think about it. There's no pain involved in loss of hearing, it's just something that catches up to you. It caught up to me a couple of years after I was out of there. I'd keep asking my family, "What'd you say? What'd you say? Turn the TV up a little louder," and it's knocking everybody's ears out.

At half past twelve, Ragin seeks out a clear spot on one of the half-dozen Rizer's loading platforms, spreads a piece of newspaper on the stoop, and sits down, facing the noisy black congestion of Pennsylvania Avenue, to eat his lunch. He unwraps a brown paper bag and takes out half a sandwich, cold cuts packed solidly into one of Rizer's submarine rolls. Besides donating large amounts of surplus bread to various school cafeterias in the Baltimore area, the bakery gives free rolls to its employees.

He eats with quiet gusto, sipping coffee and taking long contemplative bites from the sandwich. He picks crumbs from his lap and puts them into his mouth with a deliberateness that suggests a childhood of hunger more than a penchant for neatness. He is not demonstrative, but for a man with so many strong and reflective attitudes, he has a striking mellowness to his voice.

—All the people in my neighborhood are little wage earners, people just like me. They all make between five thousand and ten thousand dollars a year.

The way to get ahead is to do the right thing with the right boss. At my age, I might not jump at a big promotion, but I never was afraid of responsibility. If new jobs were offered to me, I was never afraid to take a hold of them. I don't resent the boss.

But the middle and little man has always been manipulated, while the big man has been taken care of. That oil depletion allowance is downright cheating the taxpayers. It's got to be corruption; that's the only way I can see it. Who's getting the payoff? The generals and admirals come out of service after so many years and go into these big outfits. They know everybody in Washington, all the lobbyists. I don't like it and I think I'm entitled to that benefit just as much as they are, but that's the way government is. Through history, all the way back to Caesar's time, that's the way it's been. Maybe I'd be the same way if I had money, I don't know. I hope I wouldn't, but it seems like anybody who has ever gotten up there has done the same thing, regardless of who he is.

No matter what we do, power will be abused and money will be stolen and misused. Medicare is good for old folks, but I don't believe a lot of people who need the care are getting it. There are a lot of people who don't need it or who can afford to pay. As far as I'm concerned, though, the program is basically good. I can't save enough for my old age, by the time I pay for my house, car, phone, television, a few luxuries. So it is a good program for me.

Inflation hasn't hit me hard because when I bought my house fifteen years ago, I paid a little less than nine thousand dollars. I assume it would cost in the neighborhood of twelve thousand dollars today. I still have a long way to go on the mortgage, but what is really helping us is a

4½ percent GI approved FHA mortgage. That is a big help, compared to 7½ or 9½ percent.

Food is our biggest expense item, about fifty-five or sixty dollars a week. Take oatmeal. I've eaten it ever since I can remember. That's an extremely cheap cereal, and it gripes me to pay the price they charge now. The government makes deals with the farmers not to grow this, not to grow that, not to plow their ground. I have an uncle in West Virginia who gets fifty thousand dollars not to touch his place. And the prices go up.

I make about $140 to $144 in an average week in the summertime, $107 or $108 clear. In the wintertime, I'll go way above that—about $130 clear. Everything over forty hours is time and a half. I could have more overtime, but seven hours a day in the summertime suits me fine. In the wintertime, I'll gladly work overtime. When I first started out I was making seven and eight dollars a week.

I get free bread. It's not expensive to the bakery to give it away. I don't want to be a hog—I try to take two or three submarines or a few small loaves of rye. Bread is laying all over the place. It's an extremely cheap product to manufacture, the way they get flour in bulk form. If they could make it day and night and there would be a demand, they could sell every loaf of bread they make for ten cents a pound and still make a lot of money.

After food, insurance is my next greatest expense. Car insurance alone this year cost me $266, and just my son and I drive. But more often than not, we manage to stay ahead of our bills. We use credit, but never a credit card. I don't want one around—I'm afraid of losing them or having them stolen.

I don't like the idea, but I can see the trend coming to socialism, one step at a time. Prior to 1920, no poor man and very few middle men paid tax. The rich man didn't pay much, but he paid all of it. That's why the soldier got nineteen dollars a month. As soon as Mr. Public had to start paying the tax, everything kept mushrooming— salaries, equipment, everything. There is no way to go back. Even the average person like myself, I work three or four months for Uncle Sam. I don't mind that as long as I can still get by on what I make. I don't care for yachts or boats.

Ragin crumples his brown paper bag into a ball, puts it in the empty coffee cup, tosses the cup into a big garbage can by the loading platform, and returns to the sweet shop. In the afternoon, his routine changes from mass production of cinnamon and jelly buns to French pastries—napoleons, éclairs, cream puffs. Rizer's owns a variety of special machines to roll and flatten the flaky dough and fill the shaped crusts with premixed creams. The fillings themselves are not made in the sweet shop, as they are in the patisseries of Holland, France, and Switzerland. Rizer's adds water to huge cans of ready-made powdered mixture. Instant *voilà*.

For the cream puffs, the only hand labor involves baking the delicate crusty half-ball forms. By 2:30 Ragin has made twenty dozen of them ready for filling. Another line worker then takes the empty puffs, a trayful at a time, to a small machine in the corner of the sweet shop. He pours a bucketful of prefabricated cream into a trough toward the rear of the filling device. Tawny-yellow and almost smooth, the mixture is stirred automatically to remove any remaining lumps. Thin tubes run from the trough to small horizontal funnels pointing straight out from the front of the machine. Ragin takes the puffs, one in each hand, perforates each by punching them onto the funnel tips, then with his foot depresses a lever which causes a fixed amount of cream to be pumped into each puff. The whole process takes about a second and a half. After a trayful of puffs is filled, Salomon dusts them with powdered sugar and places them carefully in boxes of six.

Ragin fills éclairs by the same process, then covers them with chocolate icing. Each time he works on French pastries, he remembers his last job and the pride he took in his work. The management at Rizer's wants to make baked goods of good quality, but when one or two line workers manufacture such great amounts, as do Ragin and Salomon every day of the week except Saturday, the monotony of their labor tends to dull their craftsmanship and its satisfactions.

By now Ragin's overalls are covered with chocolate and blackberry stains, his hands white with powdered sugar. The most complicated baking done by Rizer's involves turning out hundreds of napoleons with some semblance of traditional delicateness. Specially prepared dough, a batch of which Ragin makes up three mornings a week, has to be flattened and reflattened many times over to insure the proper flakiness. Large white sheets, each between twenty and twenty-one pounds, pass through an expensive imported flattener. Then they are stretched, rolled with rolling pins, folded, and fed once again through the machine. The device saves time and trouble. Ragin remembers the old days when he had to roll and flatten the dough by hand, and he's thankful now to do without the manual labor.

Ragin hates to work on Sunday, as do most of his friends in the sweet shop. He does not belong to a union *(you have to give part of your soul)* although Rizer's employs both union and nonunion labor. The majority of the bakers belong, while most of the truck drivers, salesmen, and line workers do not. The company has never been struck because management works hard at negotiation. Costs are inevitably passed to the consumer, but Rizer's doesn't try to convince its younger union members, who want the money, that the costs will be passed back to them. Older workers are more concerned about fringe benefits, social security, shop conditions. But Ragin remembers when he was young, and he understands.

—I was drafted on June 6th, 1942—my thirtieth birthday. My brother and I had three- or four-month deferments. Then the next time they sent us a notice, we had to go or else. We weren't really looking forward to it, but we didn't try anything extreme to stay out. They gave us time to straighten out our business, to get rid of it before they would call us. We went in the same day things were settled, to Camp Meade. Then I was sent down to Fort Knox.

I went through eight weeks' basic training, and I was in the kitchen one evening after a meal, talking to the sergeant about doing something for him, and I noticed he didn't have any desserts, so I offered to make some. He said, "My God, I've been looking for somebody." He never expected someone to come up and volunteer to do something like that. So I made him a bunch of pies. He had a whole pile of cherries there, number 10 cans, and I made about forty or fifty pies. The praise he got the next day! He grabbed me by the collar and pulled me right in there. That was it. I had no more worries. I didn't have to go out in the field or anything. I was in for four years and one day.

I went overseas in September, 1943, first to Casablanca. At the place where we were, right up the hill was a prisoner camp, and all we could hear was these prisoners counting all day, I guess for punishment or something. Closest I was to the front line was in Italy. In fact, it was so close we were getting free cigarettes, the ration that you're supposed to get for a couple of weeks. We could hear the shelling and shooting quite often. I spent almost thirty-three months in Italy.

I liked it. Well, naturally, since I met my wife there. I was working in a bakery in Naples. We used to bake a lot of bread for all the surrounding bases and camps, and she passed by with a girl friend quite often. Another soldier, he was an Italian by birth, talked to them. I couldn't understand the first word except *bon giorno*, good morning. But it wasn't long before I was trying to communicate with this one girl, and soon we *were* communicating. I was going on thirty-three and she was twenty-six when we got married. Then we came back to Baltimore.

I had a very good setup over there and I could have stayed, but of course all I wanted to do was come home. I had been offered apartments almost rent-free, but I wanted out. That's all. My brother and I had talked about going back in business but there was too much difference already in the two of us. He was still single, had no intentions of getting married, and I was happily married. We could see there would be complications. And my wife as much as said she would not care to go into any kind of a business. All she wanted to do was raise a family.

I still think that if the younger generation studies the way they should be doing, they will see that our form of government is about the best there's ever been. Students are defecting now because they don't want to face their responsibilities. But it's not their fault completely. Nixon should have declared some kind of emergency, to keep the Russians from taking one step after another. That's all they're doing, taking two steps forward and one back. They're always gaining a step on us.

This war is so different, it bothers me. The young people feel that the Vietnam War's immoral because they read and see on television that all of the Vietnamese are a bunch of grafters. I believe that, too. The only thing they're interested in is our money, and the only thing we want is to hold the Russians from taking another step. Congress should have declared war. If they did, it would have changed a lot of these young people. It would have rallied them. So in a way the young people are justified.

Nixon isn't strong, but he's smart. He knows how to pick who he needs. But there's something about the man that does strike me as being strong. I can't pin it down. Maybe it's that he won't assert himself on so many cases—good rule for a good politician.

I've often thought that Agnew could be President, but how honest is any man when it comes to power, or to the almighty dollar? Agnew appeals to me, of course, and to a lot of my friends. I think he's on the road to something. The Golden Greek—did you ever hear of a case where a man rises to power so fast? He brought a few things to light about the liberal newspapers. Even a few editors admitted they quiet certain things down and play certain things up. He's on the right line for law and order, too. At a meeting with a colored group here in 1968, he told them they're responsible for the King riots—they knew what was happening and they condoned it. He said later that what he did was probably political suicide, but he told the people right to their faces. This is what makes him appeal to me. If he keeps hitting the nail on the head the way he's doing now, I think he'll go someplace. If he doesn't swing over to the big money, the little man is going to do something about putting him in power. I'm mostly Democrat, but I'll switch if I like, if I think the other party's man is going to be better.

When Ragin goes home, punching out at 4:30 in the afternoon, the second bread shift has already been on the job for half an hour. Today he makes the front line of the evening rush-hour traffic, so it takes him but twenty minutes to reach his duplex and the family. They run to greet him, all except Mary Lynn and Susan who are away at college. Maria has been cooking all afternoon. She smiles when her husband pecks her on the cheek. Dom—beardless as a birthday present to his mother—asks for the car. Ragin says okay.

Jeannette, a bright little girl of about eleven, ushers in her two new stepsisters. They give John bashful hugs. The Ragins took possession of their foster children a year ago (*Christmas presents,* says Ragin) and have spent the time since warming the two kids up. Baltimore County Welfare helps pay for their care and feeding.

—I like fooling around in the garden after work, in the little farm I have outside. Sometimes first thing when I get home I'll look around for a new *Life* magazine or *Reader's Digest.* I love bowling, used to bowl a lot before getting married. But nowadays it's a luxury to bowl. A man has to realize that certain things stop when he gets married. Can't keep on bowling and going to the bars and bring up a family, too. I enjoy watching soccer and ice hockey, and sometimes I'll watch television. When I was in Italy, I saw a few soccer games. It intrigues me in a way why soccer should be such a great sport all over the world and such a flop here.

I get a week's vacation and if I could I'd love to have a few days in Ocean City. But I hate the traffic and driving. That trip still takes two and a half hours, driving sanely. I'd rather have somebody else do the driving. I think I'd also like to go to Alaska, if I had the chance. I've thought of it since I was a kid.

In spring and summer, when it's light long after John Ragin returns home, he spends the time before and after supper in the world of his garden. Today the dog barks a greeting. In a few square feet, sandwiched between the adjacent fences of his neighbors and around the kids' portable swimming pool, are the pole beans, squash, two kinds of tomatoes, white grapes for the wine, basil for the spaghetti. Ragin wishes he had a few acres someplace— an idle, pleasant thought which he dreams often. He knows there's little chance for escape from his postage-stamp paradise. The neighbors' gardens aren't as elaborate, but to each side the houses are alike. According to Mrs. Ragin, you can tell how much money people around here make, within a few thousand dollars, from which street they live on. She knows what the neighbors bring in each year.

Tucked into a corner of the backyard is a large metal

stagecoach frame, painted white, which Ragin salvaged from his father's farm almost a half century ago. A bit of nostalgia that seems a bit out of place, but Ragin remembers how his father was his own boss, how he always had something to sell the year round to keep the family going—chickens, whiskey, plums.

Things have changed. Ragin counts his blessings.

—Religion plays a part, and maybe a good part, but I wouldn't say it's dominant in my life now. When I was younger, it did. You hit a certain age, you move away from the church. You get to the point where you ask, "What is all this malarkey they've been handing us? Why didn't they tell us the truth in the first place?" I didn't go to high school or college, but I read enough to give me the same feelings that college kids have. Later in life you come to believe that there is a God almighty, that there's someone pulling the strings. I see there's too much good, even though there's a lot of bad, for things just to be running loose by themselves. Somebody's putting everything together. It seems preordained. Are you fated to die tomorrow? There are cases where a person was pulled out of the water from drowning, then the next season he fell in the water and drowned, this time for good. It's a funny thing. God Almighty looks favorably upon some people, more so than others. Whether these people are doing something for God, I don't know.

Ragin ponders as he checks his garden, then looks up at the sky. He gazes past the telephone poles and wires and watches the sun setting through the city's trees, before he goes inside to supper, television, and the children.

FOUR

The Coal Miner

*At last all the seams were gradually filled,
and the cuttings were in movement at every
level and at the end of every passage. The
devouring shaft had swallowed its daily
ration of men; nearly seven hundred hands,
who were hot at work in this giant anthill,
everywhere making holes in the earth, drilling
it like an old worm-eaten piece of wood.
And in the middle of the heavy silence and
crushing weight of the strata one could hear,
by placing one's ear to the rock, the
movement of these human insects at work,
from the flight of the cable which moved the
cage up and down, to the biting of the tools
cutting out the coal at the end of the stalls...*

—*Emile Zola*

The company lot is a flat red expanse set among hills that fall away to vast distances, and no one is within earshot of Elmer Tiso as he makes his way past the last row of automobiles. Far across the rutted mud several stragglers from the cat-eye shift pass through the portals of Middleton Fuel Number 11. They are for a moment silhouetted through the dimness of the sodden early morning, against the glowing open passageway behind them. Two dark figures separate from the group to be received by separate cars still waiting in the half-filled parking lot. Moving singly and in pairs, a few more men appear at the entrance. One or two are barely out of their teens, yet from a distance, at small scale, their carriage and the weariness of their gait belie their youth. Though he is the senior at Number 11 and knows most of the night shift, Tiso would be unable to distinguish among them from his vantage point in the grayness.

— To Tiso, who has drilled, hauled, blasted, and wet down bituminous coal for more than thirty years, they are all youngsters. His face could have been carved from the hills: weathered but firm, strong wrinkles sharing their predominance with a few eroding teeth. His hair is still mostly brown, matted thinly atop a narrow forehead, unruffled by the freshening air, as if he had just removed a close-fitting cap. He is a middle-sized man. There is little to suggest the long years he has spent at hard and hazardous labor, save his stooped back and the hollow in his chest, and the slight limp caused years ago by a falling timber which might just as easily have crushed his skull or staved in his breastbone.

His hands, gnarled like the knotted bark of a loblolly pine, hardened and calloused, show a blackness almost hammered in. It takes more than soap or sandpaper to clean and soften a miner's hands. The only other mark of Tiso's trade is not a physical one: he shares his fellows' pride in the strenuousness of their work and—this almost perversely—in the unremitting threat of injury and death under which they labor.

— —I was born in 1918, in Cleveland. There was a total of six of us kids in the family, and I was the second eldest. My father was an immigrant from Europe, what they call a Slav—Czechs, Polacks, Slovacks, I don't know the different countries in there. They can only speak one tongue, but they can understand six or seven dialects.

At the time I was born, my dad worked in a plant out in Cleveland, some sort of a steel plant. In '22 he come to West Virginia. I vaguely remember coming in an old-time truck, to a place down here called Crown. He went in a coal mine right along this river. But it wasn't long before he was run out of the coal mines through union activities, and we went to Buffalo, New York. He worked in a company that produced musical instruments and I started school there. Then in 1927 or '28 we come back to West Virginia.

— I remember when we came back to this coal mining outfit down here. At first we rented a four-room house from the company in the company town. It was pretty rough; outside toilets, no water, no electric in the house. We used kerosene lamps. After a while, we moved to Fairmont, into a fairly big house. I remember going to the Thomas E. Miller Elementary School. My dad quit the mines again in 1929 or 1930 and went to work driving trucks. He had this Morgantown run, a Fairmont run, and a Clarksburg run, delivering to what they called at that time the Great Atlantic-Pacific Tea Company stores. He stayed with them three years and lost out again, didn't work for two years. We lived up here in an apartment house in Fairmont.

In 1933, we moved right back down to where I am at today, into a home which had about two acres of land and a garden spot. My dad went back to work and started at Eastern Fuel in 1933. We were a pretty close family back in the '30's when we were together. If we wanted to play baseball or football, or any kind of ball, we had to go out there in the cow pasture, or we went swimming in some creek. And that was it. That was our recreation, that or a ten-cent or nickel movie. Things were rough during the Depression, but we didn't exactly go hungry because my dad always tried to hustle enough—even picking up odd jobs—to go ahead and make ends meet. We didn't have all that we wanted, but we still got by with it. A school lunch? If you had seven pennies, you could go ahead and buy milk all week for them seven pennies, little half-pints of chocolate milk. Our neighbors were hanging in there, too. They were mostly miners, what they call the hand loaders.

In 1935, I started working at the Eastern Fuel and Coal Corporation here in Morgantown. I was seventeen when they took me in, had approximately two years of high school. I liked school but I guess I had the mines in my blood for a long time. Couldn't get away from the coal detail. That was my first job and I worked for that one company to sometime in 1942, approximately eight years. They had started to hire young people at that time. They had this National Recovery Act that the Congress enacted around '35 and things were picking up a little bit. Then they put in the Wagner Labor Act, and done away with company police, told the companies to behave. Roosevelt said you let the men reorganize to have their own unions. The union meant a great deal to me.

I traveled to work with my daddy in his car. It was me and him and we had one Negro with us all the time. We had worked with many a Negro for Eastern Fuel at Grant Town in the '30's. I myself worked side by side with them. As a matter of fact, even the company would sometimes give us a Negro to work with. There was no dispute or rivalry in the work, but they lived apart in the section called Black Bottom. Up here in Appalachia the whites are a lot different from the people who live down in the southern part of the state. In their actions in handling different things about strikes and stuff like that, I think the southern part of the state is much more vicious. They'll have more violence down there. If we ever had a racial problem, it wasn't in northern West Virginia, it was down in Charleston. This part of West Virginia is awful close to Pennsylvania and Ohio, and I actually believe people are more civilized up here.

That first day at work, the men I was with told my daddy they'd watch me, and we went back approximately three miles and started loading coal with picks and shovels. We were lined up at that time where one mine foreman had maybe 100 to 150 men. The men weren't too rough with me. People were just trying to make out. I worked the three to eleven shift for about five years. I went on different shifts. When I went on what they generally called the swing shift or cat-eye shift, I had three different starting times. Some nights I would start at ten thirty, some nights at eleven, and sometimes at twelve. Then if we had to do extra work, they would call us out at two in the morning and we'd work until ten the next day. The company set up the shifts and we had to abide by what they told us. If it was midnight, we went from midnight until seven in the morning. It didn't matter that they wanted to run the mines their way. It was just a job to me; just something common. I don't know about the other men, but it never really affected me. When I was in the coal mine, I never tried to find another job. I don't know why. I just didn't.

On the ridge behind them, denuded trees are dimly visible in the outline against the sky. At intervals along the terraced hillside of Number 11 sit shuttle cars, trapezoidal bins which will be freshly filled after a night's cutting. Although there is enough daylight now for working, bluish floodlights still burn on towers and cranes at the heights. Tiso has just driven around the far side of Mountains 12 and 11, by the huge winches and breakers which move and crush the coal, now squatting in abstract-shaped masses against the heightening sky. Close at hand such machinery suggests unbounded strength or great force overcome, yet at this distance their awesomeness is lost and their noise muffled. As he moves closer, the roar of the nearest breaker grows deafening, as belts and lifts tumble fresh troughloads of bitumen into its maw.

Tiso will punch in early this morning. He has come through the hills westward from the outskirts of Morgantown, where he has owned a home for the past thirty-eight years. Like many West Virginians he takes pleasure in the countryside, but at this ungodly hour of the morning, his windows up against the chill, he took in only what was straight ahead. Long ago he stopped thinking of the monotony of this small trip, made thousands of times, five or six times a week for fifty weeks, every year for the past several decades.

It is late in the fall now, and already the low grass is tinged with rime. Far below the road, small farms and houses are cradled in bare rolling valleys.

Tiso's neighborhood is not rural. Most of the Middleton work force lives here or in developments like it, in the compact bungalows which were a hallmark of the postwar employment boom in suburban and semirural America. Not quite shantytown, but not far from it. Typically the houses are shingled and gabled, with concrete stoops and heaters fed from outdoor fuel tanks. Their design is purely utilitarian; no attempt is made to hide those parts which give heat and light. Pipes and drains show baldly in front, basement masonry is unadorned. Still, Tiso's home—small and phoneless, with a lot of land around—provides comfort for him and his wife and their twenty-year-old son. It is the castle of a union man, a manual laborer who saved his money, guarded his benefits, and educated his children, sometimes through college. Today's miners don't live in the rickety wooden shacks on stilts of the prewar company coal towns, or the dismal frame houses, each with its garden plot, that row on row formed the vast colliery developments of a half century back. Automation has increased the wealth of the mining population while reducing its size. The fruits that unionism has yielded since John L. Lewis busted into Appalachia in the early '30's make the industry look good, but they have little to stem the manpower reductions, which daily add to the growing numbers of jobless poor in West Virginia and its bordering states.

Soon Tiso will pass from the wide expanse of the rolling hill country to the darkness below, where black walls absorb light and seem to swallow space as well. As he reaches the main entrance of the mine, he sees two men with whom he'll be working: Shorty Robinson, his partner for the past several days in Number 8 shaft, and Joe Kozak. Today Kozak will be cutting with their crew. Tiso greets them in the causeway off the equipment shack that serves as gathering place and nerve center for the scattered operations of mine Number 11. Here the shafts plummet as much as four hundred feet into the depth of the mountain, then spread like tentacles rayed from a thick black core. The three punch in and walk to the newly installed locker room beyond, where the hum of voices intensifies. The miners file steadily past the partitioned check-in point and swarm along the long oak benches. The three early arrivals are soon cramped for space, but it is a feeling to which they are quite accustomed.

Two men break off a quiet conversation and sidle along the bench to their places before the lockers to the left of Tiso. He nods a greeting. With studied deliberation bordering on ritual, they climb into sturdy work clothes, their blunted fingers carefully tightening trouser straps and bootlaces. On the high wall above Tiso's locker, there's a sign—*Safety Is No Accident*—barely visible through the dirt. But the men assume the danger to the point of almost welcoming the risk. It is written into the union contract that any coal extracted in the process of rescuing a miner buried under a slide must be credited to him. They still tell the story of the veteran trapped in a crosscut; when the rescue team finally reached him, he asked that one last car be loaded in his favor before he climbed out.

Tiso makes a point of keeping his rubber-soled boots in good repair, for they will protect him from the mud and slime around the cable car tracks, and they will insulate him should he accidentally step on one of the high-voltage feed lines running to the machine cables. He is as careful of his boots now as he was fifteen years ago, on the day after he saw a crew partner stumble and die, writhing across a feeder half-obscured by the sludge of a tunnel floor.

—I wasn't afraid or excited the first time I went down into the mine. I thought that if we would have some disaster I wouldn't be there. We were under very good supervision. Before the men entered any shaft, the man making a four-hour run in there would come out and say this section of the mine is okay to work, no gas found, things are okay. Now this had to be okayed on a bulletin board, because the men would not go in unless it was. The company themselves didn't want you taking chances; they wanted you to be right with it. Your post, your timbering standards should always be right. If it isn't right, they call it to your attention and you might get disciplined for it. There were some men maimed or hurt in those days, but no mine disasters where I was.

In November of 1941 I married a neighbor girl I'd known since we were kids. I was already a coal miner six years before I married her. In all my twenty-five years underground, she has never asked what it was all about. She would never send me to work. If I would take a day off, she would not say go to work. I asked her one time later, why she didn't ask me to go to work, and she said, "Well, if I'd sent you down there to work and you had happened to get butchered up or killed, I wouldn't forgive myself."

Once I was laid off by the Christopher Company, and in the span of a week and a half I had two other jobs. First I went to the Mountaineer Coal Company. I worked three days and I quit 'em—didn't get the proper safety. What I was doing was wrong and I did not want to get burnt. They took me down into the mines and when I got down into the faces in the working places, they said, "Your machine is here, we want these places cut." When I went to cut with this mobile unit machine, I was cutting overhead and come to find out the boss said don't use no water. I asked him, "What do you mean, don't use no water?" He said, "My tipple won't take care of it" Actually, this was bad. Unless you used the water or spray system to wet down the dust and suspension, you couldn't see what you were doing. They claimed the tipple wouldn't be able to handle the wet coal. The tipple is what they run the coal over off the conveyor belts into the railroad cars, in different grades: dust, B coal, A coal. Well, I didn't get excited. I told my buddy, "This is my third day here and I quit. This is it." I told my boss, "I won't be back," and he asked me why. I said, "I'm not going to tell you. You ought to know." I mined coal for fifteen years, but I was a new man with them and I didn't want to get into more detail with them about their system.

The same day that I quit, I got another job with the Number 11 and 12 Jameson Company. That same morning I quit after working the midnight shift, I came back up, took a bath, went right down the road, and the man said, "Elmer, come out this afternoon."

Each company had their own setup for physical examinations. When you first get hired in, you have to take a pretty rough physical exam. They test your high blood pressure, your eyes, your general health, and all this. They take it all into consideration, and it keeps down the injuries.

In 1956, I was injured in a mining accident, got fouled by a 170-ton machine. It caught me by the right foot and it come near cutting my ankle off. I was up there in the hospital for twenty-two days and off work for four months. The second time I was injured, at the South Union Company, it happened practically the same way on the same leg and I was off nine months. The company I worked for was very good to me. Of course, we had difficulties in different cases, but this wasn't it. They told me that I wasn't even taken off the payroll.

When somebody gets hurt, they call out, "Stop everything on that main line. We've got a man hurt." We clear the railroad in the mine right away, the men themselves do it. All our self-rescue squads are actual miners. They are mining coal as union men, but they are backed up by the company to be trained in self-rescue. They've got several teams in this district that's all good. They're trained by the State of West Virginia and the company both.

A first-aid team would give you the seven fundamentals —or the five or six, whatever they got today in first aid— like artificial respiration, control of bleeding, control of burns, proper transportation of a person, what to do if a person's in shock. At the Jameson Company, we had a very fine team which the company sponsored and this company actually put the money up for uniforms. It costed a lot of money for the shoes and the white uniforms. These people would go to the International Contests, out there in Indianapolis, where they all meet and see who would be the champs. We come in second best one year. I wasn't on the team, but I was with the people who were. The company threw a picnic right down there at Greensburg, Pennsylvania. This Jameson Coal Company told all their employees to come down to the city of Greensburg: "We'll turn the whole block over to you." They gave you all the ham you could eat, all the beer you could drink, chicken, whatever you wanted to eat.

Fifteen minutes have passed now since Tiso's arrival. He and Shorty try their helmet lamps as they rise from the benches, girded for a day's work, and move to the elevator at the end of a concrete hallway. Kozak follows at a distance, inspecting the contents of his lunch pail. With the rest of the crew they gather for a briefing by Beck, the foreman. A dozen listen for instructions. Below it would be impossible to assemble even so small a group in many of the narrow passageways, but here, too, conditions are less than ideal. Men pass noisily to and fro, a generator drones steadily nearby, and already the radio in the partitioned office crackles with messages from down under. Beck shouts instructions: Get up a better roof in Number 7 . . . fifty loads today . . . Freeland and Cowell stay on the crawlers . . . watch the face, damn it. Okay, let's go.

Tiso and Shorty will work together again today. Kozak will be blasting on the other side, in Number 8, and already he has moved to the rear of the main shaft elevator behind Freeland and Cowell. As is his custom, Tiso is last aboard. He braces himself on Shorty's shoulder while raising a leg to adjust his trousers. Beck tugs a pull chain and the horizontal elevator doors jerk toward one another, framing briefly a band of brightness, then meeting at chest level. Lit by one bare wire-guarded handle lamp, the car is far darker than the shack with its dirty walls and rows of fluorescent strips. But the tunnels below are even darker, and when the men ascend at the end of the day they will walk half blindly to the shower room.

Beck's crew is small but efficient. An automated gang of ten or twelve men can cut and load over two hundred tons of coal during an average working day, but that figure pales against the coal reserves available. Except maybe for rocks, there is more bituminous coal than anything else underground in the United States, about three trillion tons of it. If all the reserves were built into a wall three feet thick and six feet high, it would girdle the globe 12,037 times. And some 90 percent of America's underground coal is recoverable through present technology.

The largest of the underground machines, the continuous miner which gouges the glistening seam faces, wets the coal, and transfers it to waiting shuttle cars, has eliminated much of the extraordinary physical strain of mining —along with jobs for many thousands of unskilled workers. In the past they toiled as "backbreakers," shoveling great chunks of coal on a pay-for-tonnage basis. This "coal mole" can cut and load coal more quickly than it can be carried away. More than any of the other mining machines introduced since the end of the war, it is responsible for the 100 percent increase in production the industry has had during the past two decades. This is the machine Tiso operates.

—After '35 they started to put in automation, continuous mining, and loading machines, and they were gradually doing away with the manpower. By about 1942, the hand loaders was practically done and they were putting in ten- or twelve-man units. They had maybe two or three men setting the timbers, two men laying the track, probably two men cutting the coal, and a man shooting the coal. Then this little machine would come along and load this coal right direct into the mine car from the face in the mine.

When I first started mining, I carried a pick and shovel, and a self-rescue kit. On this here mechanical mining, the company furnishes cuts and bits, the grease and oil, and all hand tools. We carry the tools right on the machine. I am what they call a coal cutter. The guys that follow me take care of that coal. I think it's a great improvement for the sake of the men that this equipment is doing the work. What I mean is there's no such thing as going down there and breaking your back trying to get coal out of the hill. Let the machines do it. I say this was a good move.

Taut cables lower Tiso's crew slowly down, past jutting pipe and conduit and luminous elevation numerals sprayed on all sides of the shaft. Through cracks in its door and walls, the car casts irregular pools of light along the tube's rough, moist surface. The miners ride patiently, silently. Through the gap where the elevator doors meet, the darkness grows progressively thicker as they descend. They are four hundred feet below the main entrance when they stop.

Tiso is the first to get out, squinting to adjust his eyes to the blackness. It is cool here, and he will be uncomfortable until he boards his machine and starts working its lever and gears. Whether because of his years or because his job is far less strenuous now than it was in the days of the pick and shovel, he finds it more and more difficult to abide the chill. It is different on the outside, above ground, where in the summer the men stand in front of the mine shafts to get the cool air.

The light radiated by the open elevator car is barely sufficient to see by. Tiso switches on his head lamp and sends a shaft of yellow against the far wall, forming a small cone just above the moist rock bed. Light shadows follow his as the crew crosses the fifteen feet of chamber leading off the shaft to the small man-cars waiting at the mouth of the tunnel. Now somewhat better adjusted to the gloom, the men ease themselves with difficulty into the cribs of the train which will carry them to their pit.

The chances are that none of Tiso's crew has ever traveled by subway through a large city—an experience similar to this daily passage through the blackness of crisscrossing passageways, broken intermittently by patches of dim illumination where other men are cutting or loading or making repairs. Subways are more comfortable, however. In the small enclosed cars in which the miners travel, they must squat with arms and legs pulled tight to their bodies, their chins on their chests. The tunnel is seldom more than four feet high, and a man may injure himself seriously if he raises his head. Even in the work areas the miners have to be careful, because helmets alone aren't enough to protect them from occasional scrapes or from the live power wires directly overhead.

Number 11 mine, which has been worked by Middleton for nearly a decade, consists of over a dozen crosscuts—passageways which angle into the mountain and swell into pits or work areas wherever they meet a face of one of the serpentine coal seams. For thousands of feet they run through the mountain's interior. The impression here is claustrophobic; this sensation, and the blackness which absorbs any artificial light, combine to create not so much a scarcity of space as a feeling of its total absence.

The train lurches forward, squealing along its track for several hundred feet. Finally it slows and stops. From just ahead come the sounds of hammer and pick and muffled voices: a small crew mending a crack in the roof. The vehicles start again with a jerk and move past the workers, who are visible in luridly outlined shadows as their lamp beams dart here and there. The train turns a curve, screeches ahead for several minutes, then stops and reverses direction, moving again around a curve quite similar to the first. For even the most experienced miners, it is impossible in such darkness to retain orientation with the world above. They are now totally detached.

The crew reaches its destination: faces 8 and 7 of crosscut Number 5. They step slowly from their cars and move through another dark passageway to an open area containing a continuous miner, three shuttle cars, and the end of a conveyor belt. Tiso operates the miner, Shorty one of the cars. Beck leaves final instructions before taking the rest of the crew to the next face. He and the others move off quickly. They are invisible save for their head lamps, tails of soft blurring light. The bluish glow of the lantern that Beck holds aloft is the last to vanish. Its flame changes color in the presence of explosive methane gas—another safety check, especially valuable in late fall when the danger of methane leaks increases.

Even in the modern automated mine there are at least a half dozen potential sources of serious or fatal accidents. Though safety regulations have reduced catastrophies, mine fires still occur often enough to be more than just grim reminders of mass deaths during the early half of the century. And despite the most careful precautions, the specter of a major mine disaster plagues the industry.

In November of 1968 at Farmington—a few short miles from Middleton Number 11—a methane explosion hurtled through the underground tunnels of Mountaineer Number 9 with terrible force, trapping and killing seventy-eight of the ninety-nine men on the cat-eye shift. Most of the bodies remain where they fell, and in all likelihood they will stay there forever, abandoned along with the miners' legendary passion to recover their buddies, dead or alive. Mountaineer Number 9 had exploded once before, in 1954, leaving sixteen dead. And the president of the United Mine Workers stood at the scene of the 1968 explosion, praising Consolidation Coal Company for its safety-mindedness, pointing out to newsmen that coal mining is inherently dangerous, and saying that disasters are inevitable.

—Two or three of my friends were in that explosion at Number 9 two years ago, and I kept reading the list of the men in the mine. They're still trying to get to the bodies, but even if they do they can't work on them. They're decomposed. They ought to put the bodies in a plastic container and seal it up.

There are different stories about that explosion. Some people felt it shouldn't never have happened in modern days. Others said I'm going right back in when they get it cleaned up. There was another explosion in 1906 that killed over three hundred. But I never thought I'd go in that coal mine and never come out; I had no fear. The thought of a mine explosion just never entered our minds, or we didn't let it.

Tiso's boot slips into a gushy puddle of clay and mine water. There's a lot of underground water in West Virginia, and the men face the constant danger of electrocution or, far more hideous, of drowning in their cramped work spaces. They may be crushed by rocks, coal, and timbers in the event of a cave-in. Rail cars and large cutting and boring machinery may mangle them. Methane gas—"fire damp"—which is undetectable under normal conditions, may poison them. Where there is improper ventilation or where there are uncontrolled build-ups of combustible coal dust, the fire damp may trigger explosion and fire. Small methane sparks can ignite coal dust in an instant, whipping shock waves through the tunnels at the speed of sound. In the presence of dense dust clouds, an explosion may be detonated by electric shorts, arcs, or open flames. In the first case, danger can be forborne by spraying the coal faces before they are cut with powdered limestone. The limestone reduces the dust's rate of dispersion and combustibility. State inspectors are supposed to eliminate electrical accidents by checking wiring and connections and prohibiting the use of carbide lamps in helmets, but the new safety lights are far more cumbersome than the carbide lamps.

—The three mines I worked for, which were all pretty big operations, were in fair to good condition. We didn't run no obstacle course. We took care of the problems before we got to them. It is more up to the individual man to talk with your foreman to see that we have the right conditions—such as to try not to get in too much water (seeing in this state you got a lot of underground water in the mines)—and to see that we have the proper timber standards or pinning standards, and that our equipment is permissible.

The federal government comes in to inspect and the state Mine Department comes in quite often. They come in with the company representatives like the superintendent and the general foreman. They are the two big men. The foreman is essential 'cause he used to be a card-carrying union man.

The coal operators operate on a simple basis. They work for maximum efficiency to get the coal out the cheapest and best possible way, without getting somebody hurt. All the power down in the mines is always a hazard. When we unload, we watch the big feeders to our power lines so we won't get electrocuted. I saw one of the men get killed right out in front of me once.

Sometimes things happen that you wouldn't expect. It happens that quick. Some of them are not too pleasant, like a runaway trip going back in the mountain, or somebody actually getting rolled on by a miner or some buggy, or somebody getting covered up with a rock fall. Now this happens, and we don't get excited, but we try to clear the way to get him out of that mine and give him aid or not. They'd come up and say a man's hurt or covered up— quick! The last man who got hurt on the crew I was working on got his leg broke. Between his ankle and his knee, he got two compound fractures. A fellow by the name of Deacon Steeple, dead now, was running the machine after me. I was cutting them wide and deep with that machine, and I cut this one lump of coal, eighty to one hundred ton in the one block. The shop foreman blasted that big lump of coal and they tried to get it on that machine and take it up to the conveyor. It tipped over on him. He tried to push it back, but the coal pushed him right down and broke his leg. They picked him up on a stretcher and took him out.

Now the company rules were to take a sledgehammer, put your goggles on, and break that lump of coal before putting it on the big machine to pick it up; the machine couldn't handle anything over forty or fifty pounds. What they were doing when that man got hurt was horseplay, cutting up. The next day, they asked me, "What the hell was going on down there last night?" I told them the best I could that it was a man-made trouble, which it was.

Wiping his face on his sleeve, Tiso talks to Shorty in brief phrases interrupted by the beginnings of a wheezing cough. Each one of West Virginia's forty thousand miners stands a good chance of contracting coal worker's pneumoconiosis, or Black Lung disease. The cure isn't known but the cause is. Every minute they are underground, miners inhale microscopic particles of coal dust, which ultimately clogs their lungs. Slowly they suffocate. The dust also gets into their hair, clothes, and skin, and the rims of their eyes become coated. Older miners never stop coughing it up. On the job they pause more often to catch their breath. In the later stages of the disease even short walks become difficult efforts.

For a long time the dangers of Black Lung were minimized or ignored entirely, company doctors told miners that they had asthma or emphysema, and the union failed to press for corrective measures. Finally, after a spontaneous wildcat strike closed every mine in the state, the West Virginia legislature passed a law that increased safety regulations and compensated workers disabled by the disease. To date very few miners have been paid for their suffering. Most of them still think that a badly shored roof or an exposed electric wire is their main health hazard.

—Once when we wouldn't go in the mine on account of some kind of safety thing, the superintendent accused me of having the men stirred up. Actually, I didn't want to get out of the coal mine, but they said to me, "We're going to fire you." So I said, "Then pay me off in full. Don't hold back for no two weeks. I want my money." One said to the other, "Let Elmer cool off a little bit; he'll be all right." I heard what he said, but then they threatened me again. I said, "That's your privilege. All I own down there is my dinner pail and coat. I'll go home, but I won't stay." You must have a very legitimate reason to get rid of a man—not carrying out his proper duties or holding back, stuff like that. But as for going in the coal mine, we got a union here and we talk. I said, "We're doing something here that's not right." The superintendent just walked away from me. He said, "Goddamn it, Elmer, you're no goddamn good." "Well, Mr. Rodack," I said, "I learned that from you. What I'm doing is not right and I don't want to do it no more. That's what I'm kicking about." He said, "You're a goddamn agitator troublemaker." I said, "You're the man that caused it; you are the sole cause. If you had come down and told us, this would never have happened." I truly set him down; I had to get it off my back. I was testing him, too, like a little child.

Shorty lifts the receiver from the radio bolted to a platform near the miner. His request for power clearance is granted from above, and he inserts the miner's feed line into the main power core. Tiso mounts to his seat.

With a roar from the throttle, the huge augers attack the face of a coal seam and chew out large chunks, at the rate of twelve tons a minute. The coal mole has eliminated the need for undercutting the face to drill and blast the solid coal; its mammoth jaws tear large troughs into the shiny black mineral. Long, steady, inexorable strokes. In order to move the greater loads more efficiently, many of the companies have replaced cumbersome and dangerous rail cars with a series of conveyor belts. The one in Tiso's pit is a tributary to the main conveyor, fed by perhaps a dozen such contraptions, as it rolls through the center of the mountain on its way to the tipple at the mouth of the mine. Shorty operates a shuttle buggy, a rubber-tired electric car that expedites removal of coal to the outside by hauling it from the back of the mines to the belt or, in some cases, to rail cars.

Such machinery has practically done away with track-layers and backbreakers. Timber-setters are equally rare, for roof bolts—thick steel pins inserted through soft ceiling slate into the rigid strata of shale and granite above—now hold the friable overhead rock more securely than the old fir columns. As a result, payrolls in medium-sized mines have dropped from thousands to hundreds. The largest now might employ one thousand or twelve hundred men.

Tiso and Shorty cannot talk over the roar of the machinery. Both their fathers hacked at the inside of these mountains with picks and shovels. It's been a long time since the initial boom days of the coal industry, when large Eastern corporations invaded the hills to buy the mineral rights under huge portions of land in West Virginia, Kentucky, and neighboring states, and to bring shades of prosperity to thousands of illiterate mountaineers. Between 1875 and 1910 ownership of some 85 percent of the area's coal passed from the natives to nonresident investors, often for no more than a few dollars per acre. This was good money to the hill people, who felt they were being paid handsomely for underground rights they didn't need, rights which weren't going to be exercised for years to come. They signed away the coal to the charms of smooth-talking company agents, whose deeds amounted to masterpieces of exploitation. When the coal operators started production in earnest, after the railroads had made the mountains accessible, they recovered from one thousand to fifteen hundred tons of coal per acre foot, a minimum of five thousand tons per acre.

As the demand for coal to fill the nation's fireplaces and furnaces increased, the hundreds of mining camps burgeoned into company towns—crude forebears, perhaps, of the low-cost welfare communities-turned-slums of a half century later. The people to fill them came down from the hills and over from the East Coast ports and up from the South. Italians, Czechs, Poles, and blacks were brought in by the operators to work side by side with the hillbillies, mining coal ten hours a day for nine dollars a week.

In 1910 the coal industry provided work for seven

hundred thousand men, but by 1927, even before the coal-market collapse, the initial boom of building and employment had subsided, and new methods of production were enabling the operators to get by with fewer laborers. Soon the immigrant population gave way to the native mountaineers. By 1970, the work force had dwindled to 150,-000.

Truck mines, easily financed small operations which could tap otherwise inaccessible outcroppings of coal, absorbed some of the overspill during the postwar boom. In general, however, John L. Lewis' prediction, that the thousands of disenfranchised in Appalachia, the Cumberlands, and Pennsylvania would find work in other industries of a boom economy, proved shortsighted. Some jobless have migrated to large cities like Detroit, Baltimore, Cleveland, and Cincinnati; others, whether through complacency or stubborn mountaineer allegiance to their homeland, have stayed to suffer the appalling poverty which recently has drawn public attention to Appalachia.

—In the old days, I had no problems with the management at all. They were very fair-minded and they paid us for what we done. We loaded this coal by the piecework tonnage rate of fifty-five or fifty-seven cents a ton. If we loaded ten or twelve tons, we made about six or seven dollars a day.

✝ I was paid at a rate of a dollar an hour for the first seven hours of a day, and $1.50 an hour for each hour of overtime, which was the United Mine Workers contract. This made ten dollars a day, which wasn't bad money in '40 and '41. In '42 they upgraded us again and we got to around thirteen dollars a day. This kept going till '60 when we got up to almost thirty dollars a day. Later on they put the differential in between four and six cents on the hour, according to the shift. The day shift got the straight time, the afternoon shifts got thirty-two cents more than the day, and the midnight shift got forty-eight cents more.

For the next three hours Tiso tears coal. Rivulets of black sweat form in the wrinkles of his face. Automation has taken away a certain dogged spirit from the miners. There is still the camaraderie, still the shared suffering, but without the air of ignorant men's resignation. You don't hear the rhythmic tap-rap of the picks and shovels any more, nor the workaday beats of the songs of labor: *Y' load sixteen tons and whatd'ya get? Another day older and deeper in debt. St. Peter, don't y' call me 'cause I can't go—I owe my soul to the company store.*

—There were some people that just didn't care whether they'd see tomorrow or the next day, or not—some live for today and to heck with tomorrow. They'd spend half their money on liquor. This was it. There were people I'd known—and it's incredible—who'd deal down through a company store to between eight hundred and fifteen hundred dollars as a grocery or food bill, and they couldn't pay that. These people pulled out of here between two, three, or four in the morning. They loaded up their belongings in a jalopy, and Ohio-bound, Cleveland-bound, Pittsburgh-bound, or Baltimore-bound, they got out of here.

But if they'd stayed, the company store would've kept taking all the money every payday, twice the month. I'd seen it twice the month, every penny was gone. I'd seen it day in and day out and I said, "Why the hell don't you guys quit working? You're not gaining nothing."

When I went to work for them, I told the company I didn't want no company house, no company water, no electric. I'm an individual and I got my own place. We had no drinking water here, but we always had our own private system, an electric deep-well pump. The well didn't produce very much, but we had enough to get by on. Some people went three miles to get water, brought it in gallon jugs and plastic jugs. About five or six years ago, they brought the city water out of Fairmont, and they put in bathrooms, showers, hot water tanks. The Jameson Coal people from Greensburg had to tell their own people to dress better and to keep clean and use a lot of water to take baths. The men got too ragged and they had to tell them to buy new clothes, like boots or a pair of pants.

I just wasn't afraid of them; I wasn't afraid of risking my job. I don't care who worked for me, or who worked around me, or what foreman I had. If I thought he was trying to give me a raw deal during that shift, I'd call attention that he don't do it, because it ain't gonna work.

I said, "Don't do it, buddy. You're making a mistake." I'm going to tell him one time, nice and polite, "Don't do it." Maybe I am a little too forward at times, and I probably talked to the super where these guys were scared to death of him. If this guy growled at you, them guys went and hid.

It has changed in the last several years because they are more and more modernized. There are some pretty wealthy men and they still work. They have saved their money. Some didn't, depends on how the person felt about it. Not many up here go on welfare, only a few families. With a lot of them it's a matter of pride. Like me, I don't want no handout. So long as I'm able to go to work, I'm going to give my employer a fair day's work for a fair day's wages. Anyone disabled and has got no income, a widow, a bachelor, anybody, I think they should help them. But if he's an able-bodied man, then give him a job, let him work.

We're good people out here. West Virginians are common as every day in the week. Even if you have no money and no coal in your coal bin at home, they'll bring it to you and say, "Pay me when you got the money." People aren't starving to death out here. I've read stories where they say they're going hungry, but they're not going hungry. Those that help themselves get along so much better, but some people don't want to help themselves. The government made a mistake when they picked them all up. They should have told them, "We either job-train you or you go out there and find a job."

A lot of coal miners spend their money as they get it, and for a lot of them it's hopeless. You got to take an aptitude test to work in the mines today. When I went down to get a job from Consolidation Coal Company, I had to go through a test that run at least three and a half hours. We had to work with a triangle, circle, trapezoid, anything you want to call it. I never had to take an aptitude test before.

They've still got the six big coal mines in the county, plus an awful lot of small ones which are great producers too. These are all rated for about forty to forty-five years of life. I think they said they had thirteen or fourteen hundred people back in the mines in Morgantown, which is enough for what they call an automative or mechanical mine. There are two big mines here that employed five hundred men, but both shut down in 1960 because they automated so fast and the markets were bad. No sales. The fellow that gets it is the little guy, but that's the way it is.

Sometimes the operators just don't care about the little man, and the unions won't back him up on his pension. A fellow I know by the name of Jud Sanders, a Negro, he sued them and didn't get to first base. He spent thirty-three years underground in the state of West Virginia, and now they have denied him his pension. I talked to Jud the other day and he cussed something profane. They sent him to work in the small nonunion mines to make up a certain amount of time on social security and on these miner's dues for his pension. After he got all that done, they still denied it to him. They said, "You didn't work a certain quarter year." We read a lot of papers or we talked about politics, but it don't do no good to talk about it. We have people in office that don't belong there, but they're still in. They don't put them out once they get in. Recently we've been reading about secret-door meetings in Congress about West Virginia. The people involved in this state don't want that secrecy. Things should come out in the open. I read in this new census of 1970 that this state may lose another seat in the House of Representatives— there you are again. They've left the average little man way behind; they're not keeping in touch with the people. If you know what it's all about, it's different, but if you don't, you're lost. I was talking to a man a while back and I said legislation ought to be like the ABC. He said it can't be changed, it's stuff above us. We can't analyze it. When you get down to what Congress is actually doing on Medicare or mining reforms, it's so complicated, you can't keep up with it. Hell, people can't digest what they're doing.

Politics is just too much for me. I think Mr. Lyndon Johnson moved entirely too fast on all the welfare and clean into that Vietnam War, and Nixon's the man hooked to Johnson's problems. From what I can understand and read, that man is going to have a hard time if he's truly trying to get out of Vietnam. I didn't vote for him, but I have no grudge against him. I just don't think he can handle our problems. I did admire John F. Kennedy for a fact. One of my boys got an autograph from him—I don't know how, but he got it.

They claim our governor's no good. Jack Anderson from D. C. put out a story about the Honorable Governor Arch Moore. It's hard for me to believe, but they say he took eighty thousand dollars in political funds and invested it in the stock market. President Nixon was going to appoint him for some kind of Health and Welfare job. They're still under investigation.

Tiso operates his machine with the assurance of a man prepared for any eventuality. He has worked continuous miners for the past seventeen years, probably longer than anyone in this part of the state. The team moves steadily, Tiso wetting the coal with a sprayer before cutting it, Shorty and the others moving the large lumps, some as heavy as fifty tons, to the nearby conveyor. When he started in the mines and was paid on a tonnage basis, Tiso labored harder than he does now at the hourly rate. But the machinery does the same work in a fraction of the time and its operators must move carefully and methodically.

Tiso makes sure that the face is properly wetted and the coal dust controlled. The bitumen he cuts from the seam falls onto the machine's bin in sizable lumps, some of which must be cut down so that the shuttle cars can handle them safely.

It is pure monotony, guiding the miner back and forth across the long seam face, and if it weren't for the money, Tiso would prefer the less specialized, more varied work he did before the mines were automated. There is little to see in the murky chamber. He fixes his gaze from time to time on the shiny face, its ever-changing surfaces reflecting his lamplight with prismatic fancy. There's a lot of time to think in the mine, especially since the constant roar of the machine makes conversation impossible. If he could talk while working, he might speak of his plans for retirement—after two more years underground he should be eligible for a pension—or of whatever a man might bring to mind whose memories, like a monochrome, extend bleak and undifferentiated into the past, relieved now and then by an extraordinary event or a break in the gray routine of his labor.

—In '42 I went to work for the Christopher National 5 Mines, and worked there until 1950. I was called into the Army around 1943, and I got as far as the induction center. There was fifty-seven of us there, and I think seven of them were rejected and they sent them out. Then they stamped us "inducted," and told us, "You fellows go back to work where you were at that mine and stay there. If we need you, we're going to call you." So after being drafted and inducted, they sent me back to the mines. They needed this coal.

I worked right in the coal mines all through the war. We got a lot of overtime, got paid time and a half. We had a little problem on contract talks, and I think they put a freeze on the wages. At one time there the men did strike, and they raised the American flag right down there in the coal yard on the company flagpole, and said, "Well, boys, you are now working for the U. S. Government." It was only token, because actually we never got no government or federal check, but we worked right on through all this skirmish. They were wanting production bad.

On April 1st, we'd have the Mitchell Day parade. That is still the big miner holiday in West Virginia every year. They go from coal mine town to coal mine town, maybe pick out Morgantown one year, Fairmont one year, Richwood, and so on. It's been going on ever since I remember. John Mitchell was the daddy of the eight-hour day. They'd get out these high school bands or miners' bands, and they'd have the poor people march with them and they have different coal companies. They kept the morale up.

Another time we got on a very good production basis and they said, "If you're hungry, Elmer, or the family's hungry, go up here to the log cabin on Route 19. Drink your beer, treat your family, we'll pay for it." This actually happened. I was often told through my superintendent down here at Johnson's Number 11 and 12 mines, that they were really concerned about you. The other people I worked for didn't hold no picnics. Although they had a first-aid team, they didn't go out in a big way for it. They weren't hardly concerned about health.

The only period I ever traveled was when I was injured. I wouldn't have gone then, but the doctor said when he released me, "Elmer, if I were you, I'd get out of the state for a while and travel." Well, I run across a beer salesman

and I drove around with him. We'd go to Baltimore once
the week, Cumberland twice the week, Cincinnati once the
week, and Newport, Kentucky, once the week. We'd pick
the beer orders up and then we would drive until we got
tired, and just find a roadside park and stay there for a
while and drink some beer. We'd get all we wanted free.

I went out to Baltimore several times, but I never found
it too good there. We were lost. We were country people
out of town. I didn't like the taxis and the mass transit,
and I didn't like that type of living. The apartment I stayed
in out there was on Old Charles Street. You'd walk in off
the street, and you had an apartment here, you had one
up there, and we're in the middle here. I'm talking a little
loud and my friend says, "Hey, people over here, people
up there, people over there." I said, "Buddy, this ain't for
me. Let's get out of here and go somewhere else." I didn't
care much for that.

Sometimes we'd get a group together and go down to
see a Pittsburgh Pirate baseball game at Forbes Field.
Three or four of us'd go on a weekend. We spent a little
time down here on Cheat Lake too. This neighbor of mine
had a little Montgomery Ward Sea-King motorboat and
we'd go up there and fiddle around one or two days, just
look around and sometimes do a little fishing. I was once
up in an airplane, just for a joy ride. I wasn't afraid, but
the buddy I was with was scared and he got drunk. Sometimes I watch the Andy Williams show or a musical show,
a mystery or Bonanza or something like that. I listen to
the news about what's going on in the world every day
at twelve o'clock, and read the Washington *Post* a great
deal, every day in the week. It's the morning paper but
we read it in the evening.

When I worked the midnight shift, I would spend my
free time in the garden. I grew corn, potatoes, beans, pep-
pers, squash, lettuce, stuff like that, and I had tomatoes
coming up. It was more for something to pass the time, to
see whether we get a good season each year or a bad
season. It's clay soil around here and you got to use fer-
tilizer and different things. But I wouldn't trade this out
here to go into some city ghetto or city apartment. I
wouldn't feel comfortable and I'd be totally lost again.
Your neighbor may be a stranger. You never speak to

him, yet you pass him a hundred times a day. I've seen that and I've seen their bars—I went in once and took a shot of liquor straight, and right away the bartender knew I was from West Virginia.

At noon the men working Number 8 face shut down their machines and join those from Number 7 in the open passageway between. After hours of continuous din the miners need several minutes to adjust to the relative quiet. They begin to speak only after all are seated on the low benches and have arranged the contents of their lunch pails. They have forty-five minutes for lunch. Tiso listens to the others talk of their families, their complaints about the union, and the new strike in a mine over the next ridge. Most of what he hears he's heard before, but he nods and laughs with the others. He knows more about the union than any of them, although there is a mixture of faith and distrust in his understanding.

On the one hand, Tiso and his companions share a disarming naiveté about both the coal operators' benevolence and the union's advocacy of their welfare. While the pick-and-shovel stereotype of the oppressed company town may have disappeared from the American scene, the owners' lingering paternalism helps keep today's miners innocently amenable to the industry literature—which paints them as "skilled, well-paid technicians who handle expensive and highly sophisticated equipment, and may drive miles to work like any other commuters." But if their insensitivity to exploitation had been dulled by so many years of company-nurtured ignorance, a new awareness had been sparked from the open frauds perpetrated by their supposed compatriots, the union leadership.

When the United Mine Workers first began to recruit members around 1915, the miners, considering themselves prosperous enough, ignored promises of even higher wages and better conditions through collective bargaining. The operators discouraged union membership by various forms of intimidation, from threatening to fire anyone who joined to more violent coercion. By 1935 the pendulum had shifted and the miners were able to document their grievances and defy the big companies. Most operators either went out of business or signed a union contract. In 1950, after John L. Lewis had stopped grabbing headlines, the cycle was completed; union leaders and coal operators, in violation of the Sherman Anti-Trust Act, sat down in secrecy and began some very friendly collaboration. Neither Tiso nor his buddies know what collusion is.

—These here miners have been upgraded tremendously since the year 1964. They work five days a week, forty hours a week, portal-to-portal travel time included. If you've got a long distance to go, they can't work you but six hours a day at the most. This portal time is something that was brought in here not too long ago when these new laws went into effect. If you're on maintenance or the mechanic force, you work a little more than that, six days, to keep this equipment up. Travel time and paid lunch hour is all new.

They put in your parking lot, your shower room, your changing room. In things like that, it's the best in the world. Some of the personnel and public relations people say the miner is the most highly skilled man in the world. Now this is what they've been telling us here recently, and yet the papers will come out and say that the laws aren't being carried out. I can't come to a conclusion about that.

The United Mine Workers had a lot to do with the changes, although I never seen a lot of them myself. We had good to bad labor management. I was down there with the Jameson Company for ten years, and if I had to see the union down there once a year, I was fortunate. If we had a local matter, we tried to thrash it out before we got up to the district level with the company. If the district and the company couldn't get together, then a guy called the umpire, a neutral man, would come down and would make the decisions, right or wrong. He'd say this is what we're going to abide by, this is it, fellows.

We struck once for seventy-seven days when I worked down here for the Number 5 Christopher Mine. We struck for the welfare and betterment of the miners, and all this, but it didn't come through. The better pension went through, but better conditions didn't, because in seventy-seven days' time, a lot took place in that coal mine that actually wasn't safe.

When the mine started up again after the strike, the day shift did not work, but the afternoon reported. There was only a handful of us that went in there. We had one representative from the union and we had one from the company. The man from the company, Lee Smithwood, is one of the men that actually owned the operation. When he drove in to his property down there, we were getting lined up, picking up our safety equipment, lights and batteries and the kits, and going in the mines. As soon as the men got lined up, ready to get into the mine crib, he come out and make us a little talk. I'll never forget it, because I was right there talking to him. He told me, "Elmer, you are going back in that mine this afternoon. This mine has been down for seventy-seven days. Your track is wet, your mine is damp. You may have loose rock on your haulage, you may have an overhanging rib, or you may have a flood in your section. Your equipment is damp and wet. My advice to you fellows is to go in there, be careful. You're not going to set the world on fire with this one day's work. We're trying to start back off where we left off at. And be careful, we don't want nobody hurt. This is the furthest thing from our mind."

He said, "Good luck to all of youse." Then he left. He had a great big Cadillac and he drove out of there.

Then our union man said the same thing, but he emphasized just a little bit different. He said to be awful careful. We don't care about a day's production, we don't care about this, we don't care about that, he said, but be awful careful. Look around, see what it's all about before you actually start back in there.

The union is supposed to protect you. The United Mine Workers come around and put an assessment on and say, "Well, Tom, Jim, Joe, we're going to take twenty dollars apiece from you to fight our cause. We want this for legal fees." This is an actual fact. They took our money at the rate of five dollars a day, or ten dollars a month, or twenty dollars for two months. You take one hundred thousand miners at twenty dollars each—that's a lot of money.

They have accused the union of misusing the funds and loaning a lot of money to small-time operators to try to keep them going, to create jobs. They have done it all right, but probably Tony Boyle's trying to do the best he can under the circumstances. A lot of the miners today are still not working. Tony and the Congressmen are having a little heck in the investigations about mine safety

programs and welfare. The papers have accused him of
being lax on safety and they have accused him of a lot
of trickery. I don't know. He was elected in there and he'd
be pretty hard to replace. I don't see how they can put
him off till the next election comes up, unless they can
declare it void now. I don't like these ways of doing
things sometimes, but there's nothing I can do about it.
I never met him.

The only one I ever met is John L. Well, you couldn't
get to him, you know, just wave at him, just "Hi, Jack"
and keep on going. It was right down here at Arkwright,
right down here about eight miles out of town. He come
into the bathhouse looking around. They claim he worked
in the mines out in Iowa. I think he had about only an
eighth-grade education. The woman he married was a
schoolteacher and she was the one that actually taught
him, according to what I read. I admire him. He was
all right.

Well, I have had seventeen years of running a continuous
miner and I told them once that I had enough of it, that
I truly didn't need that big money—I could get along with
twenty-five dollars a day awful good. I wanted a change
like somebody else and they wouldn't give it to me. We
were classified. The union and the coal operators set the
classification up. The motormen, the buggy men, the shop-
men, the drillers, the timbering people, the track people, the
machine operators—they were all classified. And once you're
classified into one job, man, you're done. They won't generally let you quit and be rehired doing something else.
The union brought it up to protect their own workers,
they claim, but it didn't protect anybody. It put a thing
on your back that you couldn't shake loose. If you wanted
to be a free agent, you're already classified and you haven't
a chance—"Elmer, you are an operator and you stay here."

I like the system we had before as being a free agent.
If you wanted to do something else for a week or two, go
ahead and do it and we'll put somebody else on that
machine. You felt like going back on, we'd trade off and
he'd go down here and I'd go back on the machine. The
automation is a good thing for the men's welfare, but they
brought that on in a slick manner, too. They forgot the
people that helped, and I'm one of them.

Beck, who has taken his lunch apart from the rest, interrupts their talk to discuss again the roof in Number 7 and to ask Tiso about the size of the coal chunks he is cutting. Tiso respects Beck's competence as a company foreman, but company men and union welfare card carriers keep their distances. The foreman is responsible for safety, his own as well as the others, so he is mindful of the electrical system, the ventilation in the tunnels, the possibility of methane leaks, and the working habits of his men. Beck's crew has not had a major accident in the year and a half he has been assigned to this section of Number 11 mine.

—They asked me one time to be a foreman, but I wouldn't take it. They said, "Why don't you join our ranks and then we'll get along much better?" I said, "No thanks, fellows, I'm well satisfied where I'm at and that's it." The foremen, the pushers, the face bosses, they've got no voice. They're told, "You go down there, take that crew of men, and shift the coal. We want lots of it. Get your coal, boys, and be safe. Bring your production up." But the foreman's a man in between. He's got no protection from either the union or the coal operator.

I wasn't afraid of taking the responsibility of the four or five men who were actually bossed. I'd done it several times, but I didn't want to lose my union welfare card or nothing by being on the coal operator's side. They get paid at the rate of one hundred dollars or one hundred and twenty dollars a month or better, and then they got different benefits like being stockholders and stuff like that. But the foreman's a man that if they kick him out, he's got nowhere to go to. They'd like to have a union, but they are denied one. They don't even participate in the Welfare Fund. They help get this here coal out of that mine and I think they should be eligible, but they're not. They tried to organize not too long ago. The company threatened to fire them.

Beck is twenty years younger than most of his men, and not very much older than Tiso's oldest son. The foreman is respected, almost liked, for the zeal with which he works and the money that he makes. Yet higher wages notwithstanding, Tiso has been careful to keep his own sons from the mine.

—I have two boys that I put through the public schools

and through college. The oldest one is a graduate from
the West Virginia University and he's working on his
Master's. He's twenty-eight and married. He and his wife
and kids stay with us about four or five weeks of every
summer.

The second boy wanted to go in the mine, but I said,
"You're not gonna work no coal mines," so he got a job
down here with a baking company, making him a little
money, and he come back this year to the College of Com-
merce. I told him, "You help yourself, and I'll help you
along, see. If you only make one hundred dollars a week,
if you're outside it doesn't matter to me." I want him to
get a certain amount of education, where I didn't get it.
If I had it to do over again, I would have stayed right
in school and forgot about the coal mines. I don't know
about college, but I would have finished high school, because I see now where it would have done me more good.
These modern-day kids, they have never had it better,
and sometimes I wonder why they kick so much and have
riots. I don't know where it's at, myself. I told my youngest son, "Don't get involved in no kind of radical crowd.
You stay away from them." They claim that the radicals
are communist-inspired, but I doubt it. I think sometime
that the whole problem is that Vietnam War. It's like having the tiger by the tail and can't turn him loose.

Once again the crew gathers to receive instructions.
Daley and Montgomery will continue rock dusting in
Number 7 section, to minimize the danger of fire or explosion, and to prepare the face for the cutting which Tiso
will begin next week. There is another day of bolting to
be done before the section will withstand the great strains
which the augers of his machine will put on the walls and
ceiling. At the end of the day the roof of Number 8 will
need even more work, for as the miner cuts deeper and
deeper into the coal seam, the enlarging cavern must be
shored, again and again. These few faces will be worked
for many months before the pits are sealed, and crews
attack the seam from new entrenchments. Everything
considered—automation, safety regulations, union benefits,
higher wages—the physical labor and emotional endurance
accepted by today's miner is not far removed from that
of Zola's nineteenth-century France. The only difference

now might be the noise. The men can barely think over the roar of their machines. The crystalline coal still falls back into darkness, there is still the monotony and the solitude, but the pickaxes striking their great hollow blows, the panting chests, the grunts of discomfort and weariness beneath the weight of the air and moisture, can no longer be heard.

Tiso's toothless, wrinkled face assumes a curious blend of friendliness and consternation when he talks about his fellow miners. To him they are brothers. (*I never in my life ran across a snotty miner or a smart aleck. They were all down there like me, making the best of the living. We're good people out here.*)

After working a large section of the face, Tiso stops his machine momentarily and glances at his watch: a bit more than an hour to go. Shorty is on the radio again taking advantage of the few moments of relative quiet to check their progress against the loading schedule kept by the control meter above. He is told that the tipple—the immense series of tilting bins which receive the loads of coal from the main conveyor and sort them according to grade and size—is backed up. They can rest for five or ten minutes or maybe more. Tiso slowly moves the miner back into position, and tears another load from the shiny face. It is three o'clock.

Beck's whistle is barely audible above the deafening reverberations of the machinery, but the men have been waiting for it, so they hear. Tiso and Shorty lower themselves stiff-legged from their rigs. Treading warily across the damp, hard mine bed—though they have grown accustomed to the gloom, they still must squint to make out smaller objects—the two of them negotiate the power cable, then join the others for the short walk back to the train which returned minutes before.

The operation has been relatively clean this time, thanks to cautious preoccupation with rock dusting. The men's faces are black all over, except for the circles around their eyes that were protected by goggles. Daley and Montgomery wear strange effects of their day's labor: above the blackness of their skin is a gray-white pall dusted on by their lime spraying, lending them a ghastly, wraithlike appearance. Through the darkness of the tunnel they all seem somehow larger than life. In a minute all are in

position, contorted, tired, and silent. Within a half hour
they will be outside.

Tiso spends twenty minutes under a hot shower, scrubbing with hard soap, to cut through the coal dust on
his face and hands. A long time ago he learned that the
more of his body he kept covered, the faster he'd be able
to leave the day's work. When he peels off his necker-
chief, which has changed from red to rust-black, a white
band appears under his chin.

Beyond the entrance the late afternoon sky is ashen, as
if hued with a mixture of limestone powder and coal dust.
A single thick cloud of black dust billows from a breaker
crushing coal on the ridge behind Tiso. Gone from this
part of the coal district are the company camps which
sprouted around the large mines in the '20's and '30's,
with their closely spaced shacks and laundry hanging
from the windows and small garden plots all covered
with a fine film of soot.

The dust remains the miner's silent enemy, but it no
longer stalks him when he is above ground. There are
other ways in which the mines spoil the verdant West
Virginia mountain country and scar the natural balance
of the land.

—Strip mining is less dangerous than a shaft mine because it's all outside work, but I don't like it at all. I
think they ruined the state. They tore the hills up and
left them. The strip companies put up about five hundred
dollars per acre—this money was meant for the state to
restore this land, but they didn't do it, neither the state
nor the operator. If they tore a ridge all up and then
abandoned the mine, actually they didn't replace it. It's
still the same way, all down through that country. I don't
like to look at it myself. I think at one time they had
legislation there in Charleston that they was going to try
to abolish strip mining. If they would reclaim it, it
wouldn't be bad. The state, and then some companies too,
have reclaimed a lot of it, I don't know how many hundreds of acres.

Nobody never raised no Cain about what the company
was doing over there at Big Indian Creek. It is really
polluted. I used to fish there and the kids swam there.
They talked about impounding that waste water in these
valleys, building a dam, pumping it in there, and letting

it evaporate or treating it, but they say it's a costly project. It truly doesn't affect me. After all, I'm fifty-two years old. The air pollution is terrible, too. That bothers me.

Freshly showered, Shorty, Tiso, and Joe Kozak leave the entranceway of Number 11. A full day of operating the mining machine has sapped Tiso, and he is looking forward to an hour's nap before supper. He steps past an oncoming car: Shorty's teen-aged son. His companions slide in next to the boy, who waves to the older man now making his way slowly between parked cars and over the rough dried mud of the lot. Several miners pass him on their way to the entrance.

FIVE

The Cabby

*The guys you take out to Queens who tell you
they used to be cab drivers themselves and
then give you a thirty-five cent tip; the junior
stockbrokers, girdle manufacturers, and
Mafia hoods with the ugly girl friends you
pick up in the supper-club belt in the East
Thirties and Forties. Not to mention the
people* outside *the cab: the little hoods who
come up to the cab to mooch some change
and also to see if you're carrying your
money in your shirt pocket, whereupon a
hand will shoot in so fast you see nothing
and rip the whole pocket off; the fruitcakes
who climb up on the hood of the cab and
walk right across it because you are poked
too far out in the intersection. Sometimes you
get it all in one night.*

—*a New York cabby*

—I love this job. I liked it from the beginning. It's the best theater in the world as far as I'm concerned. You get to know all different kinds of people, what they think, what their hopes are. Funny as it may sound, when they come into the cab it's just like they come to confession. They talk, they loosen up. And they have to listen to me, too. They can't jump out of the cab, they have to listen until they get dizzy from me. I say what I want and they say what they want, and we kill the day that way.

For example, all this turmoil in the country, I look at it as two homes in the neighborhood. In one of them you have doors and windows broken, and you can hear the argument between the mother and the father, and the daughter and the son, and the father and the son, you can hear all the arguments—as long as these people are talking, they have a chance of some day either a neighbor will

help them or they'll help themselves. And then you look at
the house next door, and there are people living in there,
but you don't see no door, no window, nothing opened.
Everything is locked up, everything is closed. Well, hell,
I'd rather live in the house with the noise that you *can*
hear, instead of living in the other house, because I don't
know what the hell is going on behind there. How else
can anybody get together, how else can you know how I
feel if I don't talk to you, if I don't scream?

The people come in trickles, then in droves. Some of
them gather in a dark cavern which smells or urine and
beer and they wait for big freight elevators to take them
from street level to the subway platform down below. They
are going from the Cloisters at the northern tip of the
island to midtown Manhattan. It's morning and part of
the rush hour, in New York City a long sixty minutes.

Finally the subway elevator opens its doors and the
people pile in, putting down their tabloids and looking
up with wooden faces. After the doors close they watch
the signs they see everyday without reading, the metal
placards on the cabin walls which say *BEWARE OF
PICKPOCKETS* and *MEDDLERS TAKE NOTICE*
and *THIS IS NOT A FREIGHT ELEVATOR* and
HANDS OFF, PLEASE. On the platform below it is even
warmer than in the elevator. The tunnel is crowded and
filled with a constant rumble, which every few minutes explodes into the thunder of arriving trains.

If there are no delays or accidents and if the walk isn't
too far at either end of the trip, subways are the fastest
means to get around Manhattan. The busses are slow, but
cleaner. When the weather's good a commuter can even
ride a bike through the morning cool of Central Park,
deserted except for other cyclists or women strolling with
their dogs. Some people choose a theatre seat for the surrounding frenzy, if they can afford the fare to hail a taxi
and don't mind darting in and out of tight traffic.

—I'm using this job as an institution, as something that
I can learn from or learn in. Before the rate hikes I got
on the average about seventy, eighty, maybe sometimes
ninety passengers a day, and they come in from all walks
of life. From prostitutes to scientists you get and if you

got your ears open, you learn. You see the one that's upset and aggravated and ready to fight the whole world, how he looks to you, and you don't want to be like him. You get somebody else who tries to beat you out of a fare or tries to rob you or something, you learn from him. You get a prostitute, you see her the way she is, fighting to make a living, you learn from her. The other day I had a man that worked with the government in the taxation department. The things I learned from him, I don't think I could have found out in five years of original book reading.

Maybe I don't know what the hell I'm talking about, but I love people. I like to talk to them, I like to see what makes them tick, how they feel, how they think. Sometimes I'm a pain in the neck, but I figure the hell with that, as long as I get something out of it without harming anybody.

Alexander Socrates Panos is one of the twelve thousand licensed cabbies in New York City. He looks a decade older than his forty-seven years, but he feels younger, and often he flashes warm smiles of contentment through irregularly spaced teeth. Gray-black hair barely covers his balding head, curling down into thick sideburns. His face looks as if it's been chipped out of rock. He has a strong Greek accent, and it is sometimes hard to tell whether he comes across more like a latter-day Zorba, or like Anthony Quinn, whom he resembles.

—From the time that I was born, we had depression in Greece and nothing else. I can't remember a day that my stomach was 100 percent full. There were three boys and two girls. I was born in 1923, in Athens. I was the oldest of the boys.

My parents were what in Greece is called middle class. My father built his own houses, where we would live; when he would sell one, we would get the hell out, and he would build another. Most of the time we were moving in while the workers were still working. His business was nothing to brag about, but it wasn't bad. We were a lot better off than most of them over there. We were eating every day.

When I was seventeen, I went to the Greek Maritime Academy. It took me a little more time than the usual to graduate because we had the war and the German occupation. It's hard to forget those days, and painful to remember. When the Germans came, the Greeks left and the English left. They went over to the Middle East. Then after the Germans we had the Italians. I was a member of the Resistance, in the meantime, before I jumped over to Malta. There I was in the army, and then I went back into Greece. Never a dull day. I have nothing real nice to remember from those days. I seen people dying from hunger right in the streets. The body becomes like a balloon from hunger and they were dying like flies.

After that I started to work as a seaman again. First I went to Italy, then to Germany, from Germany to America. The United States gave a hundred Liberty Ships to the Greek government and they were in great need of officers, so I was elevated right away into a second mate. I never did work as an apprentice officer.

I came here in 1947. I started out for a vacation, figuring to stay about a month, a month and a half, as much as my money could carry me. I played soccer—we were the equivalent of professional then—and I first saw my wife on the soccer field. She was the manager's daughter. As soon as I saw her, I wanted to meet her; don't ask me why, but I figured that girl is for me. I liked everything that she was doing—the way she was talking, the way she was sitting down. I watched her very carefully, in the half time before the game, after the game. They would take the whole team out for supper in a restaurant, spend a few dollars on the boys. I went for another trip over to Europe and then I came back again. In '49 we were married. I was playing soccer, center forward position, as almost a permanent member of the national team of the United States. I couldn't play in the Olympics because I was a pro here.

7:00 A.M. Alex Panos gets up with the buzz of an alarm clock, has breakfast with his wife, then walks the dog. That's his job in the morning, to walk the beagle. The whole routine, which he's been following six days a week for the past five years, takes forty-five minutes. At quarter to eight he sits down at the breakfast table with his children.

Marlene is eighteen, plays the cello *(she didn't get that from me, I can tell you that)*, and goes to Mercy College in White Plains. Two months ago she was going to be a lawyer, now it's an English major, maybe next week a scientist. Alex doesn't care what she chooses as long as she's healthy. But he wants his son, now at Fordham Prep, to go to Yale and be something better than a cab driver. (*When I say better, I don't mean there's anything wrong or degrading with driving a cab, but he can get a better job because I'm willing to go all the way with him, as high as he can go. No matter how much expense it will take or how much he wants to learn, I'll be here to help him. I will not hesitate.*)

While the kids eat, Alex checks the weather in the paper. He finds the *News* a lot more reliable than the radio. It's going to be warm. He is dressed as he always dresses: checked sport shirt, khaki slacks, gray rain jacket, black shoes. He owns only two suits and a few ties. Alex says good-bye, gets into his cab, lights the first cigarette of the pack and a half he'll smoke today, and drives off. He'll be behind the wheel for most of the next twelve hours.

At 8:02 A.M., Alex pulls up to an apartment building not far from where he lives, in Washington Heights, near the Cloisters. His first customer—an elderly doctor who works for the State and whom he's been driving down to Wall Street every workday for three years—is waiting.

—When I first decided to live here permanently, I worked as a waiter at night and in the fur business during the daytime, to learn the trade. In the fur business, if you don't know the trade you are not of any value and you can't get any salary. I learned the trade in about a year and by the end of '51 I started having my own business. I was sometimes making money, sometimes losing money —the blasted thing was like the stock market. Once I was way up in the sky, the next time I was down in the dumps, and I got sick and tired of playing up and down like a yo-yo. I realized that I spent sixteen, seventeen years of my life in that, so I decided that I would like to have a better way of living without the aggravation. About 1965 I started driving a cab part-time. I wasn't taking a chance on full-time because I had to see whether I would want that to be a permanent way of making a living. There are a lot of Greek cab drivers in New York who are ex-furriers, same as me.

Alex pulls down his meter flag, moves into the fast lane of the Henry Hudson Parkway, and heads toward the West Side Highway and Wall Street. The inside of his cab is neat and relatively clean though it looks as though the company which installed his equipment did a makeshift job. A lot of cabs look like this. A hole has been drilled into the dashboard where a radio might have been, and a thick cable runs through it to the meter. Attached to the meter above the dollars-and-cents indicator is a large yellow license—with a mug shot of the driver and his serial number—covered with smudged plastic. The meter provides background music; passengers can hear it ticking behind everything that Alex says.

—I like to be in the open, and I feel independent and happy in the cab without anybody on my head. Even if I didn't own my own cab, I would be free to a certain extent. Of course you always have the feeling that you're working for somebody else's pocket. But what you do to turn that around is to work a little harder and to save a few dollars. You can always get a Small Business Administration loan, and you have your own cab. A lot of people do it.

Close to half of the twelve thousand taxicabs licensed by the Police Department's Hack Bureau are privately owned. It's no small investment—twenty-eight thousand dollars for a medallion and thirty-five hundred dollars for a cab —and a number of owners go into partnership, one driving during the day and the other at night, to cut in half the cost of the medallion. But the price fluctuates, and right now it's down because of the burgeoning number of gypsies. Gypsy cabs are driven by mavericks who often overlook the need to inform the Hack Bureau of their intention of going into business, thereby saving themselves the tidy sum of twenty-eight thousand dollars.

—There are four categories of legitimate cab drivers. Very few are in the first one—people who have decided to make this a way of living, like any other occupation. They are a minority.

The majority are small businessmen that weren't able to keep up their business. They had to find a way to make a living, and this is just about as easy a thing to do for a nonskilled man as anything. That would be the second category.

You will see that more and more minority group people, like blacks and Puerto Ricans, are going into this line. I would assume that you see more of them driving cabs because here they have a certain independence. They can go wherever they want, and they feel like they are their own bosses. Of course they're working for somebody else, but while they're out they're their own bosses and they don't have to work in a factory or someplace else, where they would constantly have somebody on top of their heads. Here you take the cab in the morning or in the evening and you get back at night. You give the fleet half the money back and you take yours. You keep your tips, you get your check, and that's it. That makes them feel that they accomplished something. It's a better way of living for them.

And the fourth group is the students. Some of them find cab driving on the weekends or evenings as a way of supplementing their income, in order to get through college. Some of them have graduated already, they have their degrees, and they're still cab driving. Now how would anybody explain something like that? Some of these fellows, you know, they're disillusioned with life, or anti-establishment, or they got into the business world and they didn't like what they seen there. I don't know if it's temporary for them. I like to think that it is.

Thirty-five minutes after leaving Washington Heights, Alex arrives at a large modern office building on Wall Street. He pushes up the flag on the meter, which shows $4.50, pockets the five-dollar bill he gets every morning, and moves on. At the corner of Chambers Street and West Broadway he spots an elderly lady waving with her pocketbook and pulls over to let her in.

It's getting warmer. Traffic has already built to a peak. In New York the number of private cars driving downtown is piddling compared to the number of municipal and commercial vehicles which fill the streets to overflowing. Police cars, paddy wagons, fire trucks, garbage trucks, meat trucks, cement mixers, trailers, derricks, cranes, steamrollers, buses, grocery vans, not to mention the other cabs. Together they emit a boggling variety of noises and smells, most of them loud and noxious, to go along with the multicolored trash littering every avenue.

—If I would let the New York traffic bother me, I would go out of my mind. It's rough, but this is the way that I make a living. I don't like the traffic, but there is no way I can eliminate it, so I have to learn to live with it. I'd be in favor of building new highways or anything that would relieve this traffic aggravation and serve people in a better way.

Of course I would prefer to take people around by cab, because of my work. But a good mass transportation system makes sense, no question about it. Sometimes I'll happen to have a customer at about four or five o'clock in the afternoon, which is the peak of the rush hour here. The man tells me Queens or La Guardia Airport or Kennedy Airport or wherever, and I'll see something very disturbing. There is a big difference between the West Side Highway that leads to the Jersey Whitestone Bridge and the other highways that go over to the Island. The Jersey people as a rule pool their cars. You'll see four, five, six people in one car. I don't know whether they think of saving us from pollution or noise—I assume they do it for economic reasons. But you go on the other side now toward Long Island, and in only one out of every ten cars will you see more than one passenger in a car. Some day they will have to start banning private cars from downtown areas, during the rush hours, if these people don't start pooling their automobiles. But most of them stay in the car, bumper to bumper, killing time, aggravating themselves—bumping against each other sometimes when somebody tries to cut into them, because they get aggravated. It affects their disposition and also contributes to the traffic situation. More highways might make it worse, but this is a problem that I would leave to people that know a little better than me, people that can see what's for or against a program like that. Thinking and doing something about it are two different things. They might be thinking about it, but hell, they don't do a hell of a lot.

But there will always be traffic tie-ups. Garbage collectors that work on the truck, and collect garbage in front of the house, do you know how many times a day they hear "you sons of bitches?" They hear it about 855 times every day, that people call them son of a bitches, because they're in the middle and they don't let the other guys pass by. If I tell you that they hear the horn about three thousand times a day, it's not too much. Everybody is pushing them, everybody is rushing them. But these guys, they're working for the city and as a rule, people that work for a government, they don't break their necks. But people are forcing them to work a little faster because of the traffic, and it's a panic to see them. They don't want to do it but they're forced because deep inside they feel that they should let people go by, but at the same time they have to do their job. A woman the other day, she gets out of the cab with an umbrella, it was raining, and she went over there while they were working, putting the stuff into the truck. She went with the umbrella and she was giving them hell—why don't they let her go? The guy says, "Honey, please, we get out of here faster if you be quiet."

As a rule the traffic in New York is hard and you cannot speed, you cannot go over the speed of forty, fifty, or sixty miles an hour or you can really get hurt. All the cabs are battered up because we try to make time. After all, this is what we're selling—our time and service—and we have to make time, whether we like it or not. This does not mean that you're a reckless driver. You just try to do a little better, a little faster than the average guy. Squeezing in and out, you have these results. Four or five times, I've scratched somebody's fender or somebody will scratch me, but I've never been in a serious accident. Nobody got hurt ever. New York City cabs must have seat belts but I don't wear them. We figure we're good enough in our jobs not to have to wear them.

It always takes two people to have an accident; it's never just one man. If you don't try to cut in front of somebody else and if you give the other guy a little chance to breathe, you will not be hurt. I'm preaching now, but if you do all these things you stand a good chance of driving a little bit safely. Cab drivers are good drivers, no question about that, but the difference between me and the pleasure-car driver is fundamentally the practice. I'm trying to beat time, I'm trying to make a living, and I don't know how much in a hurry the average guy is, but I don't imagine they're in my particular situation. Therefore you can characterize me and the others as a little bit harder-driving or chance-taking or squeezing in and out. It's true, we do these things.

I can't really get too angry at other cab drivers, but I belong to a very small minority. I try to understand how he thinks, I make me him. When you do that, you find some excuse for him, because if you put yourself in his part, most of the times you will do what he does. Of course there are a few things that are outrageous, some things that you really despise. As a rule you won't do these things, but you try to understand. Some people try to beat you out, sneaking into line way ahead of you or something, a few things like that. I don't like it very much. But I guess whenever you have people, you will always have some who try the easier way to get something that you can't get by doing things the way you're supposed to do them.

Pedestrians, they're like we are, too, some of them are in great need of time. When I see them run in front of my car, I always say to myself, "Look, you want to commit suicide, that's your business, but please don't use my car for it," and I laugh. Last winter with the snow, a seventy-five-year-old man got the red light. He tried to beat the light, but the road was frozen and he slid right under my cab. I lost him in front of the hood. Thank God I didn't hit him. I guess he lost his balance and he slid and he went right down under my wheels; I prayed real hard for a split of a second. Thank God, I've never run into anybody.

Alex greets his passenger with a smile. "Sixty-fifth and Central Park West," she says. He is lucky this morning, he tells himself, to have a pickup so fast. A few weeks ago the New York cabbies won a 50 percent rate increase, and since then business has been very, very slow. (Yes, ma'am. How do you do?)

Alex finds that he misses the people almost as much as

the money, the eight million people doing their own thing in their own little worlds. They make him tick. You don't get zest from dollar bills and change. He has a clipping in his wallet from an old magazine article, the confessions of an articulate cabby, which described some strange fares. Alex laughs when he thinks about the clipping, because he's got plenty of his own stories to tell.

—Sometimes we have to play mother and father. One morning this guy came into the cab about 8:30 and said he wanted to go to Kennedy. He was downhearted that his wife was throwing him out of the house, and he was going over to Kennedy Airport. I don't know where he was headed or what kind of business he was in. I suggested that I get a container of coffee for him, but he says, "No, how about a beer?" Instead of getting *a* beer, I bought a six-pack of Rheingold. He finished five of them by the time we reached the airport. I still have the one that's left over. I talked to him for quite some time, and I wasn't nice to him—I made him admit that there was something wrong someplace, and I wasn't taking him out of the blame. He promised to call me when he comes back into the city. I don't know whether he will, and I am not going to say that I don't care. I hope that he will call, because good can come out and no harm. And then I will give him that sixth bottle which I still have. It's in the trunk.

I had another guy about three months ago, I took him out to Kennedy. When we got there he realized he didn't have his wallet with him, he lost his wallet. On top of that he doesn't have checks, he doesn't have nothing. I'm stuck with him. So what do you think I did? I gave him five dollars. I lent him five dollars to go home, and gave him my name and number. And a few days later I got fifteen dollars in the mail.

I've been stuck two or three times, but I'm laughing because if somebody is that low or that hard up, to jump into my cab and run out on me, I feel sorry for *him,* not me—I work ten more minutes and I make up the difference. But where would that leave him? Look, don't think that I was tickled pink to see that happen to me, but what can you do? Think about it. Look at that poor slob, the son of a bitch, what he has to do to think that he pulled something over.

Once I found a pocketbook full of credit cards, and one of them was a Uni-card. That is just like finding cash. I tried to call the woman up, because I wanted to avoid going to the police. When you go there, you are good for an hour, an hour and a half, because they have their rules and regulations and they have to check everything very thoroughly. I tried to call but I couldn't get her, so I had to go finally to the police department. But when I was calling her from a restaurant over on Twenty-eighth Street, a guy approached me. The word had got around that I found this pocketbook. He said, "I'll give you four hundred dollars for the cards." It was Friday evening— you know what that would do to that woman? They would have buried her, because she had no way of calling anybody. He offered me four hundred dollars to get these cards, but I told him, I says, "Look, if you ever as much as speak to me, I'm going to have you locked up." The guy is still there. He hangs around there.

New Year's day one year I picked up a woman from the Statler Hilton Hotel. She comes out, and you know she had a few drinks. She was going to Fifty-eighth Street, and she was cursing—"I'll show him, I'll show him." I says, "You're going to show what to who?" Apparently it was a company party and she caught her husband out of the room, and she says, "I'll show him, I'll pay him the same way. Cabby, you're not going home tonight." I says, "Honey, I don't do this." She was attractive, but you know you can get very easily in trouble, so I avoid this, especially when they had a few drinks. Anyway, she wouldn't get out of the cab; she says, "You're coming up, you're coming up to my place." I thought about how I could get rid of her. I says, "Honey, look, we now have the same problem." She says, "What?" I says, "We're both looking for a man, so I can't do nothing." In other words, I tried to let her think that I'm a faggot. She was cooled off after that. She told me to go screw myself and she got out of the cab.

At a corner of Sixty-fifth and Central Park West Alex deposits his lady customer and thanks her kindly. He has a special affinity for Central Park, where he can leave his cab by the rowboat lake and take a leisurely walk to a bench near the Mall. If he finds himself here on a sunny day he might pull out some old rags and polish the chrome or fiddle with the engine.

The cab is his business office, and the overhead is high. Besides the medallion, which he'll pay off soon, Alex figures on a new car every three and a half years. He paid $3100 for this one, a '69 Ford, then painted it yellow, as per the regulations. It cost another $350 to get hooked up with a meter and an off-duty sign. Every four days he puts in three tankfuls of premium, changes the oil and filter every two weeks, and fixes the engine as soon as it needs repair. During the life of the cab he will drive 180,000 miles—50,000 a year, 150 miles an average day. For this he makes upward of eight thousand dollars a year.

It costs very little to have the regular driver's license changed to a chauffeur's, but prospective cabbies have to fill out a lot of papers at the Hack Bureau and know where a hundred key places in the city are. They also have to learn the regs, like not forgetting to fill out the log sheets so the tax people know what kind of money they've been making. The Hack Bureau doesn't offer any suggestions on, say, what to do about all the broken bottles on New York's streets (Alex had two flats in one day last week) or which model car is least likely to fall apart.

Along Fifth Avenue Alex stops at a corner drugstore and buys a cup of coffee to go. In the cab, he puts it between his old clock and the meter.

—They don't get cars out of Detroit, they get tin toys. I guarantee if I kick the body of any of these cars, my foot would go through the damn thing. You pay good money, so it's not very fair. Five miles an hour, you touch something, you get out and see that your fender's gone. Hell, with five miles an hour my hand wouldn't be able to hurt somebody if I punched him. It's just another manufacturing product from an assembly line, and if the carburetor doesn't go wrong then something else does. Never a dull day with it.

And there's nothing much you can do, they won't pay a helluva lot of attention to you. When I bought this Tempest, the guy promised among other things that he would put a tankful of gas in the car. With me they usually don't say they will do this and not do it, because I will scream bloody murder. But they did not put in anything more than a dollar's worth of gas, and I trusted them so much I didn't even check it. Then I got stuck on the road, the first day I had the car.

They could do things to make things better, like taking statistics from cab drivers about the damages they suffer or about bad parts or anything like that, and working from them. But there's no such thing.

Alex glides through Central Park. The sun is bright in the sky and he feels good. According to its convention and business bureau and mayor, New York in spring is the world's most exciting city. In the official visitor's guide, John Lindsay says it's a delightful place to visit whatever season of the year. Hotels and restaurants, everywhere you look. Rockefeller Center, the United Nations, Central Park, Times Square, Lincoln Center, the Empire State Building, Madison Square Garden. What else could anyone want?

—I have my own definition of this city. New York is like an unfaithful woman whom you are in love with. She keeps kicking you and you keep going back for more. You can't stay away from her. I love New York—I would not live anyplace else but here, except maybe in the country. I've been to Buenos Aires, Rio de Janeiro, Stockholm, London, Paris, every place in Italy, France, Egypt, Saigon, South Africa, you name it. But there is no town like New York. If I lived someplace outside the city, I would be coming back as often as I could.

Sure you hear about crime in the streets. There's plenty of it. But I would not put the blame on most of these kids —I would put the blame on our officials—city, state, and federal. I'm not a policeman and I have no law enforcement ability or knowledge, but if you ask me, as a cab driver, to give you every night two hundred dope pushers and if you asked me to find two thousand dope addicts and if you asked me to deliver you three hundred prostitutes every night, I'd do it within the space of three hours. Yes sir, I know where they are, the police know, and everybody else knows. What I would like to know is why the police aren't doing anything about it.

The news gets worse every day. You hear the radio in

the morning and you feel like vomiting all over the place. You feel like driving the car right into the river and saying the hell with it, that's the end of the world, let's go. That's how it makes you feel. Every place I turn I don't see anything good. But then there is this kid in my neighborhood, a black boy, that found a wallet with $165 in it. He brought it in to the woman that lost it, she tried to give him twenty dollars. He says, "If I wanted the money I would have kept the whole thing." A neighbor takes his name and writes two letters, to the *Times* and the *News*. What happens? Did he get any answer from them? He didn't. The Federal Communications System, I wrote to them, they said they have no jurisdiction. But if there's something that's bad, if a woman got raped or something, they're happy to report that. Now I put on the news station only to see how wrong they are with the weather forecasts.

If I have a beef, anything that I think isn't right, I write letters, but I get very few answers. I wrote the newspapers about six or seven letters so far, about different things, and I never got an answer. I wrote about the black boy that returned the wallet and refused to take the reward, but I didn't get no answer. I mean in days like these, times like these, it's good to write something good about kids, you know? They're not all as bad as we all think they are, they're not all criminals. Instead of playing big a guy that rapes somebody, play up something good. What's wrong with that?

My wife writes letters, too. She wrote to Bess Meyerson and told her that she voted for her for mayor, a write-in vote, because she's the only working commissioner this city has. And she got an answer. We were happy about it. We wrote some letters up in the neighborhood to the police headquarters about the group of youngsters in the neighborhood. Nothing was done about it. We didn't get an answer.

A man dressed in a mod suit waves an umbrella at Eighty-ninth and Central Park West. It hasn't rained in three days, Alex Panos thinks to himself, so why should it rain today. The man continues to wave as Alex whips around in an illegal U-turn and, smiling, pulls up to the curb. *Where to, sir?* "Gramercy Park South, the Players Club. Do you think you can make it in ten minutes?"

I dunno, but we give it a try. The cab lurches forward and melts uncertainly into a stream of traffic. Alex figures there are about seventy lights between here and Gramercy Park, and that he can make three-quarters of them. Twelve-minute trip at the inside. But this looks like a good tip. Fancy dresser, Players Club. Alex has a sixth sense about tippers and when he adds in all the clues, it seldom fails him. (*You have to have a feeling for it, that's all. The Puerto Ricans are the best tippers. The Germans, Greeks, English, and Italians are the worst. You can usually tell who's on an expense account, especially at the airports, by those people who carry briefcases and light suitcases.*)

At 10:35 the traffic on Central Park West has slackened to a reasonably steady flow, so that it's possible to pass a dozen or so green lights at one clip. There is nothing much unusual happening in the sea of people and machines and signs that blend into a moving picture through the windshield of the cab and out its side windows. Alex takes it all in as he keeps up a running patter with his fare. He is more aware of the traffic around him, since he wants to make time, than of the small talk going back and forth.

Left at Twentieth Street. A few more blocks to the Players Club. Alex glances at the lensless alarm clock, sitting on the dashboard, and sees it's taken him twelve minutes to get here. Pretty close. He pulls up slowly to an old townhouse with black wrought-iron grillework in front, and a gold plaque with Greek masks of comedy and tragedy above the door. Alex says, "Here we are. Ten minutes flat." He puts up the flag on the meter, which reads $3.50. Across the street is Gramercy Park, a one-block square lifted straight out of an O. Henry short story. Around its perimeter is an iron fence. The park is open only to residents of the surrounding houses, who have keys. "Thanks—keep the change," says the man in the mod suit. He hands Alex a five-dollar bill.

Maybe the luck is changing, Alex thinks to himself. For the past month and a half, ever since the rates went up, he's averaged less than half his usual number of fares per day and the tips have been next to nothing. It used to be that a cabby's tips would add up to 30 percent of what he's booked for the day, but after the rate hikes,

not any more. Most cabbies don't declare all of their tips
—the government expects 15 percent of total meter read-
ings—but even that's not helping. It also used to be that
you could sort out the good from the bad tippers—always
pick up a Puerto Rican, never a soldier or sailor. Now
everybody's cheap.

—The biggest tip I ever got was when I went to Aque-
duct Race Track. As a rule when it's late in the day over
there, we stay and try to get two or three people to go
into the city, to make a few dollars more. This guy came
out in a hurry and I guess he had just won a lot of
money, because he asked me to take him to La Guardia.
Before I opened my mouth—to tell him, wait, so I can
pick up somebody else, to make it worth my while—he
says, "Don't worry, you get thirty dollars." It was an eigh-
teen- twenty-minute job, and the regular fare on the old
rates was around $3.35. And he gave me thirty dollars.

It's 11:15 A.M. Alex cruises along Thirty-fourth Street
toward Herald Square, turns north on Broadway and
goes as far as Seventy-second, then heads through the
Park and back down Fifth Avenue. He has to wait twenty
minutes before he gets his next pickup, a woman with
three children who wants to go to Hayden Planetarium.
A five-minute, two-dollar trip.

Even with the massive subway system and thousands
of buses, some eight hundred thousand New Yorkers used
to take at least one cab a day. Then the rates went up
and the average fare skyrocketed from $1.35 to two
dollars. The old-time seven-dollar total from midtown
Manhattan to Kennedy Airport doubled to fourteen. The
people struck back. A man told *Time* magazine that "those
guys think New Yorkers will accept anything. Maybe we
can take a stand here and show them." *Time*, and native
commuters, advised tourists to take the subway.

Now cabs line up in mournful dormancy outside train
stations and bus terminals; it takes a heavy rain or very
late hour to overcome the people's newfound resistance.
The taxi industry remains stoic, certain that the people
will come around, it's all a matter of time. It used to be
very hard to get a taxi when you wanted one, it was a
valuable commodity, and the drivers still feel that the cab-

taker is a special breed who disdains bus or subway.
They might be right, but for the time being the cabbies
are coming round first. Courtesy and cheer, once foreign
words to men hardened by many years behind the wheel,
are heaped forth in salesmanlike splendor. The slack
summer season is coming on, and many cabbies are
beginning to shift uneasily.

Alex accepts it all matter-of-factly and defends the strike
that brought about the rate hike. Under the old system a
two-mile ride cost less in New York than it did in Boston,
Chicago, Houston, Los Angeles, or San Francisco. Now
New York is right behind San Francisco. Alex pulls up
to the Museum of Natural History at Eighty-first Street
and points out the direction of the Planetarium. The meter
reads $1.80. The woman gives Alex two dollars even.

—Right now everything is fouled up. Sometimes people
don't tip you at all and very seldom will you find a guy
that will give you say 15 percent. Prior to the increase
you make a trip up in the Bronx, for instance, and you
invest an hour and ten minutes. You know you have
another half hour to come back before you start working
again. It's four dollars on the meter, and the guy gives
you a quarter tip. Well, you don't take that kindly, because you figure you work an hour and three-quarters
for two dollars. And you say, "Well, wait a minute." You
try to explain to him the time involved, and you tell him
that this is what you get—you get 50 percent of what's
on the meter—and you don't feel it's fair that you should
be treated like that.

I sympathize with anybody who has a grievance, a
legitimate one. I being a salaried guy who has to work,
I can understand their problems, because I go to the
same grocery store and buy the same groceries like they
do. Cab drivers' grievances were very definitely legitimate. Maybe the rates shouldn't have gone up that much
all at once, but on the whole it was justifiable. We are
just about par now. We're making the same money we
used to make some time ago, before the increase. For
the past few weeks, we're getting about 50 percent of the
fares we used to and we make just as much. We're holding our own—at least we're not getting worse. I would
classify myself among the hard-working cabbies. Of

course some days you get four or five fares more or less than the other hustlers, but on the average I mean that I work about as hard as anybody can in the number of hours I put in.

But it's not like it used to be. I had a lawyer once from Chicago pick me up at La Guardia. Apparently he was representing six or seven people that were hurt in an airplane crash and he came down here to settle the case out of court. I picked him up, he asked me how much I wanted an hour because he wanted to employ me by the hour. So I tell him, I said, "Eight dollars an hour." He asked me if I knew a quiet restaurant and I drove him back to Cavanaugh's on Twenty-third Street. I had to stay out there and wait for him to finish. They ate, and they had drinks. It lasted from 12:30 till about seven o'clock. On occasions, they would send me a drink out with the waiter. That was a good day.

I feel I pay a lot of taxes because I'm earning somewheres about two hundred dollars a week, and I'm paying about forty-eight dollars taxes a week on the average. It's a big chunk out of my pay. You get five thousand dollars a year, for argument's sake, and you can't go to the boss and say look—this went up, that went up, right? Taxes are being higher and that's being higher. All of a sudden the cab driver comes along and says he wants an increase in fares. "The hell with you," you say, "then I'll walk." You know you can do without. But what about me? I got expenses, too.

A few weeks ago my wife asked me for a ten-dollar increase in her allowance. I said, "All right, we'll talk about it, we'll negotiate." Well, I like strawberry jam. She puts it on the table and says to lift the square price tape. I lift the tape: three for a dollar—that was from weeks before. Now it's thirty-nine cents—a 20 percent increase. Three years from now I'll be picking up more people but still I'll be screaming for another rate hike.

I don't have to tell you about the ten dollars. She got it.

We don't go out very much because the budget says no. Every time you move out of the house, you have to figure the theater and a sandwich or something, it's a twenty-dollar bill, and a twenty-dollar bill could be put to better use. We're always very careful with whatever we spend. But with two kids, one in college and the other approaching college, you don't save.

While I was on strike, I took two hundred dollars out of my vacation fund that I put fourteen dollars into every week, and I haven't been able to put it back yet. While I was out, I painted all the closets. My wife found something for me to do. I did the closets, I scraped some of the floors a little bit, I cleaned a little bit. I didn't do a helluva lot. I don't know how the hell I'm going to put that money back.

Alex heads through the Park again, over to the East Side. He glances at his log. He's had ten fares so far, a slow morning, and it looks as if it's going to be a long day. Things will have to pick up in the afternoon, even to reach thirty fares—less than half his average before the rate hike. He cruises slowly along Madison Avenue until Seventy-fifth Street, then stops in front of the Whitney Museum. He tells himself he'll wait for five people to come out of the front doors.

The fourth and fifth people to leave the Whitney are a teen-aged couple, the girl swinging a camera by its strap. Tourists. Alex calls through his side window, "Wanna ride?" The boy asks how much it will cost to get to the United Nations. Alex says, "I take you there for a dollar." The couple hops in.

At First Avenue and Fifty-ninth Street Alex spots a beaten-up turquoise limousine with a small amber light mounted on one of its front fenders. "A gypsy," he mutters, and shakes his head. The gypsies are thorns that straight cabbies have to live with, but the function they used to serve—transportation in Brooklyn, Queens, Harlem, and the Bronx, where legitimate cabs tended to make themselves scarce, and when there was a great shortage of taxis in the city—has been superceded by the recent and drastic decline in fares. Now when a gypsy appears in Manhattan, the straight cabbies blow their tops. The mayor has established a Taxi Commission so that things like the gypsy cabs can be effectively discouraged, or at least regulated. But vast portions of the hack code are regularly overlooked. The Hack Bureau is supposed to police the cabbies—among other things, to check for discrimination against black would-be fares, cruising around with the off-duty sign lit, highflagging trips where the meter doesn't move. It's an impossible job. The Bureau tends to concentrate on the airports, but sometimes it's hard to tell who abuses the law more, the cabbies or the hack inspectors.

—Last August I was at Kennedy Airport and there was this redheaded cop there, I don't know his name. A woman approached me, and asked how much do I want to take her to Fair Lawn, New Jersey. I look at my book and I think it's worth thirty-five or thirty-three dollars, I forgot which one. So I told the woman thirty-two dollars. She says, "No, that is too much, I'll give you fifteen dollars." I says, "No, you'll have to get another cab that goes for fifteen dollars, I'm not." And she left.

The cop was waiting for me, he was talking with another guy next to him who apparently was a hack inspector. This guy comes over, running. "Let me have your card, your picture." He takes out his badge: hack inspector. I says, "Congratulations, you're a hack inspector, now what?" I was angry by then. He says, "What did you do?" I says, "I'm not going to answer you, until you ask me what happened—what do you mean, what did I do? Since when I've done something?" I says, "The way you're going to ask me is, what did happen with this young lady?" (Young lady—she was about fifty-five, sixty.) He says no. He says, "I'm asking you, what did you do?" I says, "You're not going to get an answer, you do whatever you want." Then I said to him, "Since when by talking to somebody I must have done something? I mean what kind of logic is that?" And then he realized, I guess, that I knew what the hell I was talking about—that I wouldn't budge. So he says to me, "All right, what happened with this lady?" I says, "You go and ask her, because whatever I tell you is no good." He takes my picture out so I will not run (because I'm a criminal), and he goes. He asks the lady what happened and she told him that she wanted to go out of town and I asked her whatever I asked her and she says that she wasn't willing to pay me that money, so I didn't take her, and that was it—that was the whole problem. So he comes back, ten or fifteen minutes later with my picture, and he says, "Okay now, take your picture back." I says, "Now wait a minute"; I says, "What makes you such a big man, to stop me from working fifteen minutes?" I says, "I lost a fare, a guy passed by and he took the next cab because I wasn't ready to go without my picture." I says, "Why did you take my picture?" Of course there wasn't any way of me arguing with him or doing anything about it.

The Hack Bureau police are human like anybody else. You usually see them at airports, except that now at the International Depot at Kennedy the cabbies have their own dispatchers. This Taxi Commission that the mayor put in will probably improve the service, but you'll get a hundred different answers from a hundred different drivers about it. There should be some kind of change. When you go to the police department, they ask you guilty or not guilty—somebody must accuse you and that person has to make a formal accusation in front of the judge—but the thing is that when he gets the case before him he reads that cab driver A, B, or C is accused of doing this or that, and in his mind this cab driver did it, period. There is no if's or but's. This guy is convinced already that you have done it—otherwise you would not be there. This is how it works.

Once I picked up a woman from La Guardia. She must have been seventy-five years old and she had two big suitcases. She had a friend with her, too. One got off at Ninety-seventh Street I think and the other on 107th. Now a seventy-five-year-old woman, you're not going to let her carry her own suitcases. So I put the car in park and I went and took the suitcases out. The woman paid me in the cab. I took her suitcases, and I swear to God, it wasn't more than ten yards away I saw the policeman, right behind me. How long did it take me to go over there, say good night, open the door for her and put the suitcases in? About three seconds? Five, seven, ten seconds? I came back, and the guy had pulled out my key, he was writing a ticket: *key in ignition, car unattended*. Now parking tickets, I get quite a few. Up in my neighborhood it's easier to find a twenty-dollar bill in the street than to find a parking space, so I get on the average about ten a year. But this one was a dilly. You gotta pay it, so why get in trouble? But I didn't want to pay. I had to wait to go in front of a judge. I was really angry. I'm not trying to justify the fact that I left the key, I shouldn't have done that. But he should have looked at it in a different way, too.

At the United Nations Headquarters on First Avenue and Forty-fifth Street Alex deposits his teen-aged tourists. They give him a dollar and a quarter. He smiles to himself. They are dressed in levis and old shirts and both have long hair but it's not hard to tell which one is the girl. *Boy, is she stacked,* he thinks to himself. They tell Alex to keep the change, man—peace. He says peace too. Good kids.

It's quarter after twelve. Alex isn't very hungry but he heads straight for Jimmy Walker's place, Forty-third and Madison. Wherever he happens to find himself at noon he usually stops for a sandwich. No more than half an hour for lunch, with maybe three fifteen-minute coffee stops during the day—an hour and fifteen minutes total, except on days when he has to hustle.

He likes the atmosphere at Jimmy Walker's. At lunch time the place is crowded with office people and shoppers. Alex waves to the cashier and grabs a big handful of peanuts from a barrel near the front of the restaurant, orders a pastrami sandwich and Coke, goes to the men's room, then returns and sits down with a cigarette. He picks a table by himself near the front, where he can look out the window. It has gotten very hazy outside. Alex Panos does enough talking during the day; he likes to think during lunch, about his kids and his wife and having a good time and other things. He looks out the window: it is a bright kind of hazy, but he cannot see the sky.

—I don't want to kick my own line out of the window, but pollution caused by automobiles is here—if I say it isn't, I would be lying. But I myself don't usually give it a thought. I know in the morning when I get up and cough I see the results of what I accumulated the previous day, and I'm sure there's a little more inside than that. There's no question that you feel it, especially in the summertime when it's hot and you don't have an air-conditioned cab. But I'm used to it. I used to say to myself it was the heat when I knew that I was getting dizzy sometimes or I felt uncomfortable. Now lately somebody else starts telling me there is pollution. There are a lot of things that we weren't aware of that existed and now we know—I think it must be that and not the heat, because (now that I think of it) I was back in Greece two years ago and it was hot as hell over there, but I didn't feel it the way I do sometimes here.

I had air conditioning in my last cab, but the way these guys are making the air conditioning, they only take your money and nothing else. The air conditioning overheats the cab when you drive bumper to bumper in stop-and-go traffic, to the extent that the life of the car becomes two-thirds of what it normally is. My last air-conditioned cab, I had a Chevy, lasted only two and a half years and these cars usually last three and a half or better.

Of course I don't think my smoking helps me any. I put the blame for that on my uncle. He told me once, never sacrifice anything for the sake of living. I smoke about a pack and a half a day. Some of the passengers tell me not to smoke, and as a rule I comply with that because usually the fares are five or ten minutes and it's not a problem. We get some people like from Kennedy Airport into the city, and mechanically I reach a couple of times for my pack of cigarettes and then I remember that I was asked not to.

The noise, too, is everywhere and I hear it and I live with it. It's very annoying, but I don't particularly beef about it or kick about it. I say to myself, well, the next guy who works on a tractor, he makes noise, and I work in the cab, I make noise. Whatever we're all working at, the other guy makes noise.

Scientifically I wouldn't be able to explain it, but I don't feel as good in the city, while I'm working and going about my business; I don't feel my lungs are the same as if I was out in the country, out in the open. There is a difference in the air you breathe here and outside. If I could get what I need in life, and that isn't a hell of a lot—if I could make a living, I would like to live in the country.

I hear in the radio all day long, do something about pollution, write to my congressman, this and that and so forth, but nothing's complete yet. I cough like a little dog all day long, but it's something that I can't do nothing about. If we all started being uncomfortable over that, then I'm sure we would do something about it. Just to give you an illustration, out in the neighborhood they were throwing things from the supermarket into the street and they weren't keeping it clean. I started with my son, who is an Eagle Scout. I told him, "What are you doing about it? You are supposed to be the troop's leader, what are you doing about it?" They are doing something about it now, because now it's clean. But I didn't tell anything to my son till I saw that we had trouble right in the neighborhood. As the pollution gets worse, they will do something. Unfortunately, like we say back in Greece, we're waiting for the knife to cut us a little bit, to see a little blood; then we'll do something about it. But we don't prevent the knife from coming into our skin.

On the way out of Jimmy Walker's place Alex buys a pack of Luckies and grabs another handful of peanuts. Business has been slow so he figures he might as well chance it and head for La Guardia, even without a fare. On nice days he likes the ride to the airports, anyway, except on Friday, when there are twenty outgoing flights and maybe one coming in, and many cabs go home empty.

Most cabbies do the bulk of their hustling and high-flagging in and around the airports. Riding the arm or highflagging means carrying passengers and not running the meter. This is especially profitable with fleet cabs, where the driver turns over 51 percent of his take to the company, but independent cabbies sometimes highflag for income tax purposes. The fleet owners know exactly what's going on when a cabby turns in twelve dollars after driving 175 miles, but a long-standing shortage of drivers forces them to swallow hard and bear it. Several fleets have installed "hot seats"—anything over twenty pounds on the back seat triggers the clock and meter.

It's usually easy to tell when someone is riding the arm, because the light on top of the taxi is rigged to the meter and switches off when the flag is pulled down; when the light's on, there shouldn't be any passengers in the cab. Most drivers don't bother to cover up their highflagging, especially on turnpikes where the cops are anxious to keep the traffic moving, but the more paranoid have a number of ways to beat the system. Although the meter is sealed and they can't break the seals secretly, they can use a strong electromagnet to jam the meter clock, and the off-duty light will stay dark while the flag is down. They can also turn the ignition key as far to the right as it will go, while the motor is running, which has the effect of shorting the light; this method is good for getting by cops in tight situations. Some hustlers have mastered a way to pull the flag arm part-way down, so that the light goes off but the meter doesn't register. Hack inspectors are supposed to watch out for this sort of thing, but they tend to concentrate on train stations and airports.

All cabbies engage in some form of fare camouflage, although the fleet drivers tend to do more than the independents. Often at the airports they charge group rates (five dollars each for three people into Manhattan) which well exceed what the fare would have registered on the meter. The fleet cabbies pocket everything that doesn't show on the meter, and half of what does—paying taxes only on the registered take. The independents have nothing on their consciences except taxes.

—There are a lot of other things going on which are against the code. For instance, you are at the airport and there is a shortage of cabs and you have a lot of customers. There are thirty or forty or fifty people waiting and one or two cabs coming in. So one guy hails you, you stop and pick him up and you see there are not a lot of cabs. You ask the man where he is going, he tells you Manhattan. You say, "Anybody else going to Manhattan?" And of course it's not the normal rate, you charge a little cheaper for each individual. But that is very definitely against the law—you can't double up and charge everybody separately. On the other hand— now this is the joke—two or three riders can get together and employ a cab. These people don't know each other, they just met at the plane—okay, let's the three of us get a cab—you know what I mean? So these guys they come into the city from La Guardia to three different hotels for a buck and a quarter each. But of course there is no law that I can say to them, "You can't do it, you know you can't double up." That hurts. It deprives another two cab drivers from getting two additional fares. But I must say when they do something like that, most people are a little more liberal with the tips and as a rule there is no beef about it.

About two years ago. I was at TWA in Kennedy Airport, and the regular flight from Los Angeles came in. At the time there were only about two or three cabs there and about a hundred people. Everybody was jumping, trying to get a taxi, so I got a passenger and then another guy came over and he asked me whether he could ride with me into New York. I asked my passenger and he said yes—you know, make an extra buck—so I took him. Then another man came around and the same thing, you know, going to New York? "Yes, all right, you come in, too," I says. By that time a soldier comes over to me and, "Look," he says, "I'm flat, you know, I have no money." I says to hop in. I figure the other three guys will pay for the trip. So he gets in the back. Now the guy sitting next to me, who wasn't the original one, says, "How you going to charge me?" I says, "Now you start already, we haven't even left yet. I'll tell you what, I'll charge you six dollars." He says that's fair enough. He says, "How about the soldier?" I says, "He pays ten dollars." He asks me why. I started needling him right away. I says, "because I pay for his uniform and his food, I'm a taxpayer." And he got mad at me and he said that wasn't fair. Then he says, "I know you're kidding me, you're going to charge him six dollars, but that's not fair, you know, you shouldn't do that." He was giving me a whole lecture, you know, he was angry at me. I didn't tell him that the guy was going in for nothing. The other two guys in the back, they talked to me and they were laughing. Anyway we reach Fifty-ninth Street, the soldier gets off, and he says, "Thanks a lot, but I would like to give you a dollar. I have a dollar, have a beer." I said, "No, you have a beer on me, keep your dollar." When the guy sitting next to me heard that, he really hit the ceiling. He said, "Why didn't you tell me?" I said, "Why should I tell you if the guy's going in for nothing?" Well, he was the last one out at Forty-first. He had to stew for eighteen blocks. He got out at the Waldorf Astoria, and he takes a twenty-dollar bill out of his pocket. I tried to give him change because I had told him that I was charging six dollars. He says, "I don't want any money from your dirty hands."

Of course he didn't mean it, you know, he was sort of laughing about it.

Alex pulls into the line of outgoing cabs at the Eastern terminal, behind three cars waiting for pickups. Business hasn't been so slow here as in the city, perhaps because the tourists are unaware of the rate hikes—or more likely because they figure New York is New York and they have to put up with it while they're here. Business is always good at the airports. Cabbies arrange their trips to coincide with the times when a dozen flights come in at once, when there are clumps of four or five harried and bleary-eyed passengers—who have probably had to sit in their plane for ten to fifteen minutes on the runway—justling for empty taxis. At those times Alex wishes he had a twelve-seat limousine instead of a four-door sedan.

Alex waits for the three cabs in front to pick up fares—about five minutes—and then opens the door for a middle-aged florid-faced gentleman who seems to be in a hurry. "Fifty-sixth and Broadway." Alex pulls a black suitcase into the back seat well. The man starts talking about the demonstrations in Washington. Alex is tired of thinking about radicals and liberals, of defending them for the most part; he's more of an expert on Lindsay and local politics, but he talks anyway. Keep the customer happy.

On Fifty-sixth, just before Broadway, construction crews are blocking the street. Alex's lips keep moving but his voice goes dead—outside the cab a jackhammer is pounding the pavement and a portable water pump is otherwise disturbing the peace.

—Nixon is not for me, he's for the big boys. I never voted for him and I never will. I happen to belong on the other side, with the little people. He put the interest up to 8½ percent, he lost business, and now he tries to revive it. But it's not so easy when you kill somebody to revive him, you know? It takes a little more.

I don't think very much of the Mayor either, but I'm a funny guy. A lot of people can blame him for this and that, and you know the guy's above these things. But he did something that I don't respect him for. We had a man that was heading the summer youth programs here named Mr. Smith, and the federal government gave three million dollars for their summer program. The Mayor withheld that money because there was a lot of discrepancies, so this Mr. Smith took three hundred of these kids and went down to demonstrate and they got out of hand —they upset some cars of officials and they wrecked them. Now, Mayor Lindsay got on TV and he said that Mr. Smith was fired and he also said that he would punish the kids that created the actual damage for they were known to the police. Whether that was hasty or not is immaterial. What bothered me was that I got up the next morning after he appeared on TV, and I read in the *Daily News* that Mr. Smith was reinstated and that they gave the million and a half dollars to them.

Now that doesn't sound too bad, but I'll tell you why it sounds bad to me. Suppose I am an eighteen-year-old boy and I say, goddamn you, I beg, I kiss your feet, I ask, I plead to get that money that was coming to me for my program and I did not get it. Now what did I do and I got it? I made a demonstration and wrecked a few cars, and I got it. From now on, whatever I need, there is no other way to do it. Well, Lindsay had no right to make kids think in that direction. If he didn't make the decision about Smith I wouldn't have blamed him at all, but once he made the decision, make it stick or be quiet about it, you know what I mean?

I sent him a registered letter, and I didn't get no answer.

Some government people are good, but not many. Henry Barnes picked a city that was upside down and he made it possible for us to drive. He did a very good job. How could he not be good? The guy was the only working commissioner the city ever had. Plus Bess Meyerson Grant—she's a working commissioner, too. These are the people you need, people that have a willingness to work, to do something for you. The present commissioner of traffic—his name in Greek means "comedian." Do I have to say more?

I have very definite opinions about our system in this country. There is a helluva lot of room for improvement, no question about it. Big room for improvement. You want to start with crime, you want to start with big business, you want to start with the judicial system, you can start from a hundred different things. But I say as im-

perfect as they might be, damn it, they're by far better
than any other place I have been, and I have been in a
lot of places. As long as we're able to talk about our
shortcomings, and about our mistakes, and about the
wrongs and the rights, we have a chance to improve it.
And you know with the younger generation now, I think
we have a good chance in a few short years to change
things around and make this country a helluva lot better
than what it is.

I get people in the cab all day, they work in the offices,
small guys who have aspirations of becoming bigger and
bigger. I hear back in the car the gossiping, how one
tears up the other. If there are three guys, one a little bit
advanced in the business over the others, the two guys
would tell the one what he did wrong. It's worse than
women gossiping in the neighborhood. You don't become big without stepping on somebody. The big executives, they only think how to get more money.

In my way of thinking, only knowledge and ability
will get you ahead, and not gossiping. If you have the
goods, you'll get ahead, unless you have a boss who
doesn't know his behind from his elbow. If a boss will
advance me because I lick his shoes, then he's not a boss,
he doesn't know what the hell he is doing. If he advances
me because I know something and I can do my job better,
I don't have to gossip, I don't have to lick anybody's
shoes.

Two in the afternoon. Alex's log shows sixteen fares—
he may still make thirty for the day. From Sixty-fourth
and Third he zigzags through Manhattan, down to
Greenwich Village, over to Chelsea, back to Chinatown,
up to Rockefeller Center. Four pickups in the hour, worth
twelve dollars and change. Not bad if he can keep it up,
but Alex knows better.

At Columbus Circle he's flagged by a bearded black
man, who wants to go to the Abyssinian Baptist Church
in Harlem. Alex nods, lets him in, and heads north along
Central Park West. Some cabbies make a rule of never
picking up blacks. Too many things are liable to happen,
especially in Harlem—which they figure is still no place
for a white man, day or night—but nowadays in most
other outlying sections as well. Fleets and independent

drivers buy specially designed Checker cabs with bullet-proof shields between the front and back seats. There's a tray fitted through the front seat which allows money to be passed back and forth. Once a driver locks the front doors there is no way of getting at him, theoretically. New Dodge cabs come with Plexiglas shields mounted on runners, which are vulnerable to guns, knives, and ice picks but still better than nothing.

—If they don't look good to us, if we feel they are dangerous, we don't pick them up. Now these people are aware of it, and it's unfortunate that out of five hundred people that would appear bad, only two or three of them might be the ones that they would do something to you. But you gotta take a chance sometimes. I'm on Forty-seventh Street and Seventh Avenue once, and a young girl, a black girl, puts her hand up. When it comes to that, I'm colorblind, I don't see no color. I stopped. Now between two cars there were two more black fellows. As soon as she opened the door and got in, they came. I says to myself, now what the hell was that for? when I saw them coming in. I says, "Where to?" One of the men says, "Washington Heights." I didn't like it. After I went a few blocks up, I said, "Whereabouts in Washington Heights? I live up there, I might be able to find the best way to get there." He says, "174th Street and University Avenue." But that's the Bronx. Right away my mind works in the wrong direction. First, the way they got into the cab. Second, they give you wrong directions. I tried to talk to them, they wouldn't talk. If that doesn't have the earmarks of a stickup, what else does? I could taste my heart in my mouth, that's how scared I was. I would stop to pick up anybody, but for at least twenty-five minutes, inside of me I wasn't right.

As it turned out, they happened to be very fine people. In fact it was $3.30 on my meter, and they gave me five dollars, keep the change. A beautiful tip. My point is if you avoid one then you penalize ninety-nine. You know it's not fair. I guess if those new glass partitions can save one life then they are good, but you are not able to communicate very well with them, and I like to talk.

I guess I'm lucky. I came close to being held up once, but I was saved by a Negro fellow up in Harlem, 145th

Street. I don't know why he did it, but God bless him, he just stepped in the middle and he chased the other fellow out. If I ever see him again, I owe him a couple of drinks.

Every day we're waking up. I'll be honest, twenty years ago I used to see a Negro person in the street, so big goddamn deal, it's a Negro, he's black and I'm white, what's the difference? I wasn't against him then. *But* I never lift a finger to help him. He was black and I was white, so I never bothered to know what makes him tick, what's his headaches. I never ask him when he goes for a job and is turned down because he's black, I never ask him what's inside of him. But now I know, maybe not 100 percent, but I know who he is. I feel for him. I'm sure other people are the same way.

Sure I have hope for the future. Twenty years ago I didn't even know that this man had any feelings, that he had a family to feed, that he had to do something for somebody, I didn't know his cares, his headaches. I didn't know. And I still don't know what it is to get up in the Goddamn morning and see that you go nowhere. That's a terrible feeling. Well they don't have that today, I mean at least the ones that want to move a little bit. I see black cab drivers buying cabs every day. They want to do something with it. This is a heartwarming thing, you see them go and fight and try to do something. We're getting there, we learn a little more, we're educating ourselves a little more. The only thing that I see wrong in some of the kids today is that they try to separate the older generation from theirs, and you know, instead of seeing that, you know what I wish I could see? I wish I could see a youngster come and hug me and kiss me and teach me how he feels, how he understands things, instead of just brushing me away, thinking I'm an old son of a bitch, and I don't know what I'm talking about. All right, I don't know what I'm talking about. You know a little better than me, you think you know—so talk to me, teach me, make me understand who you are, what you are, what you think, what you like, what you love, what you want to do, how you're going to do it. Maybe I have something to chip in, maybe I don't. You know what I mean?

Alex drives along 138th Street and heads back down-town through Harlem. The tenements are teeming. Eighty-two degrees at two-thirty. He stops for coffee. Traffic is as bad as always.

During the next five hours he picks up twelve more fares, which take him to Park and Eighty-sixth, the New York Cornell Hospital, Lincoln Center, Ninety-sixth and Central Park West, Amsterdam Avenue and Seventy-second, the West Side Airline Terminal, Carnegie Hall, Police Headquarters, the Public Library, Peter Cooper Village, Hunter College, and the Public Library again. Twenty dollars.

At seven twenty-five Alex draws his second longest fare for the day, from Tenth Avenue and West Fifty-ninth Street to Riverdale in the Bronx. During the course of the last eleven hours he's had to pull over for three fire engines, make about seven u-turns, and stop for close to four hundred red lights. An average day, except for the number of fares. Even so, he's taken in close to forty dollars and things could be a lot worse.

—I've picked up a lot of interesting people. I've picked up Milton Berle and I wish that I will not have him again in the cab. He wasn't a nice man at all, not at all. He was a guy that it seemed in the ten minutes the trip lasted, the only way that he can have fun is if he makes a jackass out of you. And yet I've picked up people like Henry Fonda, Julie Harris, I mean people that they are lovely to talk to. It's a pleasant thing to meet them and to say hello, the way they are. Henry Fonda was trying to disguise his voice and I started laughing. I said, "Okay, okay, now I know." I took him to the David Frost show, he was a guest that night. A lovely person.

You heard the expression about New Yorkers, you know about how bad they are, and how rude they are, and how miserable they are—well, I'll tell you my exper-ience with them. If you meet them outside in the street, whether they're afraid or they don't know you, they are hesitant; they don't react the same way. But you get them into the cab, you start talking to them, they open their hearts. It's funny, but I find them full of compassion and good people, good people. As much as everybody else tries to say that they are not what they should be, New Yorkers are great—I found that with them.

Last night I picked up a nurse. She was pooped. She wanted to go home, and she couldn't afford to get a taxi, but she was ready to faint she said. And I took her home. She was working for a cancer specialist and I felt sorry for her—I got jittery myself, to think about the things she sees happening in this world, what we are subjected to every day, getting sick and this or that. The stories that she told me, boy, I wish to hell . . .

The one that did more for me than anybody, I would say, was that man who was working for the government, in the tax department. He explained to me how taxation works, and these big companies how much off they get, by putting up new buildings. They get 50 percent off for twelve years. He explained the whole thing to me. There were things with him I learned, things I wouldn't have ever had a chance of learning. It just happened to fall in my lap and I was very happy.

The passengers make everything worthwhile, even the ones in a hurry. I never met a woman passenger that wasn't in a hurry. They're always late, they're always asking me to please go a little faster, or they're a little annoyed because sometimes the traffic is in front of you. Some of them unfortunately can't blame anybody else but you about the traffic, 'cause you happen to be the one who drives the cab.

I start laughing and settle them down with my steady routine: they are beautiful and good-looking, or they're very well preserved. As a rule, I say that they look to me about twenty years less than what they really look to me, and that makes most of them happy. I tell them in a laughing way, "If you didn't spend two hours in the mirror, you would have ten additional minutes to go where you're going." But I say something like, "I forgive you because you did a beautiful job—you look like a doll, so it's worth it." Anything to make them a little happier.

At 7:55 Alex spots four college kids near New York University who want a ride to Yankee Stadium. If they had flagged him five minutes later or wanted to go into

Manhattan, he'd have passed up the trip. He wants to get home to his wife and kids. But these days a dollar is a dollar, and with Yankee Stadium ten minutes away he should still make it back to Washington Heights by 8:30, maybe catch part of the ball game on TV.

Alex talks all kinds of sports with his passengers. He tells them that he's always been a Yankee-hater and that things have never been the same since the Giants and Dodgers left, the Mets notwithstanding. They are more interested in his career as a soccer hero. In ten minutes he figures that he's met them, knows them, and likes them.

—So far I told a lot of people that I don't like what they do and to go to hell and nobody has locked me up. There was a cop the other day, and he told me to shut up. I said, "Now just a minute, you tell me to shut up once more and I'm going to belt you right in the nose, and you do what you want about it. You're not going to tell me to shut up—I read a little bit of the Constitution of this country." And he looked at me and he says, "Well, I didn't mean that." I says, "Okay, I didn't mean that I will hit you." And we left it at that. As long as I'm able to tell people what I think, and as long as they would tell me what they think, we have a chance. As long as we communicate.

What I'm trying to say is we're progressing, we're learning about each other. And we'll get there, no question about it. If I don't have any hope for the future, I might as well jump in the river.

You go back in the history of the world. Some time ago the king had the right of life and death over the people that lived in his kingdon. Well, things changed later on, and we had the same thing but with a little better form. Later on people used the law, and in some cases they still use the laws today. So can anyone tell me that in all these times, they don't see any definite progress in the world getting to be better? I grew up learning and seeing Germans as enemies; today Germans are friends. Once Japanese were enemies, today Japanese are friends. I will not take life any other way. I look for the good things, something that can make me happy, something that can please me. Why should I look for bad things?

It's funny with this job. As long as I'm driving the cab

and I'm working twelve hours, I don't feel it. I'm fresh and I'm just going. When I go home, I put on the TV for ten or fifteen minutes and I pass out. Then my wife has to come and shut it off. I don't remember the last time that I saw a complete program. I never thought of retiring. Some day I'll have to, but I feel as long as you are willing to work, you can always make out. I'm not the type of a guy that wants too much. It wasn't too damn long ago that I didn't have kids or anything much else, but here I have a couple of pair of shoes and two suits. Would you believe that we had one suit between three brothers? The unfortunate part was that we were not the same height. I'm the tallest, and we go like a step-ladder. The middle one was wearing the suit, it was okay, but when I used to wear it the damn sleeves were up to here, and when my little brother used to wear it, the sleeves were down here.

Yesterday I was twenty-eight years old, today I'm forty-seven. If I were twenty-eight again, that would mean that what I've done from twenty-eight to forty-six would be erased, and I don't want that erased. It's a good period of time. I have a lot of memories, I've got a lot of things that I consider good. If you ask me if I want to prolong my life and make it to 150—yeah, I'll do anything for that, well, of course with a few exceptions. A few days I could do without in my past because I wasn't always an angel, you know. I was very fortunate with my wife, because she was a big help to me. I never used to think on how to improve or anything like that. She put that into me. Sure, some things weren't always that great in my life. But take everything as a whole, no, I won't want anything erased.

At ten minutes past eight, twelve hours after he started in the morning, Alex Panos drops the four students in front of Yankee Stadium, accepts their two dollars, and heads for home.

SIX

The Bricklayer

*Avoid idleness and fill up all the spaces
of thy time with severe and useful
employment. Of all employments, bodily
labor is the most useful, and of the greatest
benefit for driving away the devil.*
　　　　　　　　　　　　　　　　—Jeremy Taylor

—Why do I lay bricks for a living? It's in my blood. My father started, and I followed right along. I wasn't a college-type student, so I went into bricklaying. Being in business for yourself is what makes the job worthwhile. You set your own hours, work your own pace. If you want to bust balls one day and slack off another, you can.

Every summer in high school I worked laboring for my father. Same with the summer right after I got out of high school. Then in October of '60 I enlisted in the National Guard, spent six months away, and when I came back I went to work for my father again. But a year later I got married, and I wanted something more or less steady for the wife. At the beginning of marriage, girls aren't too crazy about construction work. They start worrying about winter and the time you have when

there's nothing to do. So I went to General Motors. I
was nineteen at the time.

For six months I welded car bodies at the plant in
Framingham. It was awful—they called it the jungle. I
was at the beginning of the line and they had all kinds
of welding tools hanging from the air. We were doing
mostly Chevrolets, though sometimes we would push out
a Buick Skylark or a LeMans Pontiac. I got up at five
in the morning. It took an hour to get to work and when
you finally got there, you never knew when you were
leaving because they set a line time—you worked your
eight hours and about the seventh hour the foreman
would walk by and say, "Line time is pushed up an
hour." You had no choice. You stayed. Then an hour
later, about five minutes before line time, that same guy
would come walking along again and say, line time
had been pushed up another hour. I had thirteen-fourteen-
hour days. All I wanted to work was eight. I got out
just before joining the U.A.W. because I was in the National Guard and they wanted to put me working
nights and it would have conflicted with the Guard meetings. It was a miserable job. You were doing the same
thing, over and over again, time after time, with a ten-
minute break in the morning, and ten minutes in the afternoon. I finally got out. I couldn't take it.

By 7:30 Nicholas Robert Abbruzzi is propped up on
his elbows as he sits at the kitchen table, reading the
sports section of the morning *Record American*. His
wife Diane is mixing up a quart of frozen orange juice
while the baby, locked into his highchair, raps hard on
the tray in front of him with a plastic spoon. Three-year-
old Theresa is buried in her daddy's big chair in the
living room watching a black-and-white *Lassie* rerun on
the color television. Nick and Diane paid $540 for the
set and the picture tube blew three days after the warranty
expired. (*That's the way things always work out, right?*)
Nick passes over the results of yesterday's Daily Double
at Suffolk Downs. His brother Paul mentioned maybe
catching a few races at the dog track tonight, but Nick
isn't sure—he'll have to see how things work out today
when they talk with the builder. They used to hit the dog
track one, maybe two nights a week last summer, but

now business is very slow. Nick knows that if he and
his father and brother put in ten-hour days, they could
put themselves out of work in a month. Money is tight.
If they don't score on a few more houses when they talk
today with John Venti, the youngest brother of one of
the bigger family construction businesses in the Boston
area, there won't be any track tonight. Venti is one of
five builders who has had regular work for the Abbruzzis. As nonunion subcontractors, Nick and his father
and brother live off jobs the builders can give them.
Usually July is a good month, with numerous contrac-
tors breaking ground for one house after another. But
this year Venti is the only one framing.

In the past when John Venti needed brickies, he always
called Nick's father. But this summer, the Abbruzzis
dope it out that money may mean more than friendship,
that scab bricklayers will try to underbid them on fast
one-shot jobs, and that Venti might go for it. Nick will
approach the builder personally, talk about the rumors
floating around, ask if it's true that he will build another
four houses. This time the Abbruzzis will come to Venti
for work.

—We aren't far enough ahead to be able to cope with
anything really big. Like last spring, a pair of bricks
fell off a platform and broke my left wrist. I couldn't
lay bricks for four months. Fortunately I was able to
do laboring work, and being in a family operation my
father and brother helped carry me through. But if I
had broken a leg, where I couldn't have even labored,
we would have been very bad off.

Our budget is strange. It's unpredictable. Because of
that a brickie's wife has a helluva time making ends
meet. My father and brother and me might get fifteen
hundred dollars every two weeks for laying a house,
and we split it three ways. But sometimes on a long
job we won't get paid for a month. My wife has to make
the money last. During last summer, from June to October, I would bring home an average of $225 a week,
but during the spring and fall it was $150-200 a week
and almost a month and a half without work in the
winter. This summer if I hit two hundred dollars a week
I'm lucky, and the fall and winter I don't even want to

think about. So when she gets the money, whether it's one hundred or five hundred dollars, she has to space it out to pay the bills.

We spend ninety dollars a month for rent, thirty-five a week for food. I have life insurance that is twenty-five dollars monthly. I've got car and truck insurance, $160 and $190, full coverage. The gas, electric, and phone run thirty-five dollars a month. We make a payment of twenty-five dollars a month on the truck which I'm paying off with my brother. We have one charge account, but we pay it right off. Diane and me are alike, we don't like a lot of bills. We've just finished paying off all our furniture from when we got married. Now we pay them when we get them. This year we finally kept a real good record on our income. We figure on the average I make between nine and ten thousand, but this year it's going to be less.

We have a fairly good life. I mean we don't suffer, but we can never save money by the time we pay for all the necessities. And if something ever happens like a long illness, we'll be in the poorhouse. My son was born with his left ear tucked under. It's not deformed or anything—the doctors say they can make it right with three operations when he's six, seven, and ten—but that's plastic surgery and that's gonna cost something like five thousand dollars. I don't know where I'm gonna get the money enough ahead to send both kids to school and pay for the operations. We're not starving, but this sure isn't luxury living. A brickie can always count on a tough life.

Depending on how he has spent the previous evening, Nick Abbruzzi is variously starved or bloated in the morning. At the Italian-American club late last night, he downed six or seven draft beers. He'll do without his eggs this morning. Diane pours cold juice into four paper cups, brings one of them to her daughter, and passes Nick his coffee, which he treats with two spoonfuls of sugar and a powdered creamer. He has finished the sports section. Now he shuffles quickly through the headlines on the first five pages of the *Record*, then folds the paper for Diane, so that Dear Abby faces up. It's a years-old ritual.

Nick wants to get moving a little early today, so he can have a few courses of bricks up before the builder gets to the site. He tells Diane that dinner time will be five tonight.

In his business, dinner must remain uncertain from day to day—as uncertain as the weather or the arrival of supplies or the second wind of the Abrruzzi men. If things are going well they often elect to stay an extra hour to finish up a job. Diane says they'll do the ribs tonight on the cookout, corn on the cob is on sale at the A & P.

The Abbruzzis have a '66 Buick Skylark which Diane uses for shopping. She got it for 35 percent off when she worked for General Motors as a secretary in a suburban Boston assembly plant. Nick and Paul share payments on a '68 Ford pickup. Nick steps outside and looks at the sky. Hazy, it'll be hot, maybe rain. He hops into the cab of the truck and turns the key, which has been in the ignition all night. Out here in suburban Dedham, fifteen miles to the west of Boston, people don't want to be moved by statistics of rising crime and delinquency. It takes Nick fifteen minutes to drive the twelve miles to suburban Canton, where he and his brother are bricking at a new development of fifty-thousand-dollar homes. He turns up the volume on the radio, its dial fixed on WMEX. Loud, hard-driving rock.

Nick Abbruzzi is a short, stocky man whose clothes fit tight around muscles that have been bulging and firm since the days he first worked out in the high school weight room. His skin is light rust. That, combined with short-cropped black hair and the bright orange-and-yellow Banlon shirts he likes to wear in warm weather, make him appear four shades darker than white under the summer sun. With a cigarette clenched between his lips, he looks tough, swarthy, impatient, a Sicilian enforcer who might talk a crude Brooklynese. Instead he's disarmingly eloquent. At first he stabs the air with his Camel to make a point, *see*, and then he dissolves into a sensitive *paisano*. With friends the talk is lightly sarcastic, about sports and sex and politics. But when Nick begins to spew reflections on his social and fiscal condition, he drops his eyes and shakes his head and you know it's no act. For the last six months, while the fat was being trimmed, work has been scarce and prospects have grown dim. The brickie feels as if he were peddling a luxury.

Braking heavily, Nick drops his speed from fifty to twenty-five and turns past the brick sign he and his brother laid at the entrance of the new Spring Village Estates.

Here a bedroom community of two dozen ranch styles and split-levels rests in measured comfort, on half- and quarter-acre lots. Johnny Venti began developing Spring Village five years ago. First he came with his big earth-moving equipment and divided the area along roads and sewage lines. Then he threw up twenty-five homes on speculation and sold every one in less than three months. In 1968 he was getting thirty-five grand for a split ranch fifty-four by twenty-six, with a two-car garage. Today the same house goes for forty.

Venti follows three basic floor plans—a split ranch, Cape Cod ranch, and full split-level—and he alternates the designs from lot to lot so that no two neighbors will feel as if their houses were stamped from a common mold. The trim on each is likewise varied. Some have full brick fronts, some half brick. The Abbruzzis are grateful that Venti almost always uses brick instead of stone or wood. Venti knows that he's gotten rich sticking to a good thing. Whenever Big John drives by in his red convertible the brickies kid him about the color of the water in his swimming pool. But they're careful not to rib him too hard. The Abbruzzis have a cautious respect for Venti, not only because he's made a fortune without even a high school diploma, but because he's the only one of their accounts who is still pouring foundations regularly.

Venti will have two more jobs for them after the split ranch. Their other builders are dry. Nick will ask Venti this morning about doing those four houses they've heard he will build in Canton. He is uneasy about the new approach. The Abbruzzis are used to being called in on the basis of their reputation. (*We never kiss anybody's ass. We'd rather go hungry than brown-nose with the builders, like some of the subs.*) But they give a heartier than usual response to Johnny Venti's jokes, because deep down they know if they lose him this winter, they won't lay bricks.

The newest house in Spring Village is still a shell. The outside frames have been covered with hard plywood walls and the flooring and unsheathed two-by-four wall frames are in place, but the basic plumbing hasn't been installed and the basement floor is still dirt. Before they are done, the Abbruzzis will lay more than six thousand bricks around the home. They will build a chimney with two fireplaces, two brick stairways, and a face front from foundation to roof peak, all with imitation Cape Cod-style secondhand bricks. The real secondhands cost a lot of money.

If the weather holds and the supplies arrive on time, and if Nick and Paul can put in full eight-hour days, the job can be done within two more weeks. They will be paid fifteen hundred dollars. All supplies—mortar, tarpaper, nails, and bricks—are provided by Venti. Old man Abbruzzi, now working another Venti job, will help on the chimney, steps and windowsills. Two years ago the Abbruzzis would have done the same job for $1,350, but things have gone up all around.

—This year is probably the biggest jump in our prices. They were the same for five years. We've tacked just about twenty-five dollars on every phase of work. For a small colonial fireplace we were getting seventy-five dollars, now we get one hundred. For a fireplace down in the cellar, we were making $125. Now for a wall-to-wall, floor-to-ceiling job, we get $150. Chimneys went from $250 to $275. Brick fronts vary with the type brick. Secondhand brick for as long as I could remember was $150 a thousand. This year, they jacked prices for us up to $170 a thousand. There's a tight-knit group of brickies in this town. All the subs know what each other's getting so we can all go up twenty-five dollars in price. But things are bad now, very bad. There's a lot of scabbing, union guys doing a nonunion job. They go onto a sub's job for two or three days and cut the price.

A lot of people get the impression that the blue-collar man is making a shitload of money, but that's not always true. Sure, some construction workers, union men, are getting six, seven dollars an hour, but a lot of that money is made in lump sums during good periods with a helluva lot of overtime. You get a six-hundred-dollar check say for two weeks' work, and a third of it is gone for taxes. People don't realize that we're idle a good five weeks a year because of weather. Another thing that misleads them is when they have spot jobs down around their houses. You get a brickie, for example, to fix your steps and he charges you a full day's pay for four hours' work. He does it because he has to bring in an extra man and a truck, maybe, and for him he loses a day's pay. The

little guy that foots the bill figures we make ten dollars
an hour all the time, that we're living high when we're
not. Look at some of the white-collar workers. Take an
accountant. Come tax time you go into their office and
spend an hour and they cream you. They kill you. They
sock you good for *their* seasonal living.

When Nick arrives at the half-built house, the site is
deserted. He's laboring this job as well as bricking it,
so he has to be up a half hour earlier than his brother.
The laborer keeps the other men supplied, mixing mortar
and setting up scaffolding and moving bricks. On union
jobs there are often two laborers to every brickie, who
only lays bricks. But the Abruzzis do their own bricking
and laboring.

At 8:20 Nick backs the pickup to the pile of sand Venti
has dropped at the site. He jumps out, and begins heav-
ing big shovelfuls into the rear of the truck. When he has
tossed in a good-sized pile, he drives forward, turns, and
backs up five yards away—next to the Abbruzzi's own mortar mixer. It's little more than a small tank with rotary
mixing blades, run by a two-horsepower gasoline engine;
it is lighter than a concrete mixer, with thinner blades.
The sand used by bricklayers is much finer than the coarse
granules and pebbles used to make concrete. Nick opens
the hopper on the mixer and heaves in three shovelfuls
from the truck. Then, shouldering a seventy-pound bag
of Iron Clad Cement, he walks across what will be the
front lawn of the new home, closes the cross-grating over
the mixer, and breaks the mortar bag on it into the tub,
wincing and coughing in a cloud of mortar dust.

From a fifty-gallon drum he dumps five gallons of water
into a large plastic bucket, splashes it into the mixer,
and switches on the engine. The blades rumble and begin
churning as Nick Abbruzzi, like a careful cook, alternately
drops in a shovelful of sand, a bucket of water, or more
mortar. Puffs of gray dust fly. He uses three parts of
sand for each part of mason's cement. The mixer will
churn out 250 pounds of dark gray mortar folded to the
consistency of cake frosting. Nick's arms begin to glisten.
It's getting warmer.

—The working conditions of masonry haven't improved

much over the years. Oh, it's a little different and maybe a little safer on a union job where they might have conveyor belts to send the bricks upstairs, while we still use a pulley system, but the average conditions have stayed the same for the subcontractor. Prices don't equal what we should get. Unions have gained say three dollars more an hour than eight years ago, but not us. Seven years ago we were making $225 for a chimney, now we're getting $250. And every year the houses get a bit bigger. Our prices might go up a little, but it's for more work done, so you come out the same. My father tells me that twenty years ago when he was pouring concrete, he got thirteen dollars a yard for floors and patios. Now they're making eleven dollars a yard because concrete's a fairly easy thing to grab hold of, and you've got a lot of scabs going in on it.

It's a very insecure job. All told, you lose about five weeks in the winter. That's our time for worrying. We've never starved, I've always met my bills, but there is nothing ahead, there's no money to save. You wonder during the winter when the hell everything is going to break against you. For about five weeks it gets tight in the house, things get a little tense. If you've been in it twenty years, it ain't so bad, because you've learned how to manage your money carefully throughout the year for the periods without work. But we're still unsure of ourselves.

While the mortar is mixing, Nick sets up the guide boards on either side of the house, holding the plumb line that will guide the Abbruzzis as they lay courses—rows of bricks—along the front of the new home. Yesterday Nick and his brother laid fifteen courses against the front of the house from the top of the cement foundation. Today they plan to finish the facade right up to the eaves. He grabs a ladder and measures from the peak of the roof to the topmost course already mortared into place.

Since no bricklayer knows exactly how many courses he'll need to lay in a given space, and since each space might not be evenly divisible by the brick depth of two and a quarter inches, compensations are made in the thickness of the joints between the bricks. If a space will allow him to squeeze in seven courses, he will lay a thin mortar joint. If he could get seven and a half bricks in the space, he'll use seven and gain the extra half-brick depth by using wider joints. The yellow bricker's rule tells how many courses Nick will be able to lay in a given area, and at what joint width. "Twenty-three at six," he mutters to himself—twenty-three courses at a joint width of six. He scribes off corresponding strips of brick width on the two-by-four guides and drives a nail into each pencil mark. Taking one guide on each side of the house, he connects them with a plumb line. Each time he and his brother finish laying a course, they'll raise the line to the next nail notch on each guide, giving themselves a level guide for what will be the top of the next course. Nick Abbruzzi, who almost failed high school mathematics because he was so bad at figuring ratios, can almost estimate the number of courses he'll lay just by looking at a wall.

When he finishes the guides, Nick switches off the mixer and gives three hard raps to the mortar bed—a large metal tray under the mixer that catches the mortar—to loosen yesterday's hardened cement. The brittle mortar breaks off in flakes. He spills it out onto the ground, turns the mixer in its dolly, dumps the fresh mortar into the bed, and scoops enough out to fill two small mortar pans—one for himself, one for his brother. The old man will fill his own buckets later for the fireplace job. The trays rest on a pair of two-by-eights they set up on sawhorse scaffolding the day before, when they were working the low section under the frame's big bay windows. They'll lay five or six more courses at this level, then put up some large metal scaffolding to raise them about eight feet off the ground, at knee-level with the topmost course laid so far.

Nick takes a pair of heavy tongs from a tool chest at the rear of the truck, and begins to set piles of imitation secondhand bricks beside each pan on the low scaffolding. The tongs hold a row of ten bricks. He uses shears to cut the wire bands on the brick stacks which have been dumped by Venti, carrying rows of ten at a time to the scaffolding, and setting them in parallel stacks eighty or ninety to a pile. By 9:45 each supply of brick and mortar will have been exhausted; as laborer, Nick will have to mix more mortar and carry more bricks. Last year when his fractured wrist kept him from laying bricks, he labored every working day for four months. Now the sun begins to get hot. Nick mops his forehead.

At 9:05 Paul Abbruzzi pulls up in a '68 Corvette. He is twenty-seven, unmarried, and like his brother colored a dark bronze. After a hitch with the Marines in Vietnam, Paul returned to Dedham tattooed and intent on enjoying himself for a few years before getting hitched the other way. That was five years ago. Paul still spends four nights a week in the Boston dating bars.

Nick chose the National Guard when he became draft eligible after high school. Six months of active duty, six years of monthly Guard meetings. *Average as hell* in academics, he never expected to go to college. His older brother went to business school, to become a white-collar accountant, and it was understood in the Abbruzzi family that Nick and Paul would move into the business their father had built. If Nick had the chance again, he would still choose bricklaying.

—I didn't agree with that exemption shit, I don't go for special privileges. There's a lot of guys in this country who don't have their sights set on college. It should be equal. I like this lottery idea—if your number is picked, you should go, you shouldn't get a four-year delay. When I was graduating from high school, colleges were fun factories. Fraternities, panty raids, that stuff. There was no arguing or violence. Christ, that was only nine years ago.

I really don't know what's going to happen, but I don't think the college student should have as much of a voice as he's got. That's all you listen to now is college students. I've seen a lot of guys who spent four years in a classroom and don't know how to polish their shoes. They act like big shits. I think that a lot of these people, if they had to work for a living, they would be entirely different. I mean I think they're getting a lot of help from home and scholarships. How the hell can you go to college, pay the tuitions they have to pay, go out at night to drink and buy dope and still pay your room and board? You'd have to make ten thousand dollars on the side. I think if they really had to bust their ass, know what the real world was like, then they wouldn't be so uppity, a lot of them.

I'd like my kids to go to college because it's an easier living to work with your brain instead of your body. I

hope my son goes, but I'll be damned if I'm going to pay
his way through. That would be the best way for him to
get in trouble. I'd rather see him work his way through.
He'd have to want the education, I wouldn't shove it down
his throat. Things always mean more when you have to
work for them. I don't know what the hell my daughter's
going to do. I don't know anything about a woman's
life growing up, being from a family of five sons. I don't
even know how to buy my little girl Christmas presents.
All I know is dolls, and, no kidding, she has more fun
with trucks.

This college protest stuff looks to me like some kind of
conspiracy. It seems too well organized to not be directed.
They say it's the Communists, I don't know. But as for
these characters rioting and taking over buildings, I
think we ought to start enforcing the law. Right now
they seem to be exempt. If *I* ran into a building with a
gasoline bomb, I'd get five years. These kids are being
babied because they're college students. I think the shooting of the students at Kent State was justified. I mean I
was in the National Guard and I know if someone was
throwing bricks and bottles at me, I would have shot,
too. If they give you bullets, you use them if you're being
attacked. If you're not going to shoot, you shouldn't
be using bullets. If you want to blame someone for Kent,
blame some guy way on top of the Guard. You can't
blame the Guardsmen because they're the average guys.
They've got a bullet in their rifles and they don't shoot
until someone says fire. They shouldn't have been given
bullets, but I don't blame them at all for the way they
acted.

We don't see it much out here in the suburbs, but you
read about these revolutionaries. Well, I'm not too
worried about them. I mean I always figured that majority rule would take care of things so that if a minority
threatened us, the majority would stomp 'em out and I
would go along with 'em. I can't say that I would give
up some freedoms to get security against these weirdos,
but I can't say I wouldn't. I would have to see. I don't
see revolution, the overthrow of the government. But I
could see a big stomping-down on the revolutionaries.
I think most people would buy that.

Paul Abbruzzi bums a cigarette from his brother and

asks Nick how he thinks they should play Venti when he stops by. There's no losing him as a *patrone,* or they'll be tending bar somewhere in Boston and the family business will be gone like a puff of cement dust. Nick agrees to careful handling.

The brothers adjust to each other's pace as they start bricking, because with the string guide one can't begin another row until the other has finished and they can both raise the plumb line to the next level. It takes about five minutes to lay each course. They follow a circular pattern: scooping up mortar in their pointed trowels; plopping the cement in a spilling motion to the right; dropping a brick into place with their left hands, squashing out the mortar below; sweeping back to the left with the trowel; catching the excess mortar as a child might lick off surplus jam from a jelly doughnut; then following back to the right with the trowel, dripping the excess into the crack between the freshly laid brick and the one preceding with another small scoop of mortar to fill in the joint; and finally tapping the brick down with the trowel handle. Spilling, rapping, dropping, scrapping, filling, tapping, and spilling—the Abbruzzis rarely break their continuous rhythm as they lay each course.

On this job they use a standard bond. The joint separating bricks on one course is directly beneath the center of the brick above it. In the bricklayers' lexicon, a brick laid sidelong is a "stretcher", and one with its end facing out is a "header" or "head." If the brickies were going around a corner of the house, laying an adjacent wall, they would end every other course with the head of a full brick. The short header would strengthen the corner bond. But with just a front wall being laid, Nick uses a half brick as a header. The Abbruzzis don't buy half bricks, they make them by splitting stretchers. And although the imitation Cape Cod weathered bricks are easy to lay because of their lightness, they draw curses from the Abbruzzis because they don't split evenly on a break—cracking in thirds or quarters but rarely in halves. Nick fractures five bricks before splitting one down the middle.

At 9:30 Tony Abbruzzi arrives. The old man was a laborer in his early teens, graduated to masonry when he was twenty, and has worked around construction jobs for nearly half a century. He calls all the builders by their first names, and he can tell them stories about what it was like in the building industry when their fathers were first starting out. Tony speaks to builders as equals. He is gruff, cynical, profane, but everybody respects his work. He has been getting jobs on his reputation for the last fifteen years, and has rarely had to solicit work. He's built this business up from scratch, for his sons, and he'd like to see his grandsons carry on after them. It used to be that as soon as he finished a job, he'd have more work waiting for him and his boys, but this year things aren't so steady. They have to get out and hustle. Except for the new steel scaffolding, a nonunion brickie's work hasn't changed much in thirty years. They still mix mortar and lay bricks the same way. The job is just as tricky as far as accidents go, and the winters are just as cold.

Tony Abbruzzi is sixty-two years old, but he'll lay bricks all winter if there is work for him. When the cold weather comes, his sons' hands crack and bleed. They have to stop when it gets below 25. Even up to 40 degrees, with their bodies swaddled in heavy jackets and hoods and stocking hats, they must expose their fingers to a cold made all the more numbing by the gusty Boston winter winds. Often when they first take off their driving gloves and tackle the early morning bricks, grisly patches of top-layer skin stick to the frozen red blocks. But Tony Abbruzzi's hands are like suntanned leather. He has laid bricks when it was down to zero and he will do it again this year if he has to.

Nick's wrist aches on cold days. It has not felt right since it was broken last year. Brickies usually don't work much higher than three or four stories, so not many of them wear hard hats. But a tool, a brick, or a piece of scaffolding can do damage from a short ten-foot fall.

—It can be brutal, especially in the winter. You can't work colder than 20 to 25 degrees because you can't wear gloves. The feeling of laying the brick is in your hand—you put a glove on and you lose it. My hands crack up. My father's hands don't get sore. He's more used to it. When the temperature drops it can get bad, and you start looking forward to 32 degrees. When it's too cold you look for inside work. If there's nothing to do, you look for part-time jobs. I know a guy at a dating bar in Boston, and if it turns out like it looks right now, I'll work nights to pay the bills.

I don't even think about the everyday problems, what with the winter layoffs and the summers when you lose one or two days a week because of rain. But there's the danger of falling things, like my accident, and I must step on five rusty nails a year. I guess I've got enough tetanus in me to keep from ever getting lockjaw. Still, I guess the worst time of year is the winter. When you figure you're completely out of work for five, six weeks, the mood around the house can get very uneasy. You can't blame the wife for wanting more security. Then when you are able to get outside, you have to go barehanded, which is good for a nice case of arthritis in old age. There's many an old brickie who quit with crippled hands from laying in the cold weather.

Usually builders move pretty fast during the summer, framing one house after another right up until October. Then the pace slows, and they'll throw in four or five foundations and maybe frame only two. Right now no one's putting up houses. Of our five accounts, only one is building and another is going under with a few attachments on him. If it got to the point where I had to drop my own business, I'd get out—I'd never lay bricks for someone else. Right now I've got a fairly good name for myself for being a good brickie and being married and two kids, I've got something to hustle for, but I'm still living off my father's reputation.

Sometimes my brother says we should incorporate and they should take taxes out of both of us every week. That way I could collect in the winter. As it is, we all file self-employment, individually, I just pay at the end of the year. But what it would cost me wouldn't be worth it in this trade, not unless we had one helluva thriving business in which I made big money every week. That kind of money just isn't around in the house-building industry anymore.

I'm about as independent as you can get, but the self-employed subcontractor doesn't always have things as good. Sometimes I think the subcontractors should organize or something. It's not easy because there are so many damn scabs. Like suppose we hired a brickie to work for us, to go out on some of our jobs alone and do some chimneys and a few fireplaces. First thing you know, he's in business for himself, and he's taken away the builder as a client. I don't think that we'll ever starve; as long as we're subs, we'll be in the business, but I don't expect ever to be a rich man.

Usually the Abbruzzis work two jobs at once—one of them inside, as security against bad weather. While the boys finish fronting the house, Tony will work inside on another Venti dwelling going up a few miles away. ("Gimme some mortar, will you, Nick?" says the old man. "I'm going back over on that Medfield job and finish the fireplace and steps.") The elder Abbruzzi waits for Nick to mix the mortar and scoop up two buckets. Then he picks up both pails, each weighing between twenty-five and thirty pounds, and carries them to his pickup. Without another word, he is into the truck and off.

Nick fills mortar pans for himself and his brother. He looks at his watch. It's 9:45. They each lay five more courses, then nail on wall ties—small one-by-eight-inch strips of corrugated metal that are bent into ninety-degree angles and hammered into the walls just over the top of the last course laid. The next course is cemented over one leg of the ties, to insure that the brick facing is secured firmly to the inside wall of the house. Every five courses, the brothers repeat their bending and nailing. As they move slowly upward, mortar splatters a crusting film across the brick faces. Nick and Paul brush and scrape them every few minutes, and they use a stick or a nail to carve out excess mortar between the bricks.

At 10:40, with four more courses down, the brickies stop to tack up more black tarpaper, which will act as insulation between the facing and the inside wall. Nick and Paul work together, rolling the paper onto the naked plywood of the house, cutting it with the pointed end of their triangular trowels, nailing it into place. All day long they trade small talk, working quietly for a few minutes, then punctuating the silence with jokes, batting averages, horse tips, the weather. They do not talk politics. Nick Abbruzzi knows Bobby Orr a lot better than John Mitchell. He's more familiar with the price of tarpaper nails than with oil import quotas, and he worries more about the prospect of rain than the death of God.

The brothers have been alone at the home site since the carpenters finished their work two weeks ago. Now the plumber, carrying several lengths of copper tubing, arrives in his green panel truck. (*How do you like the banker's hours this guy keeps?* "Hell with you—I been up since 7:30 getting supplies while you bastards were still in bed.")

By 11:15 Paul is thirsty. ("Hey, you want anything? I'm going for coffee. Billy, you want coffee?" "Make it light, no sugar," says the plumber, reaching into his pocket for change. *I got it this time,* says Nick, handing his brother two dollars. "Thanks, catch you next time," says Billy. *Listen, Paulie, pick up half a dozen regular coffees with what Billy wants, and half a dozen doughnuts at that place in Canton. Give one coffee to Venti's man on the dozer up there.* He points to the east of the house where a man in a yellow Caterpillar is clearing a foundation. *The others will be for Johnny and his men when they get here. We got some talking to do this morning.* "Right, be back in about fifteen," says Paul.) He lets everyone know he is driving a Corvette, gunning the engine as he moves onto the dirt drive of Spring Village, leaving rubber as he pulls away.

By the time Paul returns at 11:35, Nick has laid three more courses. A big red stake truck is parked in the dirt driveway of the new house. (*Hey, Paulie, give us a hand with this thing, will you?*) The truck is carrying a crated seven-foot blue porcelain bathtub that the plumber will install on the second story. (*The tubs go in early so they can be tiled in. Man, that's a racket I ought to get into, that tiling. Those boys make about ten dollars an hour and they come to work in a white shirt.*)

On a union job, only the plumbers and supply boys would move the tub in, but here the subs help each other out. Nick grabs a section of the crate along with his brother, Billy the plumber, and the delivery man. They all grunt as they move the 350-pound crate onto the truck's hydraulic tailgate, which lowers the tub to the ground. The four men lift it off the tailgate and move it into the house, carefully stepping up the temporary wooden stairs to the second floor. ("Set it right here," says the plumber, motioning them into the wall-less cubicle that will be the bathroom. "Ease it down, easy, easy, that's it. I thank you, gentlemen.")

The plumber signs the delivery man's receipt, removes his navy-blue baseball cap with the Red Sox B, and sits

back on the scaffolding and brick piles. Today the talk
moves quickly from the price of a beer at the Italian-American club and the Sox chances for a pennant to Big John
Venti, and work for the winter. The plumber mentions
something about the Philadelphia Plan, which seeks to
guarantee minority employment on federal construction
jobs. He's heard that the government will try a similar
plan in Boston. With the economy the way it is, the possibility of blacks being given work over whites ignites a
quiet rage in Nick Abbruzzi.

—If I was bidding a job with my money, I'd put who the
hell I wanted on the job. There's nothing else to say.
Colored's colored. If a guy was fit to do the job, I'd hire
him, but not just because he was black. You can't run a
business like that. There's not enough work around for the
qualified people to have the government take away a good
man's job for a trainee who doesn't have what it takes.
In this trade you get a guy who doesn't know what he's
doing; one thing's going to happen—he's going to get hurt,
or put you in danger. We work heights a lot, scaffolds.
You get a green guy who hasn't been on staging much
and he's scared of it. Christ, it took me four years before
I got used to staging. You've got to get a day's work
from these guys.

But this town hasn't been hit by any big rebellion
groups. We had one colored family out here for fifteen
years. I went to school with the kid and he was well liked.
He got picked best athlete and best dancer. There are a
couple more colored families now, but not that many. I'm
told by the builders that when colored moves in, it cuts
the value of your house, the people move out. This is
what I'm told. I don't hate colored, and I don't love them.
I haven't had that much contact with them.

I didn't like them when I was in the service. They were
from the deep South and Jesus Christ they were bad. They
would have no respect for you. But things are changing.
As long as they keep to themselves, I can't blame them
for wanting to be equal. Provided they don't keep me
from my equality, too. You've got people going on welfare now, and they're making a lot more than people that
are working. I know a white guy who was married and
had six children, his wife died when she was twenty-four.
He works for the county, and he don't make that much

money. So he applied for welfare help, he wanted aid to dependent children. And they refused him. He was making a little better than six thousand dollars a year. Then you've got some of these other people in the ghetto of Boston who aren't working, and they're ending up with sixty-five hundred dollars a year. Maybe I feel this way about welfare because I myself am on my own. I don't like to see some people getting a free ride from other people's hard work and taxes. I can see welfare systems for medical expenses, but I think people should work for a buck.

Nick hears an engine and looks around. It is John Venti, here in his pickup to claim the extra coffee. The Abbruzzis are a little uneasy, but they're ready. At first they spar with the Sicilian, a gentle ribbing to set up something more serious. (*Hey, Johnny, how we gonna flush the brick next to that front door if we don't have no front door to measure?* "I'll go down Grossman's this afternoon and get it for you guys." *Hey, John, when you letting us in your pool? We got to break it in for you.* "Yah, maybe when you guys get around to taking showers I'll let you in. Chlorine only does so much to kill the shit in the water, you know." *Hey, Big John. What's this shit we hear about you taking a chance on another four split-levels here in Canton?* For the first time, Johnny Venti stops smiling. "Where'd you hear that shit?" *I dunno, down the I-A club, one of the guys was—*"Maybe you know more than I do. You got any magic words for the bankers?" Nick is confused. *Hey, I thought you were the golden boy for the loans?* "What can I say, they've got the gold locked up and nobody's getting any. Even Nixon's credit would be bad with the banks today, things are so tight. I can't get another nickel out of them for any kind of interest. Besides, what are you guys doing coming to me for? Don't you do all my houses? Don't I always call you when there's a foundation going in?" *Sure, John. Sure.* Nick and Paul are slightly relieved: no scabs, at least. They are used to Venti's gruff exterior. "Well, don't believe all the shit you hear over a highball from all those retired brickies down the club. I got something going, I'll let you know first." *Listen, John, we know that. We just heard and—*"Well, now you know. You find me the capital and the customers for the house, and I'll give you an extra hundred on the job. Listen, have to catch you later, if you want that door.")

Venti crumples up his coffee cup and drops it to the ground, now cluttered with broken brick and sand and crusty cement. He knows it will be cleared up later by the landscapers. "And listen, when I get everything straightened out with the pool, I'll have you guys down. Nick, you can bring Diane, Paul, you can bring one of your prize-winning thoroughbreds. I'll see you this afternoon."

Venti moves off. The rumors were wrong, but that may be a bigger disappointment. They wish Venti would promise more work. Nobody will care much about swimming pools when winter comes.

The brothers decide to lay two more courses before they break for lunch. Nick finally hits a brick right, splitting it perfectly in half, and drops it into place. The two work quietly, both thinking about the exchange with Venti, for the next half hour. Nick sees by his watch that it's 12:30. (*You done yet, Paul?* "Five seconds." *Let's get to some food. Hey, Billy, you coming? We're going down to Mike's.* "Naw, the wife's packed it today.") At $6.50 an hour, even the plumber is learning to economize.

After Paul locks his sports car, the two brothers jump into the pickup and move out of Spring Village toward the center of Canton. In ten minutes they are at Mike's, a small diner where construction workers in the area like to stop for lunch and coffee breaks. Nick and Paul eat the meat loaf dinner with corn and mashed potatoes, $1.05. They wash it down with Pepsis. Over pie and coffee the short order cook, who lives and dies with the Red Sox, offers his opinion of last night's All-Star game. He can't understand how Weaver can pull Yastrzemski for Frank Robinson. Paul says it's all a show anyway. At 1:15 Nick hits his brother on the elbow, motioning to go.

When they return to the frame in Spring Village, they start to dismantle the sawhorse plank scaffolding and to clear the area for the network of metal piping that will elevate them eight feet off the ground so that they will be able to finish the brick fronting. They compensate for the uneven terrain by shoring each leg of the scaffolding with bricks and boards. Then they arrange two sixteen-foot two-by-eights across the second rung of the scaffolding, six feet off the ground, as a foot platform. If they set another level of planks on the platform, supported by two more feet of cinder blocks, they will be within stretching position of the house peak. An eight-foot-square shelf is set up behind the foot platform, for the mortar pans and bricks. They have built an uncertain, shaky pedestal, but they can't afford to take time to level the ground beneath the scaffolding, the way union bricklayers must, according to safety regulations.

At 2:15 Nick jumps off the steel skeleton and switches on the mixer. It gurgles and churns. He uses the heavy tongs to carry ten-brick sections over to the top platform, grunting as he jerks the bricks over his head like a weight-lifter. Paul catches the tongs and arranges the red stacks next to the mortar pans. Nick scoops the mortar buckets full, jerks them up to Paul, then climbs aboard the walking planks to help tarpaper the area about to be bricked. Each of them scribes new marks in the corner guides, drives nails into the pencil lines, and ties off the guide on each side.

By 2:40 Nick has completed his first course of the afternoon, and begins to worry about how much more he'll be able to do today. This morning the sun was screened through gray haze, which he had hoped would burn off by ten. But by lunch time the sky had grown opaque. Now a heavy circular wind has picked up, and paper cups and empty masonry bags are blowing around the site in the kind of gust that precurses a shower. Soon the sky gets twilight-dark and the drops begin coming down, scattered at first, then pelting. In a few minutes the cigarette still clutched between Nick's lips becomes soggy and droopy. Then the rain begins to sheet, as the two brothers scramble about trying to cover the laid bricks with tarpaper hung from the topmost course and weighted down with empty mortar pans. A brick won't lay right when it's wet, or when the mortar gets too soft. Then, cursing, they seek refuge inside the open frame house. The plumber, unhindered by the storm, keeps his sympathy for the brickies to himself.

A half hour later, at 3:30, large puddles have formed in the dirt yard around the house. Nick and Paul play poker for pennies inside the house. They have lost nearly an hour's work, because they finished the chimney and all the inside work they could on the two fire places last week. When it rained five days ago they had also been idled into card playing, for want of the angle irons that

Venti was supposed to bring for the mantel section on the hearth. (*Goddamn it, the second day in two weeks!*) Paul slaps down his cards. ("We'll have stuff to do this fall all right, but it will be the summer's work. I'm going to try and find Venti for those irons.") He drives off toward the ninety thousand-dollar ranch house that is Venti's base of operations.

It is still pouring at quarter of four. The plumber is in a back room soldering pipes. Nick has exhausted his Camels, and decides to knock off early. *Ain't nobody laying anymore brick today,* he says to himself. He jots a quick note to Paul, but as he is tacking it to the front doorway with a tarpaper nail, his brother's red sports car rolls up.

Paul shouts through the rain from the driver's window. ("Couldn't find Venti. I left word we want the irons and door by tomorrow morning in case there's more of this. I'm all through." *Okay, Paulie. We'll work extra tomorrow afternoon.*)

Paul moves off. In the old days, they would drive home together and hit the bars that night after a shower, but now Nick has Diane and the kids. Before leaving the house site, he walks through the rain, scooping out the unused mortar from the pans and mortar bed, shoveling it into an already crusted heap near the sand pile. He collects his tools, his level, jointer, rule, brushes, and trowels and drops them into the toolbox in the rear of the truck, along with the pulley scaffold that went unused. Then he gets into the pickup turns on the engine, and fiddles with the radio volume. Nick listens through the news about Vietnamization and Mid-East peace feelers, but pays attention to the weather forecast. It should clear up tonight. He stops at the A & P in Dedham and picks up a ten-pound bag of charcoal briquets and some starter fluid.

At home Diane is in the kitchen spooning potato salad into a serving dish. Theresa rushes Nick and he pats her on the head, but he doesn't talk. When prevented from working by injury or weather or delinquent supply men, he gets quiet and tense. It is the same kind of sullenness that infects the house when he's been idle for three or four weeks in the dead of winter, and after seven years, Diane knows enough not to push. Her mother-in-law warned her about the moods of Italian men.

Nick broods out on the screened-in porch while he cooks the ribs on the charcoal grill. He is aware of his silence through dinner. Diane talks about her day. She has shopped at a discount outlet for the kids, done a wash, ironed, visited her girl friend. Nick punctuates with mumbles. She understands. After dinner, he retires to the television and the Boston *Globe* sports section. He has not mentioned the meeting with Venti and Diane hasn't pressed him, but they're both thinking about it. Outside, the rain is still coming down. Nick flips through the *Globe,* then lurches forward to switch off the television.

In the kitchen, he sits down and watches Diane finish the dishes. Then he talks about the encounter with Venti, how he had the wrong information about the four new homes, and how Venti doesn't see framing any more because he can't get the money. Diane nods through it all uneasily, though by now she's grown used to insecurity and disappointment. Nick feels an urge to get out of the house. It's too late to get a baby sitter. Diane says she'll stay home.

He drives the two miles to the Italian-American Club, where his father is playing dominoes with some of the other veteran brickies. Nick describes the meeting with Venti to his father. The old man withdraws to another table, where he and Nick start to make plans for hustling. Beginning tomorrow they will start phoning every home builder in metropolitan Boston. It will be like the old days when Tony Abbruzzi was building his business.

Six more beers, four more hours of talk. Nick and his father mumble farewells, and drive away in opposite directions. Midnight. Nick pulls into the garage, and tiptoes inside the house. After checking on the children, he climbs into his pajamas and slips into bed. Other suburbanites might be preoccupied with the crime rate or the Panthers or the high school heroin market, but Nick Abbruzzi's insomnia relates only to money. He has never read a textbook definition of inflation and wouldn't know a commodity from a ticker tape. But last summer he was bringing home more than he ever expected he could earn, sometimes $250 or $300 a week. Cold cash. And now he might have to give up the business his father took thirty years to build, so he can make more money shaking martinis.

Diane has been asleep since eleven. Nick pushes up the little plastic switch on the clock radio, already set for 7:00 A.M. It will be two hours before he finally drops off.

SEVEN

The Waitress

*Life has no meaning except in terms of
responsibility.*

—Reinhold Niebuhr

*One of the nice things about being a waitress,—
the responsibility is not yours. If it's wrong,
it don't fall on your shoulders, it's the person
that told you to do it. So if someone tells me
to stand on my head in that dining room,
I'm going to do it, and then if somebody
comes along and says that I shouldn't have
done that, I can say, "Well, there's the lady that
told me to do it. It's not my responsibility."*

—Mary Wills

Sprawling north out of the District of Columbia into once placid Maryland countryside, the plush suburbs of Bethesda and Chevy Chase and Silver Spring now blanket the landscape with apartment houses and shopping centers and multiple-lane highways. You can take any of the three main roads linking Washington with Baltimore, thirty-five miles to the northeast, and you'll see hints of a new supercity—the foreshadows of a megalopolis —intruding among the fast disappearing splotches of farm land. It is all part of a massive urban nonplan that will someday stretch from Virginia to Massachusetts.

Silver Spring has grown so uninhibitedly during the past fifteen years that it now reckons itself Maryland's second largest metropolis. Countless residential and commercial boom towns spread north of Washington in a dizzying array of Well Planned Neighborhoods, each plotted to squeeze in as many houses as possible and still leave a little green showing.

Somewhere among the apartments and small brick bungalows of Silver Spring, James Wills and his wife Mary nestle in closely budgeted comfort. He's a government security guard, she's a waitress. Their compact three-bedroom house, painted white, is set on an angle to the corner in back of a well-kept green lawn. Mary Wills does not brag when she tells how they built this house themselves. She is a little, wiry woman with thin wrinkles on her small-featured face and strong, worn hands. She's always been an independent, bootstrap woman, a maverick, a candid talker.

—I was born on a tenant farm. My folks were poor people in the Carolinas of those days. That was 1919. I was raised on a tobacco farm, in Green County, North Carolina. I was the oldest, four more besides me.

A dollar bill was very limited to the people down there. My father never did anything else but farm. Tobacco, that's the money crop. They also raised cotton and corn. A tenant farmer means that you live on this man's farm in his house, eat his food when he chooses to give it to you, and farm his crop on shares, certain percentages of the money. In other words, you make a hundred dollars, and the farmers gets 75 percent, the tenant gets 25. Lots of times the expense and the cost going into the crop is more than the tenant's share, and at the end of the year he ends up owing the farmer money instead of the farmer owing him.

We had an average house, no hot and cold water. We had to carry water from a well. You put it in a bucket, you carry it to the house, you put it on the stove, you heat it, you put it in a pan, you wash your face. No plumbing, no electric lights, no insulation. You want to go to the bathroom, they have a little house out back about a quarter of a mile.

We had three bedrooms, a dining room and kitchen, and we had a living room. My mother, she had her hands full with the housework. She did the washing, ironing, and fixing meals, and we did most of the work in the fields, from sunup to sundown.

I was working when I was knee high to a grasshopper.

The rest of 'em in the fields had to have water—that was my job. My mother'd fix a big jar of water and I'd be so small I couldn't step over the rows, so I'd throw the jar over and crawl across the row, pick the jar up and go again. Everybody works like that on a farm.

We never had to worry about a place to live, or something to eat. We had three meals a day, had our own family milk cows, raised our hogs, our own meat, our own garden, our own vegetables. My mother did a lot of canning during the summer, so we raised all we ate, except if it was coffee, sugar, salt, pepper. Usually we'd have to go in town to get that—about eight miles, ten miles.

When I was six, I started going to school. I walked five miles there and five miles back. It took about an hour. There was no school truck on the route at the time. When we'd come home, we had to step out of our school clothes and go straight to the field. There were lots of times, especially when I got up some size, that we'd go and register the first day and then I wouldn't see the inside of a school till after the dry tobacco had been worked up and sold, and that was the last of October or November.

Then in the Depression, they couldn't get nothing for their crop. People in the cities were standing in bread lines. The farmers had no money to buy clothing and stuff that they needed, but they had plenty to eat 'cause they had raised it. We had people from out of the cities come to our door and ask for food. They were willing to work to pay for it, but we had no work for them to do. My mother always brought 'em in and give 'em something to eat, the only thing we could do. President Hoover was in the White House. When he was elected, he promised the people, he said, you elect me for President and I'll put you on your feet. And 'deed he did. Everybody that even had an old car of any kind, they had to put it in the garage, jack it up and take the wheels off it and make it into what they call Hoover carts. Did you ever hear tell of those? It's an axle with two wheels, two tires, car wheels, you know, and they'd build 'em a seat on it, and they'd put two shafts on it like that and then they'd hitch a mule up to it. That's

Hoover carts. That's how you had to get around. The cars were sitting in the garage jacked up, you couldn't get gas, you didn't have the money to buy gas, or anything like that.

We worked hard, from sunup to sundown and sometimes into the night. When that green tobacco starts coming up in that field, it's ready to come out. You have to cure that tobacco. You get up in the morning at sunup or before sunup, you get breakfast, and you get ready to go to the barn. My father used to have to sit up with it all night. And there was some other tenant farmers, sharecroppers, you might say, and they'd take turns in sitting up at night to keep the heat regulated. Then when that's cured out, we'd have to get up about three o'clock in the morning to get it all out of the barn into another building so we could get out in the field at sunup and fill up another barn of green tobacco. You repeat it, over and over. It takes six weeks to get it all out. Between that you gotta spray for worms, tobacco worms that would eat everything. Good Lord, on a real warm night you could just hear 'em eating away.

I think they were some of the happiest years of my life. I had nothing to worry about. I didn't worry about anything, 'cause I knew that I was gonna get a place to sleep, a few clothes to wear, and a little food to eat. It wasn't much but I got it.

Ten o'clock in the morning. Dressed in a green-blue flowered print that drops two inches below her knees, Mary Wills leaves for work. Bright red lipstick calls attention to the tiny wrinkles lining her face, around her mouth and small brown eyes, below a widow's peak with its traces of gray. She has on horn-rimmed glasses, ornamented in chrome, and wears short white socks and no-heeled black shoes.

—We had school clothes, yes. Just a dress. Then we'd get home and undress and put on old clothes to go out in the fields.

I only went as far as the eighth grade and had to leave school when my mother got sick. She had cancer, so me being the oldest one, I had to stop and stay home—cook, wash and iron, and see to the other kids. It took her a year to go away from here with that cancer. It took her a year to die. And then when she died I could pick her up in my arms and carry her anywhere. She was nothing but skin and bones.

With three sisters, we never dated. One didn't date by hisself. If the one had a date, and her boy friend didn't get a date for the other two, none of us went.

I never left home before Mama died. And then I left the farm for good, when I was nineteen, and never went back. I got married for one thing. He was a private in the Army. We went to New Jersey during World War II, where I worked in a factory making flame throwers, and then when he left there and went to Texas I went to Texas with him. I worked in the PX there selling Christmas cards. From there we went to Spokane, Washington, where I worked as a mechanic on airplanes, and from there to Battle Creek, Michigan, where I worked on the air base. Ann Arbor, Michigan, is where I was when the war ended. I got my divorce then, having been married for five years. Took me three years to get that divorce, but I said I was gonna get it and I got it.

When I first came to the state of Maryland in 1945, I was riding from the bus station to a friend of mine's home where I was gonna live. The cab driver, he must have known that I was a stranger from the way I acted. He kept looking at me and finally he says, "You plan on staying in Maryland?" I says, "Well, I guess so." He says, "Well, I don't want to sound too nosy, but what type of work do you plan to get into?" So I said, "Well, I hadn't really thought about it." And he says, "If it's not being too forward, could I make a suggestion?" And I said, "Well, any suggestion'll help." So he says, "I suggest waitress work." I said, "Why?" He says, "'Cause these stenographers, office help, they don't make the money that a waitress would make."

That was in 1945. So I started working at Howard Johnson's. I knew I was on my own, and I had to make a living. I was supporting three people besides myself—my ex-husband's mother and stepfather and my son. I worked there three and a half years, and then I left 'em. Got bored, I guess.

I went to practical nursing school and graduated from

that. I had my cap, my pin. But I still liked waitressing
work better. For one reason, you're on the move. There's
a turnover of people, and it's not carrying bedpans or
feeding somebody with a spoon—you're not giving nee-
dles, you're not handing out pills. After 'bout a year, I
went back to waitressing, this time at the American Inns.

Well after the morning rush hour Mary Wills drives
through Chevy Chase in her five-year-old white Ford
sedan. Across the Capitol Beltway, past Saks Fifth
Avenue and Woodward-Lothrop and the International
House of Design and Sears, through sixteen traffic lights.
It is far more pleasant here now, for the half hour from
ten to ten-thirty, than it was when the earlier commuters
hassled their ways into the sweltering congestion of
downtown Washington.

Summer in D.C. is filled with humidity and heat; you
feel them when you try to make more than two of the
poorly synchronized traffic lights in a row. Even out
here, in suburban Chevy Chase on the outskirts of
nonindustrial Washington, you can taste the smog and
smell the fumed air. It is midmorning, the sun shines
vaguely. The air is dirty and fetid.

—I get up every morning at seven o'clock to dust and
vacuum. How that dust gets in I don't know. The air
is cleaner down in North Carolina than it is here, 'cause
it's all open fields, unless you go into town. I think the
politicians are spending too much money on other things,
like going to the moon—God put that moon there to light
the earth, that's all. They should clean up the cities.

Mary Wills pulls into a gravel parking lot off of Wisconsin Avenue. Washington-area American Inns # 10 has
not been cut entirely from the standard blueprint. Perhaps
because it's in Chevy Chase, it's bigger and cleaner and
there's some landscaping in front. Broad bay windows
beneath the scalloped roof show the main dining area to
passing motorists.

At 10:30 A.M. Mary changes into her plain white uniform and checkered apron. She is not counted on the
payroll until 11:30, but she comes an hour early to
rearrange the plastic letters on the menu board near the
freezer, to set out clean silverware, and to brew fresh

coffee. She does not expect to get paid an hour's overtime. She puts in the extra time for the convenience of the younger waitresses who have to take their children to day nurseries. She takes her work seriously.

The middle shift at American Inns, from 11:30 to eight, is sandwiched in between a breakfast shift and a night shift. Schedules are slightly different for the counter girls, supervisors, and managers. Mary Wills changes in the employee's locker room, a room in the basement with light-green cinder-block walls. There are no other waitresses down here at this hour, so Mary hurries. She does not like to be alone.

—They furnish your uniforms here, and you're responsible for keeping them clean. I'd rather have it that way 'cause nobody can do my uniform to suit me. Shoes are supposed to be polished every day. Shoestrings are supposed to be clean, too, but not a lot of the girls care. You watch their feet some time. I told one girl—she's single, a college kid, got no responsibility—I says to her, "Look, Amy, don't you own a clean pair of shoestrings?" I said, "Honey, if you don't and can't afford shoestrings, I'll buy 'em and bring 'em to you if you'll polish your shoes tomorrow morning." She just stuck her head down, didn't say nothing. The next morning when she come in, that's the first thing I did was look down at her feet. And she says, "I'll have you know I put new strings in and polished my shoes." I says, "I see you did. You look nice." Now you know darn well a college student could keep their things clean better than that.

Anne Jackson, she come in there one day, and honest to God, she looked like she'd been drug up the back of a chimney and beat over the head with a soot bag. Her hair was stringing all down, her uniform was dirty, and her shoes—I took one look at her and I says to myself I can't say nothing, 'cause it's not my place. Ordinarily they wouldn't give her a station until she cleaned herself up, but this time they let her right out on the floor. I thought to myself, I hope the district manager comes in some time today. Well, sure enough, he comes in and he walked through that kitchen and he got a glimpse of her and he comes out and says, "Send that girl home now, and tell her if she can't come in better looking than that, we don't need her." Right on through the kitchen he went, I mean he don't have to stop and look, he can see everything out of the corner of his eyes. And they sent her home. She come back the next day, her hair was neat, her uniform was clean.

But if I was to come into a shop and sit down at a station and a waitress come up to me looking like Anne did that day before, I would absolutely refuse to have her wait on me. The old waitresses, they were trained that you're supposed to smile, and the customer is always right. You don't argue with the customer because after all they're paying your salary. The company's not doing it. That customer is really putting the money in your pocket.

I used to train girls, and I'd always tell 'em, "If you don't like this work, don't waste my time." I enjoy my work. There's only one waitress I work with that I don't have no use for, because she is the nastiest-talking woman I have ever seen in my life. She's a colored woman, and very well educated, too. There's no sense in her being that way. Well, you stand there and put your dish up and call for a dessert and she'll say, "Bring it on down here, I ain't coming up there, my feet hurt." Things like that, you know. And I say to myself, that with anybody's feeting hurting them as bad as yours hurt you, they should never be in this business. I think that to myself. She's just not a very pleasant person. The others, they're all right.

Mary climbs upstairs, walks to the menu board, and begins to rearrange small white plastic letters on a black felt background. If nothing else, the nation's 260 American Inns are consistent. Although Mary Wills' unit is a bit larger than most, the franchised décor requires: ubiquitous brown and orange and turquoise, formica-and-plastic tables, flecked tile, and heavy-duty carpeting. Here there are two big bay windows, one looking out onto Wisconsin Avenue, the other into a rear parking lot. Booths, tables, and counters are all arranged according to the master stereotype, while in the background Muzak lulls patrons into a carefully manufactured relaxation.

Humming to herself, Mary posts the specialty of the day: Salisbury steak with mushrooms and gravy, succotash, home-made vegetable soup, $1.95. She also puts back the sign and price for the pot luck meal that she removed last night.

The service is a bit more studied here than in most franchises. It is taught in class, regulated by handbook, inspected by supervisors, and delivered with practiced smiles. The girls are trained to keep their cool through the mass turnovers at breakfast, lunch, and supper. Everything that market research can do has been done and refined. There are special menus and chairs for the children; the customers are provided with cards and pencils to write their own orders, and questionnaires to comment on the quality of food and service. And still, despite the expert training and guaranteed fringe benefits and programmed commendation certificates and pins, there are "problems with the help."

—There isn't the pride in the work now that there was ten or fifteen years ago. I think the cause of the change is more or less the way things are today. It used to be, if a girl didn't hold down her job and do what was right, they could let her go, just like that. The dining room supervisor did the hiring and also the firing. Now it's up to the manager whether he can let a girl go or not. A girl's got to be written up three times—a bad report—and she's got to sign it. Then the fourth time, the dining room supervisor still can't fire her—the manager's got to do it. This has been now since we've been hiring colored waitresses. You know they have a representative in the company. We had one girl for instance, I guess that was the nastiest little colored girl I ever seen. You couldn't help but like her, yet she was just as nasty as she could be to the customers and she'd be fooling around in the back doing nothing. The dining room supervisor let her go three times and every time the manager would bring her back, and he'd tell the dining room supervisor that the waitress was right. It takes forever to get rid of one that just won't work. It took three or four months before the manager got rid of that girl.

I don't think a union has ever entered into it. It's more or less a current between the whites and the colored. The white waitress you don't have that much trouble with because she knows her job, and she'll go ahead and do it nine times out of ten, most of them will. Once it got so busy that I had to call for help. I told the dining room hostess. She tried her best to get some of the others to help us out, and you know what time they came on the floor? Four-thirty. They were just sitting there, in the back, looking and grinning. Now this is what the colored do. It's their nature. I believe that it's really their nature.

There's just a natural difference between whites and blacks. I think if colored people moved into my neighborhood, they would be very lonely, 'cause I don't think they would feel like one of the crowd. One Christmas, one of the girls at the restaurant had a birthday, so I thought we'd have a combination birthday plus Christmas party at my house. Now we had a little colored girl, Mary McDermott was her name. Everybody thought the world of her. I invited her over, I was very sincere, and she came. I had one heck of a time trying to get that child to relax and enjoy herself. This is what I mean—they feel they are out of place. Once I got a couple drinks in her, though, next time I looked around, Mary was up out on the floor jitterbugging with my husband. That's right. Coupla drinks in 'er relaxed her. I just read in the paper the other day that a colored family bought a forty-thousand dollar home in a forty-thousand dollar neighborhood, and the lady was complaining that she had no neighbors—nobody ever said hi. I was born and raised with colored people, and I like colored people, but I still wouldn't feel right in a place with only colored people.

Sometimes they are hard to work with. I had trouble one day in which nobody would fix a fried fish sandwich. I told the manager, "I gotta have my sandwich, my customer's waiting and I want it pretty soon." So he went back and asked Mamie to fix it, and I heard her tell him that no white man's going to tell her what to do. It's something that's back down in them, you know. They resent the fact that they are working under a white man. But I told Mamie, I said, "I don't think the color of the skin has anything to do with it." I said, "We have colored managers. If you're not satisfied with working under a white manager, then work under a colored manager. That's your privilege. I don't think it has anything to do with the color of the skin; you're here to do just like I am."

There are some nice colored people. I believe that if a person qualifies for the job, first come, first served. If he's qualified. But I don't believe in taking someone who has been on a job for thirty years or more, pulling him off, and putting a colored person there just to equalize or balance things. It's happened right here in Rockville. My sister was telling me about a man that had been working thirty years for an outfit and it wouldn't be long before he retired. Well, he was never allowed to retire—he was displaced by a colored man.

About quarter to twelve, customers begin coming for lunch—first a few, then many. Most of them are office people. People who eat on the run seem to keep the waitresses running even faster. Mary Wills, who often sees the same hurried faces, every day, does not mind staying on her feet. Her first customer today is a regular, a floor manager from a nearby department store. He orders his usual, a large hamburger with baked beans, and a Sprite. On her way to the kitchen, Mary stops at another table to pick up a young couple's order slip. Two tuna on rye, two Cokes. Automatically, as she passes other waitresses and customers, she repeats the two orders to herself.

—Our lunches are fast turnovers—everybody's in a hurry. They've got a certain length of time to eat, a certain length of time to get back to their jobs. We got a couple that comes in every day at a certain time, and ever since I've been here they've never had nothing but coffee and two grilled cheese sandwiches—every day at lunch—and a small and large ice cream. They sit there very nicely and read their paper and drink their coffee and not a word. They're happy as long as they've got their coffee and their newspaper. People that come in every day is home folks to us. We have one blonde that's a regular, we call her Myrna. We take time to talk with them or tease them or something like that. They're just home folks, that's all.

I don't have much problems with my customers. If I get hold of one I can't handle, I call over to the dining room supervisor, because I'm too busy to stand and try and work out a solution. That's what she's there for.

If she can't do anything about it then she takes his check, voids it, and says she's sorry.

I told the manager, "The first drunk who puts his hands on me, you're gonna have to fire me 'cause I'll knock the hell out of him with my tray." He says, "You wouldn't!" I said, "Oh, yes I would." But I very seldom have any trouble with my customers. If they come in like they want an argument or anything, I just read their check, go get what they order, put it on the table, and go on about my business. Most people are very nice. If they have to sit and wait for their order a little while, they know it's usually the fault of the kitchen. They don't get mad at the waitress.

Sometimes the customers don't act proper. I had a man here the other day, who'd just gone next door to the drive-in to get his sandwich. I thought to myself, well buddyo, I'm going to tell you in a nice way what I think of what you just done. He comes over to my station and he wants a cup of hot water. Well, I charged him twenty cents for hot water—in other words, I gave him a message. I don't know whether it sunk in or not. I didn't appreciate the fact that he'd go over there and buy the food and come eat at my booth and keep me from making a sale. We have to make money off of our customers. We depend on our tips.

It's not easy work. It's a grind. Sometimes people come in here with a chip on their shoulders and you work extra hard not to irritate them. You have to keep moving all the time, and you're under tension and stress every moment. But that's the way it is.

Mary Wills returns with her sandwiches and asks her customers if she can get them anything else. As in most chain operations, American Inns' food is basic and unexciting in spite of the glossy colored descriptions printed and pictured on the placemat menus. Every dish has its category (Appetizers/Salads and Cold Plates/Features/Luncheon Entrees/Beverages/Sandwiches/Desserts) and everything is easy to read and quick to serve. Only one item (Friday's Feature: Golden-Brown Deep-Sea Scallops) costs more than two dollars. Food tastes have not changed much in the twenty years that Mary Wills has been on the job—marketing, packaging, seating, lighting, and menu printing have. The restaurant promotes one dish over another only according to what it feels the market will bear—the customer supposedly still gets what he wants. Mary Wills understands that health standards are for the government to establish and enforce, and that the chain's prime motive is to turn a tidy profit. She could never think of the American Inn's managers as evil people, as indeed they are not, but she vaguely realizes that they are altruistic in direct proportion, consciously or unconsciously, to corporate earnings.

Mary Wills keeps on moving. She likes to serve as fast as she can, not to get it all over with but because she has to, to be able to handle the volume. Since sandwiches are all custom-made by the five full-time kitchen staff members, they must be requested by special order; if they're put together in advance, they dry up. Other things, like peas, spinach, potatoes, and broccoli, are kept steaming through the day. If asked, Mary Wills suggests what she thinks is good. When she serves she brings out everything at once, again to save time, and she totals the check before dessert is ordered. That way there's no waiting if her customers decide to do without dessert.

—I know the food, and that helps with the tips. I mean, if you treat people nice, nine out of every ten will leave you a little something anyway, and at the end of the day it counts up. It also makes a difference how the silverware is placed on the table. You don't just throw it on there. That placemat goes down square, your napkin here, your fork on the outside, your knife in the middle, and your spoon on the inside. It's got to look neat. I don't like to see a dirty dining room either. That gets on my nerves worse than anything in the world.

Mary Wills waits on a dozen more customers between 12:15 and 12:45. In her time, she has served more than fifty thousand lunches. The flow of customers today is slow but steady. It is impossible to predict accurately how many people will eat lunch on any given day. Too many factors are involved, like the weather, the number of tourists, the time of year. One week the restaurant may be filled with people and commotion, and a few days later she has to count toothpicks to keep her mind occupied. But the routine seldom changes.

Of the several facets that form Mary Wills' personality, the most characteristic is her contentment with what she and her husband have accomplished. On slow days she thinks about what she has. It is a self-satisfaction without smugness, perhaps because there have been too many years lived with the realities of self-improvement. Despite her long journey from tenant farm to a house in the suburbs, she has no desire to move any further up the ladder or out of the caste. Responsibility for her assumes ogre-like dimensions. It is enough to wait on customers.

—I don't have any ambition to be a dining room hostess. I had my chance a long time ago and I told them, "You can have it." I said, "If you start that, I'm going to be out the door and gone." I wouldn't want it because when I go in there in the mornings, I've got a couple of things on my mind; I'm going to do a job, I'm going to do it the best I know how, and I know what to do and how to do it. But when I walk out that back door in the evenings, I'm going to draw a complete blank—wham, just like that. I call it complete amnesia. I walk out that back, I forget it. A supervisor can't do that. She's responsible for anything that happens in that dining room whether she's there or not. The waitress isn't going to hear about it, *she* is. And she's going to get chewed out good. That's the reason why they got ulcers and I haven't! I seen men coming in there young and going out old. I wouldn't be one of those managers' wives for no amount of money, because they never see their husbands. If they do, they're so tired they never do anything but just fall in the bed and go to sleep. They never get a chance to take their family anywhere.

This is one of the nice things about being a waitress— the responsibility is not yours. If it's wrong, it don't fall on your shoulders, it's the person that told you to do it. So if someone tells me to stand on my head in that dining room, I'm going to do it, and then if somebody comes along and says that I shouldn't have done that, I can say, "Well, there's the lady that told me to do it. It's not my responsibility."

As the flow of lunch customers declines, the dining room

supervisor gives the signal to close the rear dining room. It is shortly after two o'clock. Mary Wills, still on her feet, walks from table to table at her station, restocking the sugar, salt, pepper, and ketchup. Then she washes down her tables with vinegar water, which cuts the shine and dissolves the stains, and begins to set up for dinner. This requires different placemat menus, the same stainless steel. At 2:30, she goes downstairs to the employees' washroom, changes make-up, climbs back upstairs and sits down to a half-hour lunch, provided free by management. It's the first time Mary has been off her feet since arriving at work. She is entitled to a full hour, but this way she is able to leave for home a bit sooner. And even when she has no one to serve, Mary Wills finds that she has to keep moving in order to avoid getting stiff in the knees and hips.

When there are no customers to talk to, there are other people, like the kitchen help or the older waitresses or the dining room supervisor. Mary Wills delivers her opinions as one might savor a steak sandwich, smothered in everything, well-seasoned, compliments of the house. She is casually exasperated with Vietnam, disgusted with the new morality, befuddled by Women's Liberation, aggravated with government.

—The government should leave the dern people alone. They're telling us you've got to do this, or else. They've got their hands into too much of people's personal lives. For instance, they have this gun law business where they want every gun registered. Well, I've got enough guns at home to start a small war. My husband used to be a gun collector. He used to love to deer hunt, but he hasn't been now in three years. They're hanging on the rack. They're dusty. They've never been out of the house. Now why would we want to register 'em when they're not harming anything? We paid for 'em, they're ours, we haven't used 'em in violence, they're personal property, they're in a home. Why should we register our guns for the police to come here and take them, after us paying good money? A man on the streets who intends to do something—commit a crime or kill someone—he's not stupid enough to go and register his firearm. From what I can understand, you're not allowed even to protect your own self. It's a natural instinct. But the government says you can't do it.

Look at this case over in Virginia, where that colored boy—I forget how old he was, but he was a child—went in and was caught stealing a man's personal property. The man caught him and asked what he was doing, and the boy pulled a switchblade knife. Now what would you have done? Wouldn't you have tried to protect yourself? Well, that man killed that boy, and now the law has him locked up. He'll probably end up in a penitentiary, for defending his own property. I don't think it was the child's fault at all. I think it's the parents that's teaching him to steal, telling him, "You go in there and get it, and if whitey say you can't have it, you take it anyway." They caused their child to get killed.

In the course of the next few hours, Mary Wills passes on her thoughts that the President of the United States is nothing more than a yes-man, that the country should not have been in Vietnam in the first place *(But why drag it out? We should have gone in and got it over and got out, it would have saved lives)*, that students should not bother with government but should return to their colleges *(and get those doggone radicals and Communists out of their schools; it only takes two or three to get the whole college in an uproar—then they burn up the buildings, tear up the college equipment, and people like us have to pay for it. They're not responsible citizens yet. They're not paying taxes)*, and that most young people today have gotten away from the churches *(I believe in holiness, old-time religion—that was Christ's religion. Holiness, that's the name of the religion)*.

At five o'clock, when the sun begins to cast long shadows on Wisconsin Avenue, the dinner people start arriving. Sometimes it does not get busy until 5:45, and the pattern of the last few days indicates to Mary Wills that she will have a few free minutes. She goes to her menu board, changes the offerings of meat and pudding, and removes the pot luck sign. There is never any pot luck for dinner.

The regimen starts once again. Move 'em in, move 'em out. The whirligig continues. Sometimes Mary Wills can grab a bite on the run for supper, but not often. She knows now, after the first few tables fill up by 5:30, that it will stay busy until she leaves, and probably, for an hour after that.

—I can't see how women don't have the same freedom that anybody else has. I used to hear my mother say that they were not allowed to vote at one time, that their husbands wouldn't allow them to vote. But that's been taken care of. Women can vote. My husband never tells me what to do. They got that old saying down home about keeping women barefoot and pregnant. The people in North Carolina are about fifty years behind in their thinking, and it burns me up when I hear them down there talking like that. I don't think most women want to be dominated. I couldn't stand a domineering man. I don't think a man wants to be dominated either. Equality. I mean after all, you're one person after you're married. You're supposed to talk, act for each other, work together, and figure things together—otherwise you're not going to have a marriage at all. That's what marriage is.

I think a marriage license should be just as expensive as getting a divorce. Nine out of ten don't have that money to buy the license. It cost me $250 to get my divorce. And if they had to save up that money to get married, they'd do some serious thinking in between.

I am still as far as morals is concerned, very old-fashioned. Men haven't changed that much, I don't care what these people say. When it comes right down to it, a man is going to look for a woman that doesn't sleep around with everybody, because actually, deep down in his heart he may examine hisself, and say "Aw no, it don't happen." But when he goes out that front door and down to the office all day, he's going to start thinking where's she at, what's she doing, who's she got at the house while I'm here working, who's she sleeping with? It may not happen when you first get married—that wedding bliss and all that—but after you start settling down to a real married life, those doubts are going to crowd in your mind. It's human, you can't help it. A man can go into this sex business, and he can walk out of it the same man. But once a woman gets into it, it's hard to stay away. Your emotions is hard to control. Emotions is a very powerful thing.

I knew one time a case about a girl who lived in North Carolina. She got pregnant and had an illegitimate child. I know her mother well, and she came to visit me when I lived in Gaithersburg and I asked her how this girl of hers was getting along. She says, "Fine, I guess. She's getting ready to get married." I said, "Well, Bertha, let me tell you something, honey. Once they get involved in sex, it's hard to get away from it, particularly for the single girl. Your emotions is hard to check. I bet you a dollar when you go back you'll find she's pregnant again." "Oh, I hope not, for my sake," she says, "Where have I failed that child? I have given her everything I possibly could—raised her the best I knew how." I said, "Well, maybe you gave her too much. Maybe you didn't make her earn it."

So sure enough, she hadn't been home two weeks when she wrote and told us, "You're right. She's about ready to have another baby. And when her father finds out I'm afraid he's gonna just about kill her." She wanted to know if I'd bring her up here—let her have the baby, and adopt it out. At the time I was a nurse. I said, well, I didn't want to become involved in it, but I'd do it for her safety. I knew her father was that way. He drank a lot and he was capable of hurting her if he found it out. The mother told me that many a time she had to stand between her husband and that child—it was an innocent child, she didn't ask to be brought here. I said, "You tell her to get all the money she can get her hands on and I'll come down and bring her to my house. I'll make all the arrangements up here." And I went to my own doctor in Gaithersburg and I asked him if he would consider taking the case. He says, "For your sake I'll do the best I can by her, but she should have been under me all the time she was pregnant."

So right after that I went down to see that girl, she had herself laced up with two girdles, just as tight as she could get it. Her father to this day never knew that girl was pregnant and just about ready to deliver. Now that's how dumb men can be down there. If it had been my husband, he would have known it right away. So the first service station we got to, I made her get out and go into a bathroom, and I took a scissors and I cut that damn corset off of her. The closer I got to Washington, I kept looking at her and the bigger she got. I said, "Oh, suppose it happens on the road!" Well, she had already dropped, but we managed to get back to Gaithersburg and she was in my house for four days before I had to take her to the hospital. Didn't wake my husband up or nobody. I just took her in the car and then called a doctor from the hospital, and she had a baby boy.

My sister knew a couple that had been trying to adopt a child from the welfare. They had their order in but they didn't have one. Virginia says, "I've got the right family that would love to have that baby and they would give it anything in the world its little heart desired. They would raise it right. They're church people. They have plenty of money." So, the adoption papers were sent and the girl signed them. But when she left home her mother says to me, "Joan is not to see the baby, because she can't keep it. It would only hurt her worse." I had to pass that information on to the doctor and he would not even let *me* see that baby.

I wouldn't have seen him at all if it hadn't been that he contacted yellow jaundice after he was born. So the new parents had to wait. When they got here I took one look at 'em and I said, "Ye gods, that baby couldn't have picked a more handsome set of parents if he'd have picked 'em hisself." The father was kinda tall, he had real coal-black hair and brown eyes, and a dark complexion and the whitest teeth—he was a handsome man. And his wife was just as blonde as he was dark. They were a nice-looking couple. She come in with all of her baby bottles, diapers, and everything, and she was all excited—just like she had given birth to it herself. It cost these people over a thousand dollars to get that baby out of the hospital. The girl—the mother—paid for the bill.

At 7:30 in the evening, nine hours after she arrived, Mary Wills makes ready to leave. She changes out of her uniform in the employees' locker room, where she talks with other waitresses whose work is done and with a few who have arrived late for the evening shift. The hot sun, which Mary Wills hasn't felt all day in her air-conditioned quarters, is fading over a skyline of apartment houses and storefronts.

At this hour, as in the morning, there's not enough traffic to curse at on the trip up Wisconsin Avenue toward the Capitol Beltway. Mary Wills drives through Chevy Chase where tree-shaded eighty-thousand dollar palaces set far back from the main road suggest nearby serenity.

Except for an occasional black doctor or diplomat, the area is ivory-white. The Chevy Chase Country Club refused admission to Arthur Ashe, once ranked the country's best tennis player. Ashe has never forgotten the snub, although the membership would probably like to.

It takes Mary Wills thirty minutes to drive from the restaurant to Silver Spring, another white haven. Washington proper might be 70 percent black, but that's not proper Washington.

—Johnson is the one who signed that Civil Rights Act. Bobby Kennedy went way back in the dead files and pulled that out and placed it on his brother's desk, but his brother didn't sign it. I don't think that our late President would have ever signed it. But he got killed, and Johnson took over, and went before millions of people on television and signed it. I said then, "Well we fought and took this land away from the Indians, we fought, died, and everything else, and he turned around and gave it to the colored people which have been sleeping for over two hundred years! They had no ambition. And what went on in the country could have been nothing as far as they were concerned."

I'd like to see George Wallace make it to the White House. He believes in turning these schools back over to the states, get the government out of them. I believe that, too, that if they leave these schools alone, let the states run 'em, they won't have the problems they have. Wallace is more of a poor man's or a middle-class man's choice. I would say he's a poor man himself. He works for a living. I heard him speak on television when this civil rights business started. He was so mad he was bouncing up and down like a ball.

You know if you go out here to buy a home, if you were married and looking for a home, what's the first thing you would check? How close is my school from us? That's the reason you'd buy the property. But you can't do that today. You buy your property for the closeness of your schools, convenience, and then you're gonna find your kids bussed ten miles away. That's not right. Wallace is the only one I ever heard say that.

But if John Kennedy were running against George Wallace, I think I would vote for Kennedy. One thing

Kennedy did that I admired him very much for. This was when Cuba had those guns trained on the United States. Now, he didn't know anything about it. Our planes in the area took pictures when they flew over. They got back to D.C. and still didn't call him or get him. They had to get the pictures blown up to be sure that they were seeing what they thought they were seeing.

And they got John Kennedy out of bed at one, two o'clock in the morning to show it to him. And I think it took a smart man to figure it out, to do what he did, to stop it without a gun being fired. My husband, who was driving a bus for D.C. Transit, saw him right after that. Kennedy wasn't the type of man to pay attention to bodyguards. He often said that if someone wanted to kill him, it wouldn't be hard, which was true because he wouldn't listen to his secret service men. Jim saw him one day walking in front of the White House and could have reached out and touched him on the shoulder. Here was Kennedy way up here a block, with his head down, and the bodyguards way back here running to catch up with him. He didn't know there was any traffic going, he was just deep in concentration. Right after that, he turned those ships around and sent them back to Russia. He told them if they refused to let you board them—sink 'em. They turned around and went back. And he did that without a shot being fired. You've got to admire a man like that. I don't think his brothers, none of them, would measure up to him.

Mary Wills arrives back home, parks the car in a rear driveway, and enters her three-bedroom bungalow. The interior is neat but exceptionally plain. In the living room, a mustard-colored rug sets off a coffee table, atop which sit two gaudy red leaf-shaped ashtrays and a poised white porcelain panther on plastic doilies. There's a mirror above the television set, which reflects a religious picture and photograph of relatives on adjoining walls.

Outside, a sprinkler plays fine spray on the grass. James Wills takes a father's pride in his lawn. He speaks softly and clearly when he says, "I'll tell you one thing, I've got sod and grass that thick, I mean it's really flourishing. But I'll guarantee you, you move a colored person in this house, with two children, there wouldn't be a blade of grass in this yard anywhere. Now, I don't know why, I swear I can't explain it, but a colored person just would not take care of it. It's in their nature, they just don't care, the general majority of that race just don't give a damn. I mean if the roof's leaking, the water's running in their face, they'll stick a pan under it. They'll say, 'Maybe tomorrow it'll stop raining. And if it stops raining, why fix the roof?' Now I'm speaking of average. There are exceptions. The average colored person thinks, anything I get ahold of, I'm gonna tear it up and ruin it.

"There's homes down here in southwest Washington that I know of, they were shacks down there that they tore down, the colored people were living in shacks that in my opinion weren't fit for a good canine to live in, but they were living in 'em anyhow. They went in and tore all the shacks down, which was a good deal. They built 'em up on Nichols Avenue. They built three-hundred unit brick apartment buildings—I helped build it—and give it to 'em with free rent, free utilities, lifetime leases for their property they were taking away from 'em in Southwest. You go down there on Nichols Avenue now and look at those apartments. First thing they did was call their folks from Carolina, Tennessee, Alabama, and where there was once a one-family apartment, there are now nine families living in. Sleeping in shifts. It's true, I know this for a fact, I'm not just talking through my hat. It is in their nature to live like rats. I mean the average.

"I been working for this thirty-thousand dollar property ever since I was sixteen years old. That's right. This goes deep. Where you could move out of your apartment tomorrow, all you would lose would be your lease and maybe a couple hundred dollars. If you would move a colored family in this house right today with two children, I guarantee you within two months' time there wouldn't be a blade of grass in this ground anywhere around here. I don't know why. But when the first blade sticks up, somebody stamps on it and drives it back into the ground. I don't know why. It's just their peculiarities. They're stuck with it, there's nothing I can do about it, or anybody else."

Mary Wills calls her husband inside. Evenings are generally quiet affairs: supper and television, with whiskey and water to help sip down the day. Home for the Wills is a place to be enjoyed. They no longer have any children around. Two sons have gone off on their own, spurred to independence five years ago.

Mary puts a platter of cold cuts and a bowl of potato salad on the kitchen table and fills two tall glasses with ice and ginger ale. Through the screen door she sees the sun lowering behind the small brick houses across the street, and a balmy breeze wafts in the smell of honeysuckle and rose bushes.

—Jim and I, when we first started, we were living in a sleeping room. We'd go to work, put in our eight hours a day, come home. He had bought this lot up at Gaithersburg when he first got out of the service. He paid cash, otherwise he wouldn't have had that. The first thing we did instead of paying rent, we went out there and started building a house, ourselves, doing the labor ourselves on our two days off. He knew a little bit about laying block, a little bit about carpenter work, and the extra money that we had after paying expenses we'd take and put in material. The lot was fifty-foot wide and two-hundred-foot deep. We built a three-bedroom house, with bath, utility room, a kitchen and a dining room and a basement, and we built it ourselves. We couldn't get sewer or water, which suited me just fine because we had the best well of water there ever was, it was that good. And we had a septic tank. We dug that thing in July with a pick and shovel.

The problem with the young people today is that they got so much given to 'em free and clear with no responsibilities or strings attached. Children nowadays, they want a new suit, all they got to do is jump up and down in the middle of the floor and stomp their feet, cry a little bit and beat their head against the wall, and they got a new suit. They have their tuition paid by their parents, they have their books paid for, they have their entertainment paid for, they've been given everything. They have nothing in life to work for, so they're like oysters—whatever drifts by, I'm gonna snap it.

There's a kid down the block here who will burn his

house down if he doesn't get a new bicycle every year. A white family. So the mother says, "Look, father, you sit over there and keep your mouth shut. I'm gonna buy the child a new bicycle every year, to keep our son from burning our house down." It's true. Four doors down. There's another one over here, a girl, says, "Look, if you don't buy me a certain amount of dresses, and pay a certain amount of money for my schooling, for me to go to college, I'm going out and get pregnant. I'm gonna disgrace the whole family."

If the young people today had to work as hard as we did, they wouldn't have no damn time to do all this demonstrating. But they don't have anything to do on their hands, they have nothing to do with their idle time. They should get a newspaper and look at the want ads. They're that long, jobs wanted, men and women wanted. But the young person today won't take a job asking a dollar an hour. Short-order cook or scrubbing floors in a restaurant or washing pots and pans, they won't take a job like that. They want aristocratic jobs paying seven dollars an hour on a part-time basis setting up there telling some full-time employee what to do. That's their idea of employment. Now I'm a damn fool and all that, but that's what they're looking for and they'll never find it. We have part-time employees and they're not a bit satisfied because they're not on the top telling the full-times what to do. They're students.

When supper is finished, Mary and Jim go over the bills that have just come in. Sometimes they have to work adjustments on their budget, but mostly they pay cash, so there aren't too many painful second thoughts about purchases made on credit. They have no feeling of class or economic inferiority. Some people are luckier than others, but if you work hard you'll be satisfied enough.

At nine P.M. they go into the living room, turn on the television to *The Beverly Hillbillies,* and sit on the couch. At the first commercial, Mary goes into the kitchen and after a few minutes comes back out, bringing some ice cream, which she sets carefully on the coffee table.

—Last week I spent thirty-six dollars for groceries. I expect I spend each month about a hundred dollars. On a budget you only buy what you have to have. All that money I spend is not just on groceries—it's on cleaning fluids, washing powder, bleach, starch, and things like that. Ever since we've been married I have always handled the household budget 'cause he knows I'm not going to throw anything around. I coulda ruined him—that's another thing a woman can do. A woman can run a man far into debt by being extravagant.

I love pretty things, too, but if I can't pay cash for it and see my way ahead to get my necessities next month, I'm gonna forget it. I got a dress upstairs, chiffon, and I paid $125 for it. I got it in a plastic bag, only wear it on special occasions. My husband's never said anything to me about the amount of money I spend because he knows I'm not gonna buy it unless I really want it. We manage between the two of us to keep right around thirty-five hundred in the bank, in cash.

I have hospitalization insurance, but that's not gonna pay household bills. If I'm out longer than the hours that I've got, then I don't get nothing. And anyway, the small amount the compay pays wouldn't cover the household expenses. I pay all household expenses with what I make. I pay the phone bill, light bill, gas bill, trash bill, water bill, and buy groceries, too. Jim puts his money in the bank, and I usually have a little left over to give him for operating expenses. I had charge accounts. I closed them out. If I don't have the cash, I don't get it.

Other waitresses, they probably use credit cards a lot more. But you figure that the credit company has to have a lot of people to keep those records straight, sending out bills, and everything. They've got their overhead expenses and they've got to have a little bit of extra charge to cover that. But of course it's you who is paying for it. Now a person really doesn't *have* to go and buy something on credit. I don't know of a thing that I have to have so desperately that I got to go out and pay down on it, and then spend the next three or four months or a year running back and forth to make those payments. But from what I know, just about everybody uses credit cards, billfolds full of them.

At 10:30 Mary asks Jim if he wants more ice cream or anything. He says no, and she says she's going up to bed. "I'll be up later," he says. Mary goes into the kitchen to wash up the dishes before retiring for the night.

—I been living for quite a few years, and as far back as I can remember, those three classes—the rich, the poor, and the middle class—have always been separated. Now rich people have so much idle time on their hands, they have nothing to look forward to. But, a person in my category, middle-class-income people, they're working toward a goal which they hope to achieve. A rich person has no goal, because they've already achieved what they want. It's not only money that separates the rich from the poor, it's the way they live. Most of our alcoholics you'll find in our rich people, because they're society, they do a lot of entertaining, a lot of drinking. A middle-class person likes to live as well as they can, and in as nice a neighborhood as they can possibly live in. A poor person can't afford it. Nowadays, it takes somebody earning ten thousand dollars a year to be middle class. Anything under that would be poor, if they got any family, because it takes quite a bit of money for a family to live on. Everything has gone sky-high—clothes, education, everything.

You're working together with other people like you. Now you take a bunch of people that works together for an amount of time, you come to know each other and you like them. I wouldn't even consider myself in the class with a rich person. I'm the type who likes to be on her own, to make my own living, my own way. In the first place, if somebody hands you something, you don't appreciate it enough to want to take care of it, or respect it. But if you get out here and earn it and work for it, you're going to appreciate it more. If someone offered me twenty-five thousand dollars free, first thing I'd say is, "You're nuts! I don't want it, it must be hot." 'Cause nobody's going to hand you twenty-five thousand dollars today for nothing!

If I had a million dollars today, I'd still be the same person I am right now. I'd just have my new furniture and I'd probably buy my old man a new car, which is about to fall apart, and I'd still work. Because I've never done nothing else. I wouldn't be happy.

EIGHT

The Cop

The police in their conduct and deportment must be quiet, civil and orderly; in the performance of their duty they must be attentive and zealous, control their temper and exercise the utmost patience and discretion. They must at all times refrain from harsh, violent, coarse, and profane language. They shall avoid all religious and political discussion, either at the station house or elsewhere when in uniform. The police shall not while on duty enter any place in which intoxicating liquors or drinks are sold or furnished. [They] are required to speak the truth at all times and under all circumstances, whether under oath or otherwise. The police shall not endeavor to obtain admission improperly for themselves or others to theatres or other places of public amusement.
    —*Manual of the Boston Police (1892)*

— You know when a kid's father is a plumber, then the kid wants to be a plumber. That's the way it was with me. My father had been a guard, and one of my grand-uncles was a captain of police in Chicago. I'd always wanted to be a policeman. I joined the force in the fall of 1957, because I felt it was a chance to do something for people, and the job had good security. It was something I always wanted to do.

At 7:15 in the morning, the streets of Boston are still empty as suburban commuters close their garage doors to begin the long trip into the city. The first big wave won't hit the central business district until eight o'clock, just after Terrance Galvin and 138 other white hats of the Traffic Division have dug in at their traffic light trenches and made ready to direct the daily invasion.

Galvin pauses outside Precinct House Number One and lights the first of twenty-five Pall Malls that he'll smoke today. He is back on the job after a vacation of two weeks, one of which he spent working overtime with the police. During the other he lay in the sun with his family at the tiny summer cottage he owns on the south shore of Cape Cod. Now back in the hazy heat of the city, he passes through the tinted glass doors of the station house, grunting preoccupied hellos to either side. He has things to think about, and he doesn't have to steel himself for another eight hours on his feet in the bowels of a congested metropolis. He learned early how to swallow tedium and hard work.

At 7:45 he moves past the bulletin board with mug shots of Boston's six most wanted men, takes the elevator to the fourth floor, and passes through the Duty Room to his locker. He has come to work in full uniform. Many of his friends on the force conceal their police identities from neighbors and even relatives, but Galvin arrives in his blue-black pants and shirt, no jacket, wearing the white hat that distinguishes members of the Traffic Division from other patrolmen.

He is thirty-eight years old now, but he hasn't aged visibly for ten years. Six foot three, 260 pounds, a football player's neck and two sides of beef for arms. His headful of red curls began to recede about fifteen years ago, but stopped later at an uncertain line three inches above his forehead. Small blue eyes peer from his massive Irish face, which like his red-brown arms and untanned legs is dotted with freckles. Thirteen years of squinting on street traffic duty—Galvin rarely wears sunglasses—have formed crow's-feet at the edges of each eye.

He lights up a second butt and, coughing a smoker's cough, brings up phlegm that has been in his throat all night. He has had a mild case of bronchitis ever since his childhood, spent in an unheated flat in Roxbury.

—I grew up in a semighetto, what is now mostly the black section of Boston, with my three brothers and two sisters. We lived in a cold-water tenement. I guess my father earned a decent salary considering it was during the Depression, but we never saw the money. He had his problems—drank too much, lost his check on the horses.

He wasn't home that much so my mother had to keep us straight.

Roxbury has been the springboard for all of Boston's immigrant minority groups, from the Irish to the Puerto Ricans. Today the 'Berry is Boston's Harlem and Watts and South Side Chicago. It stretches from suburban Mattapan, where Black-Jewish relations have reached another boiling point, through Boston's South End, to the Combat Zone, where Terrance Galvin directs traffic. Tensions in the Combat Zone are always volatile, even when there is no July heat. The newspapers use words like boiling point and volatile, but Galvin doesn't have to read the papers to know what it's like in the streets.

As a child in Roxbury he learned to shout if he wanted to be heard, which is probably why his voice now sounds strained and gravelly. That and cigarettes. Galvin takes another drag, flips away the butt, and moves into an open line-up room. Other cops are there sitting on benches, waiting for the roll call.

At 8:05 a loud bell sounds over the Division intercom. A department deputy enters the room and makes a perfunctory inspection of the men and a sergeant calls the roll, spelling out the traffic assignments after each man's name. Galvin waits at ease with the others until the final name is called. Meanwhile, another sergeant moves through the men to pass out the wanted list for street crimes committed in Boston the previous day:

> Wanted by District Nine for Rape at Westminster Avenue, Roxbury: A colored male, 15 to 16 years, dark skin, thin build, processed hair, wearing a dark-colored woolen overcoat.

> Wanted by District Nine for Armed Robbery (razors and club) of a taxi driver in Kineo Street, Dorchester: A colored male, 19 years, 5'11", thin build, medium-brown skin wearing sunglasses and a long brown coat, with Afro hair style.

Most of the policemen fold the notices into their pockets without looking. Terrance Galvin takes a few minutes to study his copy because in 1959 he captured a child molester whose name he had seen on the wanted list, and you never can tell.

—I remember that animal real well. When I looked at the crime sheet on the guy, I got sick. He burned this little girl all over with a cigarette, then raped her. That preys on your mind. You can't forget it. I stayed on the lookout for him because he'd been seen around the Combat Zone. Sure enough, three days later he came by, and I got him. That kind of shit sounds pretty bad, but working with it all the time seems like a picnic compared to what the cop is faced with today.

When I first came on the force you didn't have the problems we have now. You never had a riot of any large proportions, you had better contacts with people. But today the policeman's job is getting more complicated. He's dragged into almost every situation—race relations, community relations, everything. He seems to be the whipping boy for campus unrest. There was never any campus rebellion before, you never had Watts or the Harlem riots. Today you have different problems, and people try to blame it on the policeman.

It all started with the goddamn war. It's draining us, and it's giving the radicals food to pounce on. You end that war and 90 percent of what the radicals are screaming about would be over. We can't win it by holding back, so I say let's get the hell out. It started all the way back under JFK, God rest his soul. He sent in the advisors. Then under Johnson they asked for more and you had Tonkin Gulf. Mario Savio started screaming, and the black people in the South started pushing for the rights they deserved. Things didn't change fast enough and groups like the Panthers and SDS began feeding on the people's unhappiness, and the cities exploded in riots. So they pushed us in to try and clean up what they had allowed to become rotten ghetto slums. We had to do the dirty work for the Establishment.

The war kept getting worse, and then when Kennedy and King got killed the young people began listening even more to these radicals. You have to give these animals credit for eating off the suffering, but they're out to destroy us nonetheless. So the young kids start trying to forget everything with drugs. I saw a survey that showed in a forty-block area of Harlem there are eighteen thousand narcotics addicts. Now here's where I worry—that's scary. We've got to do something to rehabilitate these people. But then there's more rioting—not just the blacks, but upper-class white kids—and after they get disillusioned and start throwing bricks, we're moved in to quell the thing. Again we're the scapegoats.

We've lost touch with the people in a lot of areas. Back in the '50's the policeman was on the beat, but today he's more mechanized. He's left the streets and is part of a mobile force. Squad cars are needed for mobility to fight crime—the beat man just couldn't cover enough ground. But the direct contact with the average people is lost, like "Hi Officer Kelly, hi Officer Smith, oh hi Mrs. Jones." We live in a mechanized society, men on the moon, but you can't take the place of the contact between the beat patrolman and the people. Something's missing today.

The men break ranks and within minutes Galvin is turning the ignition key on his 1966 Ford Country Sedan station wagon. He's driven the car 56,000 miles but it looks almost new, and he wants to keep it that way because he's got to make it last another three years. He steers over to the four corners of Federal and High Streets in the financial district, where he is to direct traffic until after the rush hour. There is a nod from every beat man on the way over and at one stop light Galvin starts talking to another cop about the proposed use of auxiliary police. He doesn't finish what he has to say. When the light turns green, he calls, "I'll catch you later," and drives ahead. Seven blocks later, he rolls the car into a parking lot at the corner of Federal and High, past the bank where his father once worked.

—When things went really bad at home we went on welfare. As a child, that branded me. We wore "welfare knickers," which were like cheesecloth. They had a flap with a button on them. But if your father worked, you had elastic in your knickers and you wore ankle socks. Uncle Sam branded us, because with our union suits, they knew who we were. I remember going down skinny-dipping and stripping, and the kids would say, "Look at Terry Galvin and his welfare underwear." This kind of thing worked on our minds. The social worker who was supposed to help us did more harm than you could imagine. I remember my mother buying a little radio and having to hide it because this obnoxious bitch, who was probably a political appointee, used to come into the house without warning, lifting up everything and snooping around in our private things to see if we had taken too much. There was no such thing as dignity then.

My mother tried hard to make life normal but we had nothing. I never got a Christmas present in my whole life until I was in my teens. I remember on Easter Sunday how I used to feel. My two friends Billy Keough and Tommy Ryan had new shoes from Flagg Brothers. I had nothing—I had to wear last year's. We used our mother's old stockings as socks to wear with our knickers. In the winter the ice would form inside the windows. I remember my mother heating up bricks for us to keep at the foot of our beds. We would line up and race to see who would get the hottest brick.

I really wanted to learn as a kid, but the schools were no good. Finally I gave up and they sent me to a discipline school. It wasn't a reform place, it was part of the regular public school system. They shoved you away in another city school if you were screwing up. They still carried you on the rolls and you read funny books until they farmed you out to high school. By the time I hit high school, I was completely unprepared. I mean you can't have a kid drawing cartoons until he's thirteen years old and expect him to be ready for higher learning. So after two years I quit and went to work.

At sixteen I got a job—illegally, because I was five years underage—as an ambulance orderly at City Hospital. We used to go on the contagious disease runs—smallpox, consumption, things like that. I used to give all of my pay check to my father except for about ten dollars. I stayed there at the hospital for three years. Then I worked as a carpenter's helper. My wife laughs, because to this day we don't own a hammer. Later, when I was about twenty, I worked as a furniture mover and then I worked double shifts at a factory that made floor tiles and linoleum. After the Marine Corps, I signed on as a cop.

On his feet now, Galvin keeps a steady line of cars moving from a ramp off an adjacent expressway. A pedestrian swinging a large transistor radio passes by, and Galvin hears a helicopter report tell commuters,

"Traffic is heavy on the main arteries but moving well."
Galvin keeps his eyes moving, distracted occasionally by
leggy young secretaries who bounce among the crowd of
early shoppers and businessmen. Will you look at *that*,
he inhales, pirouetting to ogle a pretty young blonde. He
knows he is all talk and no action, a good father who
secretly worships his wife. But at nine A.M. every morning
this is one way to get the sleep out of his eyes.

By 9:15 the commuting business traffic is exhausted; in
less than an hour, downtown will be engulfed by a tidal
wave of shoppers. Galvin drives his wagon about six
blocks to his regular beat on Washington Street, in the
heart of the Combat Zone, near Hayward and Avery.
He stops outside the Avery Hotel in a towaway area.
At fifteen dollars a week for a garage spot, there is nowhere else to park.

On Washington Street—in a two-block area just up from
the bistros and pulp joints, small drug stores, curiosity
shops, movie houses, and banks—the traffic has picked
up. Galvin steps off the curb to control it. This is his
beat.

—I was assigned to the Traffic Division from the Academy, but I wouldn't put in for a transfer. I'm out in
the street, I meet the people. I know everybody in my
area. I prefer it to the cruiser. When I'm out there,
I'm protecting the walking public, and I have a feeling
of accomplishment doing my job. We have a good rela-
tionship. A traffic officer anywhere in the country is as
much a policeman as someone on a crime patrol. He
prevents crime by his very presence, people feel safer when
they see him. Some critics say, "he does traffic in front
of office buildings. We should put civilian directors
out," and that bit. But there's no substitute for the visible
policeman, no matter where he might be. How much
crime he deters in a given three-block area, no one will
ever know.

Galvin seems to pull the cars by him with short jerking
movements of his arm as he curls up his right-hand fingers, extends his arm from the shoulder, and snaps it back
in quick, staccato motions, cocking his head with each
backward thrust of his thumb, like an impatient hitch-

hiker. He performs this exercise for periods lasting up to five minutes, as long as he can keep the cars moving up Washington Street. The minute the "foot public" wants to cross, he stops the cars and rests his arm.

The traffic moves by steadily with a brief lull at mid-morning. There will be another at midafternoon. From somewhere along the brick and asphalt horizon they come; thousands of them, twenty cars a minute, twelve hundred an hour, each hour, every working day. When the movement of vehicles slows to the point where the spacing between cars is three or more car lengths, Galvin lets the lights take over. Two big yellow standing signals on opposite sides of Washington at Hayward and Avery blink continuously, regardless of a policeman's presence. Green for one minute, amber caution for five seconds, caution and stop for ten more, forty-five seconds of red, then green again—an electronic cycle that Galvin has come to rely on for the small measure of security it affords.

The lights, at least, will always be there to back Galvin up if he has to leave. In February, 1958, with the snow piled high in dirty little drifts on the curbs, he happened to glance up at the top of a neighboring office building and saw a young girl on the ledge, her feet dangling over the side. So he rushed up to the rooftop, and ten minutes later coaxed her out of suicide. This brought him the Department Medal of Honor.

—Because of the medal, I get an extra fifty cents a week on my pay check. Until a few months ago I made $159.50 a week, but now, after our raise, Boston police are the sixth best-paid cops in the country. I'm making $10,300. That's $198.60 a week, but that isn't what I bring home. There's something like thirty-four dollars chopped out— eight a week for Blue Cross, eight for the Patrolman's Pension Fund, two dollars for the Patrolman's Association dues, sixteen to the City of Boston Credit Union. Every city employee is in hock. We can take out loans at only a few percent interest and take years to pay them back. I get the loan paid and I take one out again. That's how I started with my house and bought my car. The Credit Union is a good thing.

From what I've got left I go and put sixty dollars a week into our checking account to pay off the bills.

We've got two charge accounts. One bill has $221 in it from clothes for the kids and we owe two hundred dollars on the other bill for a living room set we bought, so we've got about $420 to pay off. By the time that's taken care of, there will be more bills. So I have to get that sixty dollars in each week. Then there's the food. Kay shops every two weeks and the bill is never under eighty dollars.

You have other expenses, things like insurance. Because I'm a cop, I'm insured for twenty-five thousand dollars. That costs us fifty dollars every four months. The house insurance is another $137 a year and of course in Massachusetts with the car insurance what it is, we end up paying three hundred dollars a year to keep the Ford on the road. Then we got our house payments. Back in '64 we got a good deal on our place. It went for $22,700, not bad for a two-family house. We put four thousand dollars down on a Credit Union loan from Boston, and now we owe the bank about eighteen thousand dollars. My mother-in-law lives with us, and she helps out with fifty-six dollars a month as her share of the rent. We put up the other $130. We're going to have to pay even more, with this new tax hike—I figure another twelve dollars a thousand on what we pay now a year for taxes, which is $135 a thousand. That extra two dollars a week that I'll have to add to the taxes will force me to cut down what I put in the checking account for the bills. After gas, electricity, and telephone bills we haven't got anything left—especially when you figure we still have to pay off on the cottage.

About six years ago, we bought this little cracker box down in Marshfield near the water so the kids would have some place to spend the summer. The whole thing cost seven thousand dollars, at five hundred dollars down. It might seem like a luxury but goddamn it, I need the place in the summer when I get off work, to leave the city and have some little place to go to. When you spend all day breathing in the shit air and eating the carbon monoxide, when you're on your feet all day in the heat and the rain with all the noise, you need a place to run to at night. It's costing us extra and we have to give up other luxuries, but I don't know what I'd do if we didn't have the little place.

With what it costs us, we wouldn't have anything left for other luxuries or emergencies at the end of the week, so I work details. It's just some overtime work that cops do to supplement their income for a few extras we can't afford after we've taken care of the basics. Before the pay hike I worked two details a week just to keep the kids fed. I was away from my home every Friday and Saturday night for four years to make ends meet. When some bar or dance wanted police protection, I worked it at the rate of $4.50 an hour. I used to take the details no one would want because in my division I couldn't get the good ones. I worked lousy hours, from ten at night to two in the morning, in the stinkingest holes in Boston. I never took my wife out once in four years. But that's over now. With the new contract we get $6.75 an hour for details, so I can work just one a week. God help me, I'll never leave my family home again on weekend nights. But if I was ever transferred to a division that's poor on details, we could be in very bad shape.

Galvin continues to walk his beat, stopping for five-minute periods to keep the cars moving. He is a traffic cop, but he carries all of the side arms of a policeman working a high crime area—a Smith and Wesson .38 police special; six 156-grain .38 bullets visible in his holster; and a dozen more in black leather bullet cases on his belt. He'd like to be carrying .38 Super Vels—bullets with recessed slugs—but they're against the regs. In his wallet is a laminated list of warnings and rights that is read to each apprehended suspect. This is a "*Miranda* card," named after a minor felon who argued all the way up to the Supreme Court that he was unconstitutionally interrogated. The Court agreed.

—The liberals call them "dum dum" bullets but they have the kind of stopping power that would keep a gunman from shooting back at you once you hit him. I've never shot a man. I once fired a warning in the air after I heard two shots and saw two men running. It turns out they had snatched a bag, which is a felony, and some officers fired warning shots. I didn't know if they were killers or not, so I chased 'em and cornered 'em in a blind alley where they were finally apprehended, but not until after I had to fire that warning shot. I was making out reports for the next three days. I've never had to shoot at a man, thank God.

You have to make a decision in two minutes out in the street that they'd spend nine months deciding in a court of justice. Sometimes you read in the paper that it takes the Supreme Court a whole year before they'll hear a case. For us, two minutes is a long time. We might have a few seconds to decide whether to shoot or to use a nightstick on a criminal, but the Monday-morning quarterbacks say, "Oh, gee, they should have done it this way." Well, it's tough being a Saturday-night guy in a gun battle and having the Monday-morning quarterbacks criticizing what you should have done.

The Court decisions—*Mapp, Miranda, Escobedo*—have made the job a lot harder. But they're the law and we live with them. Sure the policeman feels lousy about it. Sometimes you get a guy cold turkey, you know he did the job, and wher you read the *Miranda* card to him, the guy clams up and it's a long legal battle that costs the public money. You feel bad for the victim, too. But we took an oath and that's the law handed down. I mean if they came in with a test case tomorrow and repealed *Miranda* or altered it, that would make it that much easier to protect the innocent public.

Sure, many of the do-gooders have put a muzzle on the policeman, but they protect a few at the expense of the many. I'm not saying the spirit of *Miranda* is bad, but instead of our being a defense attorney for the criminal, I'd go for some changes. Like in confessions. Say a guy bumps off his old lady tonight and he comes into the station house and says, "Jeez, I just killed my wife," and he wants to make the full admission. We advise him of the *Miranda* decision and the next day, after he's cooled off in the cell, he says, "I didn't mean it. I was under duress." In other words, voluntary confessions should be allowed to stand without us being forced to discourage a guy by announcing he has the right to keep silent.

One police station I could think of, there was a sign outside the detective's room, "No Confessions Accepted Here." A guy could repudiate it tomorrow. Many cases are thrown out on technicalities. You think you'd like to see them alter some of this stuff, but then you get the do-gooders crying that we're going back to the olden days with the rubber hose and overhead lights. Some people today see the policeman as an enemy because of a bygone era.

You can't live 1920-style in 1970. In 1920 you had speakeasies, much more brutal and bigger crimes. Sometimes interrogations got rough. But it's a different ball game today. Due to all the dissidents, civil unrest and such, we're more concerned with people's rights. I mean this is good, but the people are getting shortchanged. Nobody's ever hollering the rights of the victim who's entitled to the same rights. I don't believe you should take a guy and hold him for seventy-two hours without sleep or water. That's for the birds. But these extreme examples of misuse hurt things for everyone.

Galvin spots a tarnished nickel by the curb, and bends to pick it up. His dark-blue tropical weight slacks are slashed in six places to accommodate pockets. The top-left hip pocket holds his bulky traffic ticket pad, half-empty of violation coupons. It is gray and frayed and curling at the corners, but this is not from overuse. Galvin goes easy on illegal parkers. (*I might give out a ticket every few days, but I know there just aren't enough garages down here to take all these cars. The shoppers have to go somewhere. I can't see hitting up a guy for a ten-spot who's spent half his pay check on clothes for the kids.*) He also knows that the cars he passes by won't be overlooked by the two meter maids who work this area, and that one reason he is lenient is because he can identify so easily with the two characters parked in the yellow curb zone.

The pants' sleeve behind his gun holds a small eight-inch hand baton, a junior nightstick meant for handbag snatchers who want to scuffle. A white whistle hangs on a silver chain hooked to a pin over his breast pocket. But Galvin isn't the kind who depends on whistles. When he wants to get the attention of a motorist, he uses his bellows of a chest to blow out a gravelly shout: "*Hey,* pal, y'wanna be an *angel?*" Patience is reserved only for pedestrians. Galvin has a short temper with people who wrap themselves in two tons of steel and think they own things. If a driver cuts a corner short or jumps a traffic light,

Galvin stops him with his voice, bellowing the anonymous titles of street people: Mack, Charley, Captain. He is kinder to women. (*You have to make up your mind, madam, you can't go in* both *directions.*) For the ladies he bends over with great ceremony, pushes his face inside the driver's window, and serves cream puffs powdered with dainty sarcasm. (*Pardon me, dear, but did you see the two little red lights in front of you?*) Then he breaks off by tipping his hat, which bears a small circular red-white-and-blue pin next to his badge; it is embossed with a tiny gold pig, and inscribed *Pride, Integrity, Guts.* He is easy on the ladies, because he enjoys teasing them and knows that a dose of gentle humiliation is as good for the soul as a forceful reprimand.

—The first time I ever heard "pig" used against the cops was by the left-wing radicals and it originated in Berkeley. Bettina Aptheker—her father's the chief theoritician of the Communist Party—and Mario Savio used the word. It was later picked up by the Black Panthers. They use "pig" as a slur—they see a lowly animal that eats garbage. Well, I look at a pig and I say, "Jeepers creepers, I go to the store and spend $1.29 a pound for bacon. That pig is a pretty expensive item. Look at the price of pork chops." The kids picked it up because the news media publicized the word used by the kid who's against the Establishment or is raising holy hell.

It's like advertisements. You see a name brand advertised every ten seconds on a major TV show and you'll find yourself going to the supermarket and saying, "I have to get X brand." The word doesn't bother me. I may be a pig to some people, but to most I'm a police officer, I'm their guardian, I'm their saviour. The guy who wants to call me a pig, I have to take him for his low mentality.

But I have to admit I'm a little older now. I've had a lot more time to see things in perspective. If I'd heard it thirteen, fourteen years ago, when I was a rookie, I don't know. The younger cop today may snap. On the other hand he's better educated, so he may take it with a grain of salt like me. I don't know.

A lot of these well-to-do kids grow up confined to their little lace-curtain homes, and all of a sudden they go to the university in the big city and they have to get into the swing of things. If SDS is having a big shebang, then three hundred other kids who aren't members but are bored silly want to get in the act. All of a sudden, they're growing long hair, wearing dirty clothes. "Hey, I'm on my own, Ma. I'm on my own, Pa." They go to the demonstrations, but that doesn't mean they're radical. I go to a demonstration, I see eight thousand people, I don't say they're all SDS. I look for a certain small little rat pack.

I honestly think ten thousand kids from all over the country went to Chicago to do their thing, and fifteen hundred radical nuts went there to instigate. So most of the good kids who wanted to demonstrate peacefully got shafted, got the raw end of the stick. The police were aggravated. They had to use force, which the news media branded as excessive—never playing up *police* casualties, never showing the injured officers. I think 174 cops are still out of action. Fifteen hundred hard-core radicals went to Chicago and took decent American kids and made them come back chanting "Pig, pig!"

Galvin wears other unofficial adornments on his uniform. Pinned to his collar is a small metal replica of the stars and stripes. The pig decoration is against regulations, but the flag was sanctioned after the Boston Police Patrolman's Association lobbied for the right to wear it. Together the two pins offer the only color against the dark-blue uniform, except for a circular baby-blue Boston Police patch and inch-wide blue strips on the outside of each pant leg.

Four doors down from Galvin's corner is the Patrolmen's Association office. Traffic is lighter now, so Galvin steps into the plain doorway and takes an elevator to the second floor. After a few minutes trading stories in front of the air-conditioner, he comes back down to walk his beat. It is 10:00 A.M.

—I don't want my kids to stereotype me as a flag-waver. The construction workers sometimes go too far with the red-white-and-blue routine. It can be healthy, but it can also reach extremes. When you see these radical kids desecrating the flag, it hits you in the gut. Those hard hats are just everyday guys. Some of them are veterans. They fought under that flag. And when they see desecration, something inside them snaps. I can understand that.

At 10:15 A.M. Herb Markham arrives. He will work the corner until six P.M.; Galvin, who came on at eight, will leave at four. They will keep these shifts for two weeks, then alternate. Until they got the new contract, they used to work from eight to six on staggered days. Markham has been Galvin's sidekick for almost a decade. He's a heavy-set man with curly gray hair, bumblebee sunglasses, and a belly that hangs out over his belt and holster. Herb is a very shrewd guy. *(Quiet, but shrewd,* says Galvin.) In uniform, they are a tight-knit team, periodically relieving each other on the corner as the day moves by.

Two old ladies in silver hair and blue silk dresses approach Galvin as he crosses Avery Street. They are smiling like grammar-school teachers talking to a cute child. ("Officer, where might we find Red Cross Shoes?" *Up Washington, ma'am, corner of Temple Place*.) He tips his hat. A pair of anxious businessmen step into the street in front of him. ("Which way to Lockobers?" *Winter Place, three blocks up, left on Winter Street*. "Thanks very much, Officer." *Thank you, sir.)*

Markham relieves Galvin, who by now wants very much to get some coffee and get off his feet. Galvin goes into Dalton's, a converted chain cafeteria and his street base of operations. Here, under gaudy electric candelabras and oversized-flower wall decorations, it costs $1.15 for "three country-fresh eggs, any style, with bacon or sausage, home fries, and toast—the Farm Special." The Charbroiled Steak Dinner is $1.49. But Dalton's is a Combat Zone eatery that shoppers avoid. Its clientele are the people of the streets: go-go dancers, small store owners, derelicts, peddlers. And policemen.

Galvin pulls the nickel he found out of his side pocket and drops it into a plastic charity box at the counter. Then he sits at a table in the back where he can be near the pay phone for any calls from the Association office. The seat also allows him good avantage to survey the pedestrian traffic along Washington Street. He looks over his cup as he sips black coffee, his eyes always moving, charting the throngs outside.

There are the determined shoppers, in from suburban

Boston to steal a bargain at Filene's basement, and the miniskirted secretaries in their pastel blouses who always seem to look into the cafeteria at Terrance Galvin as they move by. But Galvin sees that their glances go no farther than the big plate-glass cafeteria windows which serve as huge mirrors. The faces move on soon enough.

Old men in gray suits, the benign septuagenarian outcasts who tour the streets of the Combat Zone each day, some limping, some with canes, check the area to see what has changed from the previous night. Many of the old-timers, Terrance Galvin's "forgotten people," live in neighboring rooming houses and stop at Daltons two or three times each morning and afternoon, as a stopover during their listless daily inspections. Most of them will need a pint of muscatel to get them through the day. Galvin makes it on four cups of coffee and a sandwich at noon. Right now, as he finishes his second cup and watches a pair of streetwalkers in silks and knits move by, he mutters quietly to himself. They're out early.

Across the street, Galvin sees a plump woman with two shopping bags weighing bananas at Sal Aliano's fruit stand. During the summer, peaches go for forty-nine cents a half dozen and grapes are three pounds for a dollar. The stand is protected by the steel-skeleton relic of an old subway entrance; less than five years ago there was a four-story office building here. Now the whole block has been razed for a street-level parking lot, except for the corner where Sal sells his plums and pears. For three dollars, you can park in the lot from eight A.M. until six at night. During the morning hours, motorists jockey for spaces in the twelve-story parking garage adjacent to the lot. This helps create Galvin's biggest traffic problem—how to keep a steady stream of cars moving north up Washington Street while shoving another lane right onto Hayward and left onto Avery and up to the Boston Common. Somehow pedestrians must negotiate the three-way traffic, and Galvin is their chief arbiter.

Sitting over coffee at the rear table at Dalton's, he never takes his eyes off his corner. Traffic has now slowed to a level where the lights can take over. The University of Avery Street, Galvin calls it. When he leaves the trenches of heavy traffic for his outdoor classes in field sociology, Terrance Galvin changes from soldier to full professor.

Back in the street again, a few minutes after taking over for Markham, he catches four young tow-haired boys darting across Washington Street. A loud *Hey!* freezes them in their tracks, and they turn. He holds his hand up and curls his index finger for them to come toward him. He smiles. *(Listen, fellas, if you shoot out into the street like that, one of you will get it.)* He puts his arms around the smallest boy. *(See this little midget here? If he gets hit by a truck, he'll be this small for the rest of his life.)* Laughter. *(Next time walk between those white lines, okay?)* The boys bob their four heads silently, then turn and move on.

—When I was six years old, I began going to the Boys Club. I guess that was as much a home for me as the real place. I learned to swim there and I swam every day, five days a week. I lived to swim. From three o'clock after school to six at night, then home for supper and back at 6:30 to swim again until the place closed. I swam on four championship teams, but neither of my parents ever came to see me. Later, when I was eight, I worked in the convent near our house emptying garbage for twenty-five cents a week. We lived right across from St. Brenden's then. My mother used to prick her fingers stretching curtains to dry for the nuns, at fifteen cents a pair. She used to starch their habits and iron them for free. The nuns really could use you if they wanted to.

As lunch time nears, traffic thickens. A Pontiac GTO convertible stalls at the corner. To Galvin, the shortest measurable time is the millisecond between the time a car stalls and the time the horns behind start honking. He explodes at the cacophony, and yells over the din. *(All right, all right, cool it, turn it off, turn it off!)* Water pours from the GTO's overheated radiator, as the driver appeals to the policeman for assistance. *(You stay on the driver's side and I'll help you push it over to the corner near the fruit stand.)* Two passing boys help Galvin, pushing from each side of the convertible as he presses from the trunk, and the intersection is cleared. Over at the side of the street the young driver removes his sunglasses and requests dispensation. ("Can I leave it here until I get the radiator filled?" *Listen, Mack, as long as I'm here,*

*you're okay, but I can't promise you that you might
not have a ten-spot ticket on the windshield if I'm off for
lunch and one of those meter maids comes by.* "Fair
enough, Officer. Thanks." *Leave the hood up to show
she's broken down, and down here I suggest you lock it.*
"Right.") The young man walks down Washington Street
to a nearby garage.

—The job can be gratifying. The decent, law-abiding
person still respects the policeman, he still cares. He loves
the police because they are his protection. But the dissi-
dent students, the guys who think it's police brutality every
other minute, they're the people who don't respect you.
What the hell—you represent authority, they hate the law.

Galvin can measure his day by the flow of traffic. It is
11:40, and the cars start to come by in fours and fives
instead of twos and threes. Washington Street in July
teems with men and metal. Early-morning shadows cast
by the five-story buildings have withdrawn, and the sun
moves directly over the street canyon. Galvin removes
his white hat and wipes his brow with his forearm. This
time he uses two hands to thumb the cars and trucks by,
jerking them straight up Washington with his right arm,
stabbing out at ninety degrees with the index finger of
his left hand to point them down Hayward. More than
half an hour of this passes before Markham makes another appearance.

Galvin uses the first part of his lunch hour to gather the
morning's scuttlebutt at the Association office. He leaves
the office after fifteen minutes and stops in at a pizza
place at the corner of Washington and Essex, a greasy
twenty-four-hour hangout where, after dark, the Combat
Zone comes alive in rock music and neon. (*They have
the best subs in Boston there, if you can stand the smell
of the place.*) Even during the day, the stench seems like
a commingling of vomit and beer. But Galvin takes his
lunch to go, like the scores of interns from nearby New
England Medical Center who stop there. Egg salad on
rye with a can of Coke. He carries his lunch in a paper
bag to the Astor Theater on Tremont Street and climbs
to the balcony, where he eats quietly, and alone. As a
modern-day policeman, Galvin is allowed free access to

the cinemas, and he often takes in a full-length picture in
half-hour segments during successive lunch hours. Sometimes it takes a week to see an entire film. Up in the roped-
off balcony, he can unloosen the strings on his shoes
and relax. The Astor is one of six or seven reputable
theaters in the Combat Zone. Galvin steers clear of the
sleazier skin-flick emporia on Washington Street. *(I couldn't
take the stink inside.)* Today he passes up LAND OF THE
1001 NUDES and DRAGSTRIP GIRL in favor of GET-
TING STRAIGHT with Elliot Gould and Candice Bergen.
*(It's about this campus radical who was big during the
ban the bomb days, but who's been away for a few
years in the Army. He comes back ready to pick up his
Master's. He wants to play it straight now, get his degree
and teach, but the campus extremists won't leave him
alone.)* Professor Galvin gets hot when he thinks about
extremists. Then he rasps out with a passionate articulate-
ness that belies his lack of book learning.

—Radicals won't destroy this country, but we'll destroy
ourselves if the left wing clashes with the right. Both extremes have to be contained. Let the government adhere
to the will of the people. If a guy comes along and he
has hair down to his knees and looks like Abraham Lincoln's mother, so what? If he's working through the system,
more power to him. If our Association sees a law that's
going to hurt us, we're going to do our thing about it
and petition our Congressmen to get it changed. I hate
to use this phrase, because it's a left-wing slogan, but
we need "Power to the People." The people by their apathy
have let the power slip away. We've got to get that power
back. This country is really in bad shape. People don't
trust each other, they're living in fear. We've got a
fucking war that we shouldn't be fighting, and it's ripping
us apart.

How are we going to solve problems and improve things
unless the good kids wake up? If they really want to
change the system, they can do it the right way, by voting, goddamn it. But if they don't get their man elected
the first time, they go home, cry like babies. The truth is
I'm kind of a radical in the police rank and file myself.
Working on the Association, I have to play politics. I've
had my downs, but man, I've had successes and reforms

working through this system—lobbying, organizing, using the power of that voting booth. They should get out and do it the American way. Not by burning Wall Street, not by blowing up the Pan American building or the police station.

The radicals are the people these college kids should be fighting. Let's face it, the good college kids don't get the credit they should. The news media caters to the rabble, the garbage, because they make news. Nobody hears about the college kid who stopped to give mouth-to-mouth breathing to some old lady who had emphysema. But with the few breaking windows and looting, every college kid in the country is put on trial. Why? Just like if a few policemen lose their heads and overdo it, why brand all of the men in blue around the nation? We're not all like that—only an infinitesimal fringe. You have rotten apples in every group.

The system needs rejuvenation, a shot in the arm. I mean we can't have the fervor we had in 1776, when we had a revolution that made us the United States of America. We've lost the fervor. You go to a hearing that benefits the public, up at the State House, and you see apathy. You see ten people in the stands where there should be ten thousand up there making themselves heard. Voices are heard when they're in numbers. Let them be heard in the Congress and in the Senate and the legislatures. People want the government to do so much, but for years there's been this apathy. A long time ago in the major Northern cities, the Irish voted for the Irish, the Italians for the Italians. That's gone out the window. You vote for the guy who's going to do the job. What happens is that these liberals who want to achieve change start working through the system—but they get beat down once and they scatter. They don't stick around to try it again. Look at Eugene McCarthy. He did an amazing thing. He came from nothing and went to knock out Johnson and make people think about the war, but because he didn't go all the way and get elected, he's withdrawn now. He's reading poetry instead of staying in and fighting.

The air-conditioning in the Astor is not working well, and the old theater is musty. Galvin finishes his sandwich, waits for the climax of a bedroom scene with Gould and Bergen, then gets up to leave. Back in the street he relieves Markham again, and Markham heads for Dalton's.

Even during daylight, eight hours in the Combat Zone is a true test of equilibrium. For most Bostonians, the Zone is a place to move through quickly. There's no lingering here, except by the city's maimed and outcast, veterans who know the ropes.

The Combat Zone becomes garish after dark as transients come seeking a dose of honky-tonk recreation: students drawn to the perverse, sailors set free from the Charlestown Navy Yard, and suburban White Hunters, cruising through in expensive cars, searching for a black prostitute who will cost them fifteen bucks—if they're lucky. Police have found more than one well-to-do businessman lying in the gutter the morning after he chased some erotic black fancy and ended up beaten and robbed. You can have your fortune told or score on some heroin in the Combat Zone, four blocks along Washington Street, from Stuart to Avery.

But Terrance Galvin sees this every day, and his senses are affected in other ways. After the first half hour at the corner of Federal and High, his ears begin to throb—from the continuous explosions of the pile drivers working the basement of a new office building, from the jackhammers, the automobile horns, and the jets that use the corridor overhead to enter Logan International Airport, from the drone of revving motors and the rumble below from the subway cars, heading out of the MBTA Orange Line through Roxbury.

By early afternoon the smells begin to irritate Galvin's nose and throat, as carbon monoxide fumes cause a steady soreness in his respiratory passages, and bring on shortness of breath. The janitors have opened the barroom doors, letting out the unpleasant odor of stale beer. Pedestrians pause to light up cigarettes. Galvin backs away from the curb, chatting with Sal at the fruit stand, gets a whiff of burning tobacco, and ignites his eleventh Pall Mall of the day. On the side streets, the restaurant air vents tell what's for lunch: tomato paste and pasta at Vince's Spaghetti House, pepper steaks at the Hi-Fi Deli.

By 2:30, it is the walking that begins to bother Galvin most, an aching sensation, tendons strained from continuous hours on his feet. Galvin has been working in this congested atmosphere for years, through every element. He doesn't even hear the noises anymore, and he's learned to breathe the air. More than anything else it's an unconscious inurement. He's not inclined to worry about something he has been putting up with for fifteen years. But there is nothing unconscious about the pain he feels in his ankles during the afternoon, which now shoots up into his calves and thighs. At three o'clock he ambles over to the white police telephone standing on the corner of Washington and Hayward, and leans against the pole.

—By the end of the day, after you've been in the Zone moving traffic eight hours, you're about ready for the straight jacket. It hits your lungs, your head is buzzing, your legs ache. I really get it in the legs. So when my day is over, I run for the car and just about hit the traffic moving south. Every day I get caught in a nice half-hour jam. During the summer, with cars inching along, and the heat from the sun beating down, and the engines roaring around you, it can get brutal. By the time I reach Route Three—fifteen, sixteen miles from Boston, away from the real traffic—I feel like I've just been flushed out of a cesspool. I still love the job, because of the people, but in a crowded city downtown even the friendliest old ladies can get pissy after a couple of hours. Early in the morning it's cool and great, but as the day goes on, you really want to get out and dive into a good breaker or something. So when I get rolling down to Marshfield, I'm in heaven.

By 3:45 the street action has picked up, as executives begin early flights to the suburbs. A massive retreat is in full swing by 4:30. In the next two hours nearly two million people will leave Boston to the six hundred thousand who sleep there, withdrawing along the Southeast Expressway toward Cape Cod, the Massachusetts Turnpike to the west, the Mystic River Bridge to the north shore of the state, moving in all directions away from the city.

The diaspora will take a few hours and work itself over thousands of square miles, but at 4:00 P.M. everything is still concentrated in a nine- to ten-block area. Shoppers, meaning to beat the rush, scurry back to the garages for their cars. Galvin can't see it: all these thousands of cars that could hold at least five people each, seldom with more than one or two occupants—it seems like a waste of his time. *You could get the same amount of people in here every day with one-third the cars.*

Galvin is relieved by Markham for the last time today. It is three minutes to four. He half runs to his car. During the summer months, Galvin spends a half hour each night driving out to Route Three, heading toward his summer cottage in suburban Marshfield. Tonight, after he has escaped the traffic knot, he spots a hitchhiker and pulls over to the side of the road to pick him up. The shaggy youth is startled when he spots Galvin's uniform. (*Don't worry, pal, I'm not gonna bust you.*) The boy gets in. (*Where you going?* "Plymouth." *I'll drive you as far as Marshfield, then I get off.* "Okay, if you want." *No problem, I have to go that way anyhow. You in school?* "No, I dropped out of Boston State." *The Army on your ass?* "Yeah, I'm trying for a C. O." *Hope you're luckier than I was.*)

—I was twenty years old when I got my draft notice, and I went down to the Boston Army Base. There was a Marine sergeant there—the Marines were drafting in '52, with Korea and all. He said he was looking for volunteers, and I started laughing. He said, "What are you laughing at, boy?" And I said, "Hey, screw this volunteer shit, I'm not down here because I want to be. I don't want no part of this war." He said, "Hey, boy, you better straighten up." And I said, "Hey, pal, you don't have your hands on my ass yet and you ain't going to either." He said, "Don't talk so big, we might just draft you into the Marines. The Air Force quota is filled up and so is the Army's, the Navy's and Coast Guard." Well, I had a friend at the Air Force who moved my name up on the list and I enlisted. One month later, I was heading for Air Force basic at Sampson Air Force Base, New York. Later on I went to baking school at Fort Devens, Mass. I spent my hitch as a baker at Ramey Air Force Base in Puerto Rico. I graduated first in my class at baking school and won the Outstanding Airman Achievement Award at

Ramey, but I had to drop out after two years on a hardship, because my father died of cirrhosis of the liver.

Galvin slows the car just before the Marshfield cutoff. (*I'm turning here. Listen I mean it, good luck with the C. O. If you can serve in some hospital, it's just as good as getting your head blown off for nothing.*) The boy, his dark-blond hair waving in the breeze, says, "Thanks, man," and gets out.

Galvin moves off toward his summer home, foot pressed hard on the accelerator. He is anxious to put the city fast behind. When the oceanside beach becomes visible, he almost utters a sigh as his fingers relax their grip on the steering wheel and he sucks in a healthy gulp of Marshfield's summer air.

—My God, I love this little place. The ocean, the atmosphere. But also 'cause this area's where the little people live, the average guys who busted ass all their lives and finally scraped up just enough for a little cookie box. You won't find any executives and vice presidents down here. Maybe a few with college degrees, but mostly the working stiffs, the blue-collar man. They're good, average people. My kind. The silent majority, maybe.

But I'm in fear of that majority someday getting very loud, and then we get a major confrontation between left and right. You'll have a battle right in the street. A big move to the right is very possible in this nation, and it has to be stopped. I don't think we should have Kent State, or anybody taking a life, because life is sacred. But at the same time, we can't let these animals tear up cities. Even if the system turned around tomorrow and did everything they wanted, they still would hate it. If the hard core of left-wing radicals were controlled, the right would stay silent.

We're just playing into the hands of the Phuey Newtons and the Rap Browns and the Jerry Rubins who are preying on the malcontent. Look at the hard-hat construction workers—good Americans, hard-working, they're the lifeblood, putting up buildings, paving roads. It seems that radicalism from the left is pushing people to the right. After years of organizing and struggle, the hard hat is making good money—six, seven bucks an hour—

and he earns it. Now when he sees these kids burning, he feels threatened. His six bucks an hour is in danger, his house and family are in jeopardy. He's just had these things a short while, and he thinks someone's going to take them away. The black people—not the crazy Phuey Newtons, but the great majority of the black people—deserve the rights they've been waiting for for centuries. I go along with the Court there. The average guy deserves a better shake, too. His taxes are too high, he gets clipped when he goes to the store, the dollar isn't worth half a buck any more. And look how dirty Boston is. God, I'm directing traffic all day in the guts of the city and taking in poison with every breath. When I go down to this place on the Cape, I can *feel* the difference. All this environmental shit is good. We need changes. Big changes. And the guys that are in power have done a shitty job. The lace-curtain families have spoiled their kids. They get divorced or go on drunks or gambling and their kids grow up and don't know them. Used to be heroin was something the blacks used in the ghetto. Now it's in the suburbs. The well-to-do have fucked up the economy, the government, the countryside, and their own kids.

But when the mistakes which have been neglected for years boil over into a riot, who do they send in to stop the thing? Who goes in to put on a Band-Aid when the situation calls for major surgery? Who ends up beating heads to quell the disturbance to restore the order? Who in the end has to make the Constitution work? Us, the goddamn policemen. The guy who hasn't got the education because he isn't getting the pay. The guy who has to make split-second decisions that affect human life and take the courts years to decide. The guy who has to deliver a baby one second and stop a riot the next. The guy who can't go home from work at night, because his job stays with him in his mind. The guy who usually hangs around with other cops because other people can't understand the way he thinks. The guy who lives in danger every time he puts on the uniform. The guy who catches hell in the Jewish suburb for not being tougher on guys that hit a store, but who gets his ass burnt by the civil liberties boys if the next day he roughs up some looters in the inner city. The cop.

But I say there's still a chance to change things within the system by the voting box. I wouldn't change my job if I could. I love it. You rarely hear about cops quitting. If the policemen are starting to look bad to people, they should think for a minute that maybe we just reflect the kind of job we have to do. Maybe we stand for how bad things are in this country, because we see the sickness first, we're on the front lines. We see the crime and delinquency before it gets out to the nice white suburbs.

Galvin parks his station wagon outside the small red three-room frame cottage that he works overtime to maintain. He takes a deep swig of the sea breeze as he walks through the yard, cluttered with beach toys, past the American flag on the pole he set up himself. His wife is at the door. He gives her a quick kiss on the cheek, then goes to the refrigerator and snaps the top on a Budweiser beer.

NINE

The Telephone Operator

*Those petty operations, incessantly continued,
in time surmount the greatest difficulties.*
                    —Samuel Johnson

—The way the company used to be, that's how I liked it. Service was more personal then, you could talk to the customer, help him, and the girls had pride. Working for the telephone company was a good job in those days.

Now the girls aren't interested, they don't like information. Everything is speed. My supervisor told me, "You give very good service, but you go into too many unnecessary questions." I feel if I can help the customer better by asking another question, I will. Telephone Company policy is to look up what the customer gives you and that's it. But what good is that if you're not helping?

Five signal lights flash simultaneously on the front board. It is 9:30 in the morning. Dotty Neal turns into her station, adjusts her headset, and plugs in. *(Directory*

Assistance, may I help you?) No answer. Seven seconds later she repeats the phrase. (*Directory Assistance, may I help you?*) To her they are words wired together and delivered by rote, hundreds of times every day. This time the speaker on the line asks for a number. Dotty Neal punches at the page corners of the telephone book, pushing through the layers of K with a pencil eraser. Kean, Keane, L. Keane. (*The number is listed in your directory as six four three, nine eight oh nine . . . You're welcome.*) Dancing like bumblebees, her fingers move in a well-trained rhythm to locate and relay information rapidly and accurately. She can get to a residential listing in under ten seconds. She's been timed.

Despite the continuous look-alike rows of women strung to their answering stations, Dorothy Patricia Neal stands out. At fifty-one she is thirty years older than the average information operator. She is five eleven, big-boned, a hundred sixty-two pounds, and her frame dwarfs the three-sided stall she occupies. A two-foot umbilical wire connecting Dotty Neal's headset with incoming calls attaches her to the five-by-six-foot switchboard station. The big bright room looks as if it houses thirty-five cages, with thirty-five animals trained to react to a green- or red-light stimulus, repeat "Directory Assistance," and locate a series of numbers. Seven anonymous digits.

Dotty Neal doesn't normally think about the content or purpose of her job. That's it, a job, nothing much save conveying seven numbers, every ten or fifteen seconds speaking to a different stranger.

—When I first came to the Company, I couldn't get day hours. The only shift open was the ten o'clock swing so so I ended up working all night. I couldn't go back and forth or afford to pay someone to mind the children. Both my mother and dad worked at the time. After the war, I needed a job. I started here because telephone operators make good money. They put in crazy hours, usually Saturdays and Sundays and holidays, but they get paid very good—double time, double time and a half, and things like that.

I started at twenty-eight dollars a week. That was quite a drop, after a hundred dollars a week at the war factory. I'd be coming in in the morning just as my mother would be leaving. I'd be home to eat and look after the children, and then leave in the dark for work. I didn't get much sleep, but I guess I got used to it. I didn't have much choice then. It was one of those things you had to do.

I had always wanted to be a long-distance operator but there just weren't any openings when I first started at the Gilmore exchange. Long-distance operators handle fewer calls and they get to stay with the customer for a longer time, until the call is completed.

Course this was when they still had what what they call manual-and-dial. I used to love that. People dialing would come up on the board and the operator would press a button and a light would appear on like a little window frame. Where I was, I would get the local operator and plug in the call, that was much faster. I could handle four calls at a time in that position. And at ten o'clock when I came on I used to take over the whole board. All the day girls would go, and the night girls would just be coming on. After twelve o'clock there weren't that many calls coming through.

I was at the old Gilmore building where there were only three operators and what you did was wear a headset with a cord that stretched the length of the room. There was a board on one side and a board on the other. They used to have what they call patch cords all along the board. I'd go down when the light would appear and plug my patchcord into this huge board, which would throw it up to the center where another girl would answer the calls. Then she'd transfer it back to me and I'd find the exchange and take one of those big trunks and plug in into the right exchange number. At that time there were about three thousand possibilities.

I was in that office ten years. They were starting to change to all-dial. I had put in for several other jobs and I didn't get them. It's like every place else, certain people get certain things. But in this particular office the chief operator, who was Catholic, was very good to me. If you were Catholic you got the job, and if you weren't you didn't. That's how it was.

I didn't get the first transfer but I reapplied, and finally after a year they gave it to me. I went to the Light Street office. After a year there they made me a supervisor. I was a supervisor for ten years.

The old system required at least two girls, except at night. In the Light Street office, before dial, they had what they called an A-Board and a B-Board. The A operators were the girls who first answered the customers. When you picked the phone up, a light would appear in the office and the operator would take the customer's call and pass it over to the B operator, who would put the call up. I would have my headset and this huge multiboard in front of me, and I would just put these cords in the different numbers. We used to wear these long, heavy headsets. I would run these patchcords back and forth and up and down.

But I still liked information best. I love talking to people and each call is a challenge. It's sometimes hard to understand people and get out of them what they really want. Foreign accents can be hard to handle at first, when you're a new operator, but you learn to catch on pretty fast. Colored accents are also hard to understand, sometimes even by the colored operators. Once I had to take over a call from a colored man that a colored operator couldn't even understand, but I did. You have to have a good ear. And you can't have rabbit ears—a lot of people, especially Italians, get real angry if you can't understand them. When I first came to the Company I met a woman named Mrs. Carey, who had been an operator since 1910. She told me never to get upset by a caller. "Kill 'em with kindness, and it burns 'em up," she said. I've never forgotten that.

Another time I got a call from a colored man and I couldn't understand what he was saying at all. It so happened that I had a colored monitor standing behind me, listening in. Her name was Bella, and she couldn't make him out either. Well, this man started to complain about being discriminated against, people making fun of his colored accent. So I said, "Sir, I happen to be a Negro—now how can I help you?" That cracked Bella up.

Then there was this other colored guy who had a problem with his dog, and a friend of mine got him on her board and she couldn't understand a word he was saying except that he wanted a veterinarian. Finally, without thinking, she said, "Sir, why don't you put the dog on the line and let me talk to him?" She didn't mean to be facetious, she just got mixed up.

Information service is one job where I think a girl has

to know what she's doing more than any other. You get customers on information that don't know themselves what they want, and you're there to try to help them. Common sense is really all that's necessary, but we've had girls with college educations that weren't as good as girls that were only sixteen years old. They had common sense and knew how to go around and ask these people questions, to pull out of them what they really wanted. If you put a girl on information who doesn't understand the system, you're bound for trouble. How can she help others if she doesn't understand?

Right now we give terrible service, because people are no longer conscientious about their jobs. You used to get fired if you so much as said "hell" on the job. Now they get away with a lot more than that, like even cussing somebody out over the phone. I heard one girl use an obscene word, and she was promoted a few weeks later. There may be a lot of monitoring now, but there are so many calls that the quality of the service is still lower than it used to be. Customers aren't getting the help they need. The other day my husband called information, and he had to wait ten minutes for help. Even then he finally had to go to a directory.

In New York City the service is so bad that they have to send up engineers from Baltimore—we have some of the best down here—to sort out the mess. They have too many overloaded cables up there, and making a local call is sometimes as hard as long distance. They get two and three people on the line at the same time. But then we get some New Yorkers on the phone down here, and they ask for an address trace or something. Well, the Chesapeake and Potomac is a different company and we don't offer address traces. So they say, "You don't get this kind of service in New York"—as if we think they get good service up there.

Half the time you can't find things through the Yellow Pages, but the phone company doesn't put them out here. An advertising agency does. I once wanted to help a customer and I went to four different places in the Yellow Pages and finally the last place referred me back to the first.

Dotty Neal gets up for a second to stretch and look around the big room. For the past twenty-three years now she has been an operator with the Chesapeake and Potomac Telephone Company—a length of service that was not unusual when she began working at C & P. Now the Company's turnover rate approaches 51 percent every six months. Only four workers in this office have been employed over one year. But Dotty counts the advantages offered by her seniority: she is allowed to choose her hours and work regular shifts.

During the working day, the country's telephone operators have more than twenty-eight million contacts with customers. That makes "twenty-eight million chances to promote the company image," according to one of the Bell System's recruiting brochures. The image of the Company is of no little consequence to its corporate well-being, and it in turn tries to glamorize the operator's position. She "is one of the most important people in the telephone company." She must be "talented, capable, and resourceful—a service specialist." For some reason there are no longer any "information operators," but "directory assistance operators." Many of them come directly from high school, and some work part-time while still studying. "The Telephone Company insists that school work comes first."

The image-builders are concerned with the sounds of voices, and what they say, more with function than with decor. Dotty Neal works in a large, dull, rectangular brick building; except for glass-and-aluminum doors at the small entranceway, it could be a warehouse. Visitors to this area of east Baltimore barely know that the telephone company has one of its main switchboard operations here. What they can and do recognize, two blocks away standing in the old-fashioned outline above the rubble of a vast slum-clearance project, is the Johns Hopkins Hospital.

Dotty Neal turns to her board, waits for the familiar light and beep, and responds. (*Directory Assistance, may I help you? . . . I'm sorry, there is no K. Speile. Could it be S-P-I-E-L-E? . . . Yes, the number is listed in your directory as two five four, seven three seven eight . . . . You're welcome.*) Ten seconds. Light and beep. (*Directory Assistance, may I help you? . . . The number is listed in your directory as seven six four, nine eight one three . . . . You're welcome.*) For the next hour she continues like this; the

only variations from her routine are one unlisted number
and one disconnected number.

—I like it busy. That's the reason I do all these extra
jobs. I asked to do them because I get bored when it's
not real busy. I always find something to do. Usually I
check reprints—they're new listings that get posted and inserted every day. Sometimes the girls really mess them
up. They'll use their fingers when they're actually supposed
to use their erasers to turn the pages, and they tear pages.
We have extra ones and I go around and check positions,
to change classifieds if they're torn, take them off and put
new ones on. There's always something to do. Every
hour on the hour I take the pay count for the girls who
are stationed in the room, figure out the number of calls
each one is handling, and average it out for the supervisors. Any little thing like xeroxing and typing they
have, I do that, too.

Of course, any time it's busy I stay on the board. Each
office has an answering average it has to maintain—this
many girls to do that many calls. So if it's busy, I
answer.

(*Directory Assistance, may I help you?*) Dotty Neal
looks through the C's for a law firm. (*Yes. In your directory the number is seven two seven, two eight hundred.*)
The supervisor walks by. The group chief operator or
the supervisor checks in all the girls. They usually start
two minutes after the hour or the half hour, because there
are girls coming in every half hour. The supervisors
check to see if everyone is in her proper place, and if
she's not, they check to see if she has changed with
anybody.

They check in Dotty Neal at eight o'clock every morning. She used to come to the Fayette Street office by bus, a
ride that consumed at least forty-five minutes on a good
day. The city of Baltimore has recently purchased its
transit system—a fleet of largely antiquated buses—from
private ownership, and established its first Metropolitan
Transit Authority, but the improvement in service is
barely noticeable to the system's daily commuters. Sometimes Dotty Neal would spend two hours a day on the
bus. Now she's in a car pool.

At eight o'clock, at the entrance to the telephone company building, she stops to chat for a minute with Alfred Baker, who's been a security officer for thirty years. He knows all of the regular operators, even the new ones, but he won't let anybody pass unless he sees his official Company badge. He checks visitors' bags and briefcases carefully. Sabotage is a very real word to the Company.

Dotty Neal takes the elevator to the third floor and passes through a thick wooden door which opens into two large rooms enclosed by glass panels. In one of them there is a large array of machinery, blinking lights, multicolored wires. In the other are two long rows of switchboard stations, a young girl connected to each of the thirty-five stalls. Dotty hangs up her coat on the rack outside and withdraws her headset from one of the pigeonholes lining the wall. Sometimes various plastic and rubber pieces are swiped from one headset and put on another. Dotty does not like anyone to fool with her headset.

She enters the switchboard room, still full of chatter from the midnight shift, puts her headset in one of the emptying stations, and looks for the addendum sheets. If the new daily listings have not yet arrived, she sets up the pay-count sheets instead. The job takes about five minutes. Then she gets on the board and operates.

The addenda come in at 8:30 in the morning. The supervisor calls Dotty Neal to take care of them. It doesn't look like a very responsible job, but to Dotty it is. She knows that addendums are very expensive for the Company, and that people have actually lost their jobs because of them. Occasionally operators are caught stealing addenda and selling them to outsiders. Businesses use the new listings to reach fresh customers for whatever they are marketing. (*What they used to do, instead of taking a whole addendum, was to take a page from each position. Now what we do is count. I give the new ones out and collect the old ones, count them and make sure I have every page. If not, I find the missing page and match it with the girl's position.*)

Around 8:40 this morning the flow of incoming calls begins to increase. Dotty Neal returns to her board then and stays until the nine o'clock girls come. About five minutes before nine, when the businesses start opening up, the stations begin to flicker and beep. Most stores don't open until ten o'clock but a lot of the businesses open earlier. At nine she moves over to watch the master box for a few minutes. As soon as there are more than three lights at one time, she returns to her board. Except for when she does the hourly counts, Dotty Neal remains there.

Two years ago a mild stroke forced her first extended absence from the Company in two decades, and for a time the right side of her face was partially paralyzed. She recovered, but the line of her mouth was left slightly asymmetrical, catching and freezing an unintentionally winsome smile on her large pleasant face. She wears her age well under a frosted black hairdo, always well-kept, and looks almost studious behind horn-rimmed spectacles. She's grateful to have recuperated and returned to work, and she shows it through a continuing cheerfulness. The only thing that bothers her face now is an extreme in temperature, like very cold air.

—It's an outlet for me to go to work. When I was out sick and I wanted to go back to work, my boss said, "Are you sure?" I said, "If you don't mind looking at me, I'd *better* come back to work. It's getting on my nerves staying at home." At work I have something to do, and it keeps my mind off problems.

The Company was good to me then. Sometimes I get irritated, but it's not the Company, it's the office. When I was out for six months, I got my full salary every week and then after I went back I had to go to the doctor's four times a week to take treatments. I had laid the money out myself and it came to about four hundred dollars. The Company has something called "extra medical expenses" and they reimbursed me 80 percent of that. They have group insurance for us.

We also get phones half-price, little things like that, although I don't much care for special things like the Princess phones. They slide all over the place. After thirty years' service or if you reach management level, the phones are free and you get fifteen dollars a month toward long-distance calls. Soon I will have been here for twenty-five years and I get to choose a watch. They used to give you a dinner, but not any more. Then

every five years you get a special symbol—a pin or a
necklace or a charm bracelet—with different jewels. For
my twenty-fifth I'll get one with a diamond and two
emeralds. The benefits are good. After twenty-five years
if you want you can retire with a pension.

It was especially good to get back to this office because
it's just like a family here. In some offices it's different. If
you're in personnel, it's like your nose is up in the air
because you make a few more dollars than the others.
But in this office, it isn't. Everyone is treated alike, and I
think that's the reason I enjoy it.

Dotty Neal fidgets with her pencil as she waits for her
board to light up. The room has been carefully organized
for maximum efficiency. Two long panels, each divided
into seventeen stalls, form the general switchboard
areas. Dotty is working at the end of one of them. Special-
service operators are situated at a center table, and in
the back corner a small glassed-in space separates the
office of the group chief operator. Smaller, open desks
along the wall are used as supervisory stations.

(*Directory Assistance, may I help you?*) The customer
asks for the train station and Dotty Neal responds, almost by reflex. (*That number is eight three seven, three
one one seven .... You're welcome.*) At times Dotty wishes
she could spend more time with her callers, to lend more
of a human touch. But that is not the job. There is no
excessive camaraderie among the operators, mainly because of the nature of the work—one talks to one's board.
Still, the constant shift of personnel and position creates
an informal atmosphere. Girls get up and walk around
as they please, always carrying their plugs and wires
and wearing their headsets. As in an old Chinese school
everyone is reciting; the voices vary, but the words and the
routine are identical. A steady chorus—constant, repeti-
tious, chattery—contradicts the visual image of a quiet
office. Here there is no clack-clack of a typewriter or
drone of Muzak to drown out a silence. Somewhere beyond the surface pleasantness—the efficient, programmed
responses in thirty-five different tones—human voices pay
unconscious tribute to the winking, flashing, buzzing
boards which they address.

—I don't really notice the noise; you get used to it.

You're calling out numbers just like everybody else. But I remember when things used to be different. I hated it with a passion when they first changed from letters and numbers to all numbers. It sounds silly, but if there's two letters in a number you can remember it better than all these numbers. They just stick in your head. And now if you have a problem you have to flip the call over to the supervisor. You can't make any outside connection to solve a problem. You used to be able to call out yourself and it was quicker and more personal. Company policy now is to help the customer as much as possible, then turn him over to a service assistant. We used to give a lot more help.

I remember once, this was before we had integration in the office, when people if they were colored couldn't get help. I mean nobody—police departments, taxi cabs, City Hall—no one would help. This particular night, it was about two or three o'clock in the morning, I had a call from a colored guy. He was so excited I could just barely understand him. He was on a street corner, his wife was expecting a baby, and she was in labor. He had called three different cabs, but because he was colored they wouldn't come. He told me this. I said, "Mister, where are you, what corner are you on, and where's your house?" He told me. I said, "You stay right there and I'll call you back." So I called the Diamond Cab and I said, "Look, I'm burning up, can you help me?" The operator there asks why and I told her I have a man calling for a taxi and he can't get one and his wife is in labor. And I said, "I don't care if she's white, black, pink, or what color, she's expecting a baby and she has to get to the hospital. Can you get me a cab?" She said, "Where do you want it, honey?" I told her and said, "Would you please call me back when your driver gets there," because I thought they probably wouldn't do it. She said yes she would, and she did. Later the man called back. He was so thankful, and I was still sorry for him because he had been waiting at that phone so long.

The big round clock on the far wall says 11:30. Dotty Neal has been aware of the time throughout the morning, but she hasn't been counting minutes. She overcame that addiction many years ago. She watches her board, spins her pencil eraser, untwists the coiled wire of her headset. She thinks of what she will have to pick up at the supermarket on the way home tonight. On Thursdays everybody in the car pool takes a half hour to do the week's shopping. Dotty Neal has learned to think about her shopping and her home and her family, as she looks up numbers and talks to seventy-five strangers an hour. It is second nature to her now. She thinks about mending the fence around her house, and about buying something new for the inside.

Ten years ago her second husband bought a large wooden-frame building situated in a lower-middle-class section of Baltimore, near a major artery leading into the downtown area. Dotty Neal grew up in the city, and though she's traveled to parts far and wide on vacations she has spent most of her life here. Her second husband is another native. He works for the advertising department of a local newspaper. Their children, three girls and two boys, are all out of school, so now there is time for bowling on Tuesday nights and club meetings on other days. The Neals live comfortably in their old house, which they have furnished over the years with all manner of French Provincial and Italian Renaissance chairs and tables, so that now hardly a nook remains unfilled. The family eats and watches television back in the modern maple-paneled kitchen; the front rooms are for visitors and the cats, one white and one black.

(*Directory Assistance, may I help you? . . . That is a new listing, would you care to make a note of it? Two three five, seven eight three one . . . . You're welcome.*) Light, beep. (*Directory Assistance, may I help you? . . . I'm sorry, I show no listing for T. Fahrine, could you check the spelling? . . . F-A-H-R-I-N? Yes, the number is three five eight, one five two five . . . . You're welcome.*)

Dotty Neal glances at the clock again. Noon. She gets up, unplugs her headset and walks out of the room for lunch in the company cafeteria. Most of the other girls will leave on different shifts. They see Dotty Neal walk out but cannot talk to her because they are busy at their boards. She puts her headset in the slot over which her name is taped. It is hot in the hallway. The air-conditioning is one thing that never works right, even in the new telephone buildings. Here the supervisor was able to rent two portable air-conditioners, now situated in the bank of windows facing the parking lot out back. But today it feels to Dotty as if the machines aren't working, even with two auxiliary fans blowing.

—I can't deny some good things come with these changes. Today we have room, and we can relax and even talk, if there's a lull in calls. In the Light Street office it was real bad. The board where you were stationed was no wider than the telephone book. You would sit right by the next girl, so that her book would actually hit your book, she sat that close, and when you had to look down the corner, your head was in her book. This particular office, they had something like forty-four positions on one side and forty positions on the other side. The girls worked that close together all the time. We had a lot of trouble, but they're still using that office.

When I first started we had the oscillating fans that went around up above. They used them in the center of the floor, and would have a rope around them with strings flying out. They didn't even have fans at first, and then they finally got those. The women before me, they didn't know what fans were like. They used to have some exhaust fans up in the ceiling but it didn't do any good because the women were still crowded underneath all of them. I used to get cramps in my shoulders and back, but after all these years, I got accustomed to the sitting. Now we can stand while we work, if we want to.

I guess what I miss most is the working together as a team. In the old days, there weren't as many people and there was a closer group. Telephone operators just aren't like they used to be, especially with the bigger offices. We used to do so many things together.

This was before we had integrated offices. I think the Company started hiring blacks about thirteen years ago. Some of the older women resent them, although generally everyone works fine together. Of course, now it's more black than white, but to me this doesn't mean a thing. The only thing that I do resent, and one of the reasons that I gave up supervising, is that they hire blacks because they *have* to hire them, whether the girl knows what she's doing or not. I believe in integration and I think that everybody is entitled to a job, *if* they can do the job.

But to push it just because they say she's colored and she must be given a chance—that doesn't work. I say give them a chance. But to me information is a job where you're helping people that can't help themselves, and if you put someone in here who doesn't know as much as her customer knows, she can't help him at all. We've had more errors and complaints recently than in the last ten years put together. I believe in colored people getting an education but I don't believe in forcing a company to hire them if they're not capable of doing the job. We have never had the low quality of service that we have right now.

Not all the problem is hiring. People just don't have any interest in the job. A lot of young people nowadays—well, not only young people, older, too—think to themselves, I'm going to give just what they ask for—if it's not there, that's their tough luck. Even people working in other public service jobs are reacting irresponsibly. I just don't believe in striking public services. That's the reason I belong to my union and not to the CIO. There are other ways of settling things, especially when it's a public utility. Actually the Telephone Company has three or four different labor groups, but in Maryland we have this independent union which has just about as much influence as the others. We had one strike when I first went with the Company, but that was really just to be recognized.

I still think that we need unions, because without them the everyday person doesn't have a chance. The boss can bring his favorites in and they get all the good jobs. I just passed a test for a new position, but I didn't get it because they decided that the Telephone Company's not making enough money and the new boss wants to cut down on expenses. So I took up a grievance. All of our bigger bosses have just gotten a promotion. They had enought money to pay *them*. That's our argument. The union representative said, "After all, you have a good fight, because you were promised the job, they weren't just talking about it. You took a test and you passed and you were told that you had it." So right now I'm waiting to hear.

One of the reasons I applied for something new, even though I like information, is because I understand it's busy all the time. I still like to keep active, especially on the job. I always wanted to be a physical education teacher, but I just never did. I met a boy and got married and I regretted it afterward. I was foolish.

At two minutes before one o'clock Dotty Neal returns from lunch. She picks up her headset and goes directly to her station. Thirty seconds later she catches the light buzzer, a split second after it sounds, her arms and fingers and mind coordinated by reflex. (*Directory Assistance, may I help you? . . . There are a number of different "A. Freemans" listed. Could it be F-r-e-e-d-m-a-n? . . . What about F-R-I-E-D-M-A-N? . . . Two N's? Yes, there is an Aaron Friedmann on Redwood Street. The number in your directory is seven two seven, three five one six . . . . You're welcome.*)

All directory assistance operators are trained to pick up names with alternative spellings. The older women know them by rote. They also know the numbers for airlines, hotels, train stations, utilities. During April, when five hundred callers a day ask for "the income tax bureau" or "the tax people." Dotty Neal glances at a card taped onto the right wall of her station. All of the stations have the same white card taped onto the same wall. In other months, the operators know to look under "U.S. Government-Treasury Department-Director of Internal Revenue." There are a few other clues for quick searches, but most of the short cuts are learned by experience. Dotty knows that is why it sometimes takes a long while to get information. By the time the younger girls master the technique, they're ready to quit.

Out of the corner of her eye Dotty Neal catches a figure standing at the station to her left. Mrs. McGuiness, a supervisor, is monitoring calls at random. She marks things like voice tone, courtesy, efficiency, length of conversation. The Company's policy is for "a minimum of fanfare." There's little glamour to being an operator. Dotty Neal can tell you that. She has been at it a long time now and she can count on the fingers of one hand the number of calls that have been out of the ordinary. There aren't many emergency calls. Operators used to be able to make emergency connections through a free line, but that system was abandoned when the Company found that a lot of the free calls were not emergencies at all.

As with the other monotonies of her life, she's used to handling simple figures all day long—adding them, subtracting, counting, averaging. But most of all there is the reading and repeating of numbers. Somewhere, deep down, the paralyzed yearning for change refuses to die. At the new position that Dotty Neal has been fighting for, she would work directly with installers on the outside, and she would be busy all the time, doing different things with different responsibilities. Under her dominion would be one full exchange, like Lexington (five three nine). She would handle all the connects and disconnects that are fed into that office, and would talk only with installers who phone to ask whether any cables are available in the area for them to put in new equipment. It sounds to her as if it would be interesting.

At three o'clock the changing of the guard signals the hour, and Mrs. McGuiness begins to check in new girls. The operators can almost tell the time by the amount of chatter around them. The voice level rises and falls with the hour and day. On Monday morning the noise reaches its most deafening peak. Thursday is a slow day.

—Noise doesn't bother me because I'm so used to it. That makes everything easier. The house where I live is on a corner near a main highway, and across from a hospital. There are always cars and big trucks rushing by, and of course the ambulances for the hospital. The commotion doesn't bother me.

Sometimes the fumes get to me a little, especially from the big trucks, but we really don't have a bad problem in our neighborhood. Still, I don't remember the air itself ever being as polluted as it is, and the way those smokes stacks around the corner belch that black stuff is pretty terrible. But working in the office with the air-conditioners and everything, you don't take notice. You're away from it all day. That it, when the air-conditioner works.

Sometimes visitors to the office here remark about the noise, but it's my job. I think noise is part of living. It gets bad once in a while, but I accept these things. Sometimes it bothers me, like when they start cutting down trees to make roads, but that's progress. They have to have the roads for the cars. Lots of those things are out of our control, so much is changing. And we can't stop change.

Some things do strike me as really unfair. Like if you have a good lawyer you can practically get off with murder. Justice isn't what it used to be. The middle-class person, he pays all his taxes and he can't get away with things like the rich man. Our telephone company is a perfect example. They say we have to raise our prices because look at all these new buildings that we are putting up, and this is costing us money. But what they don't say, and most people don't stop to think of it, is that they can claim a lot of this on their income tax. So it's really not all coming out of them, but they try to give us this impression.

One time I claimed something on my income tax that wasn't allowed, and they called me in, and started checking all my deductions. Now I give a lot to charity. But that man tried to make a liar out of me, like I was claiming too much. I know there are people that do it, but I'm somebody that doesn't make a pittance compared to what some of these rich people make and the loopholes that they get away with, and he was inferring that I was lying and cheating. I told him, "Mister, you're looking for the wrong person." I know the government needs the money, but I still think there should be some way that if the rich can have these loopholes then the poorer people or middle-class people should have them, too. I think we're being taken advantage of. I wouldn't say forgotten, but taken advantage of.

I get the feeling that people are more unhappy or at least more irritable today. The number of complaints and difficult callers has really gone up, especially over the last year. The Company encourages you to try to handle hard calls nicely. If you can't—if like for instance you tell them something twice, or maybe you don't have the information and can't help them and they still insist—you say, "One moment, maybe the service assistant can help you." I always try to push it over, instead of getting irritated. It used to bother me when I would go out of my way for a customer and he wouldn't even say thank you.

But if you let things get to you—and sometimes they really can—you might say something you're not supposed to.

I remember one time, when I had just finished taking a pay count and had answered about ten routine calls. It had been a normal day. Then this man called and started ranting about the Communist Party and spies taking over all the mass communications. I tried to calm him down, but I finally had to turn him over to the service assistant. He wanted me to bring guns to work for all the non-Communists to defend themselves. Normally the only breaks in regular routine are the unlisted and disconnected numbers, or when you just can't find a listing at all.

On Saturday nights there are a lot of calls for the police, and occasionally we get obscene phone calls. Like when we had a man who kept calling in and giving the younger girls filthy language. The Company assigned some of the older married operators to talk to him and try to hold him on the line while he was being traced. Well, it took two weeks but we finally caught him.

I must answer about seventy-five calls per hour, which is above the office average. When I don't have trouble, I'm pretty fast. Sometimes I take the pay count and get away from the board, but like most of the girls, I usually just stay at the board.

Dotty Neal turns back into her station and tries to get comfortable. Before she leaves, she'll help with the five o' clock rush of calls. About thirty women fill the room, standing, sitting at their stations, calling out numbers. (*Directory assistance, may I help you? . . . The number is listed in your directory as seven six four, three three eight one . . . . You're welcome.*)

Now and then a call is transferred to a service operator. Names and faces come and go, but the scene itself doesn't change—the women wired to their three-sided cells, plugged into their blinking boards, stimulated to reflex action by buzzers, scrambling through layers of telephone pages, and smiling into their headset at faceless, nameless number-seekers. That doesn't change.

—Nearly everything is routine, either I know it or I don't. I like information. I feel like you should want to help somebody. If there is someone there, you should be able to help them.

Most of our girls, they're young and colored, and they don't especially like information. But at least it's a job. Welfare's one thing that bothers me. If you really need help, then you need it, but they could give a lot of people jobs, to make them feel like they're earning the money. The Telephone Company does it, and there could be other jobs, like cleaning streets. Remember when we used to have street cleaners? We don't have them now, and our streets are filthy dirty. If these people who are on welfare and who can't do a hard day's work could just be put out to push a broom in a couple of places, it would clean our streets up. You would feel like you weren't just giving people money, and they wouldn't feel like they were taking advantage of you. To me, we aren't helping people like that by just giving them money, and it just burns me up.

Disconnecting her headset, Dotty Neal straightens her station and proceeds to take her tenth pay count for the day. She adds the numbers carefully, sometimes counting on her fingers, rechecking and marking the numbers at the top of the page.

Her mind wanders back home again, and the dull glass-paneled switchboard room becomes a houseful of antiques, some of them genuine. She asks herself whether she remembered to feed the cats before she left this morning, and thinks about even smaller things, like tucking in the draperies behind the big exhaust fans in the windows on either side of the dining room. Browns, grays, greens. Lace on the table. Out one window, across the road, is a Catholic high school and just beyond it a hospital. There is the sound of an ambulance siren, but this one is going to the Johns Hopkins Hospital up the street from the Telephone Company building, and it brings Dotty Neal back to the office.

—After all the pay counts I've made, I should be a lot faster at this, but I still make mistakes. I like to do it, because it gives me a break from the board—used to be women could only do information, then secretary work. Now, we even have some male operators. Not many, but a few. I guess we'd have more if they wanted the pay. All operators get $78 a week to start, $109 tops. That's information or long distance. Really throws me to see a man doing this job. The customers always comment on hearing a man's voice.

Of course nowadays women can do men's work, too, and we're even in management. Before, it was just something that women never did—we just had to teach these men that we could do it. And eventually they're going to learn. We have our first girl wireman—what do they call them down there?—frame hops. This girl wanted this particular job and they said no, it was a man's job. She went to the union about it and she got it. It's the wiring part that men always do, but she was capable—she had had an engineering course—and they hired her.

Dotty puts down her pay count and goes back to her board for five more minutes. It has been ninety years since the first woman plugged in for the Bell System. In the early days there were relatively few long-distance phone calls and a small number of full-time operators. They all wore long dark skirts and white blouses, sat in high chairs to reach the switchboards above them, and carried heavy headsets. The walls in many offices were painted tan, the floors were dark-brown linoleum. Over the years, according to the Company, there have been "at least as many changes in the operator's job as there have been in women's fashions. Her job and its rewards have kept pace with the dramatic changes in telephone equipment." She works "in a bright, cheerful room . . . at her fingertips a few cords and key . . . a sort of push-button dial . . . relatively little reaching."

Dotty gets up for the last time today. She straightens her station, takes off her headset, and goes to tuck it into a pigeonhole marked *D. Neal*. Then she leaves. The other girls still on the boards gaze good-bye. On the ground floor, Alfred Baker nods. Nine hours earlier he had been the first to check Dotty Neal in, at eight A.M. That was one hour after she used to leave, twenty-three years ago, when she worked the night shift. Eight o'clock is an important time at the information office. Pay counts, addenda, the morning rush. But all the hours, days, and weeks seem to blend together. Twenty-three years. Dotty Neal sometimes finds them hard to add up.

—Now we have room, we can talk when there's a lull

in the calls, and we can even stand or sit while we're working. We used to have to wear gloves, and we had to have on a hat and stockings when we came in. Then you had to be a lady, everything was just so. Now we can wear anything. Today it's all speed and organization, just look up what the customer asks and tell him a number.

I still like information. It's a job, you have to look at it that way. The noise, the chatter, none of that really bothers me. I just got used to it.

AFTERWORD

by Ralph Nader

*And to love life through labor is
to be intimate with life's inmost secret.*
                              —Kahlil Gibran

The quest for meaning in work—as distinguished from the quest *for* work—is one of history's least charted courses. Man's struggle to make a living has always overshadowed the interaction of humans with their work and what it does or means for them.

In all societies, different social status has always been attached to different kinds of work. In our country, the principal division has been between blue-collar and white-collar work, with the latter gaining ascendancy earlier in the century when the trend to a service economy became clear. The parallel denigration of blue-collar, manual labor has taken numerous forms which combine to produce a mixture of resignation, boredom, irritation, desperation, and a sense of depreciated self-worth on the part of many manual workers.

It is dismaying how the major institutions which have

an impact on blue-collar labor persist in ignoring so many of the issues relating to the worth of the job beyond wages and fringe benefits. Government concerns itself with unemployment rates and aggregate wage rates and labor-management strife. Corporations stress productivity increases and favor highly centralized union bureaucracies. Union leaders emphasize bread and butter gains at the bargaining table. Who concentrates on the relation of the worker to the job and how outside influences—such as inflation, taxes, traffic congestion, the breakdown of community organization, and local citizen expression—affect attitudes and efficiencies on the job? Or how the job affects what workers can do about these and other matters off the job?

Even though there are as yet no enduring answers, these questions have at least been asked with increasing insistency during the past two years. The answers are more likely to be forthcoming when the important issues are identified and made concrete with the facts and feelings of workers as major touchstones. Several of these issues will illustrate the need for a new evaluation of the meaning of work as a human experience rather than a clocked means to simply earn the dollars for afterwork ends.

1.   The sense of worth perceived by most blue-collar workers on the job is minimal. Historians explain this as principally a reflection of the shift from craft to assembly line. The laborer often works on but a fraction of the product over and over again with a mind-numbing drudgery. Pride in workmanship disappears. Moreover, blue-collar work is considered "dirty work" compared to office work. Such is the popular attitude.

How estranged this view is from the relative values of blue-collar work to society! Economists have long shown that production work is a condition precedent to most service work. In recent years the country has had to learn the importance of blue-collar work the hard way, when strikes virtually paralyzed normal living or threatened to do so if the stoppage were allowed to continue very long. It is ironic that workers were reported to have gained a sense of pride when they saw the effect their absence had on a society that deprecatingly had taken them for granted.

Even creativity outside the line of duty receives little recognition. Corporate employers rarely publicize beyond their plant's confines the significant productivity and efficiency gains which frequently result from employee suggestions. Yet these same companies urge and pay for such suggestions.

There are many other signs of a society going out of its way to ignore the blue-collar laborer. The motion picture and television industries operate as if the manual worker didn't exist except as a prop for advertisements or for the well-to-do, or as an intruder on the public scene when he strikes. Although as early post-World War II European films taught Hollywood and its extravaganzas that the lives of ordinary people make subjects of great dramatic interest, blue-collar workers are rarely treated in modern fiction. This is no mere neglect of an indulgence in the activities of over thirty million workers. It is an absence of communication between them and other citizens about their hopes, agonies, fulfillments, and sense of pride or indifference in doing the job that has to be done. In short, being off-stage deprives a group of recognition, dialogue, and a sense of identity.

Blue-collar work need not be romanticized to free it of any stigma or stereotype. As portions of the portraits in this book indicate, even the most routine jobs involve a wide scale of competence with which they can be accomplished to meet valued human needs. Anyone who questions how important those needs are should consider how important the crisis would be if these needs were not met.

2. There are very few outlets for the development of on-the-job citizenship. Every blue-collar job involves an industry or trade whose impact on the public can be improved. Workers know an enormous amount about abuses which they encounter, endorse, observe, or try to avoid every day. Moreover, they often know about them far earlier than their ultimate disclosure—or emergence as public scandals or disasters.

For example, workers know that there is virtually no difference between different brands of gasolines of the same octane level. They know generally which factories dump what pollutants into waterways and that there is more pollution under cover of darkness. They know how car manufacturers fudge inspection on the line. They know how government inspectors tip off coal mines of their impending arrival or how their coworkers smoke in prohibited areas. They know which meat and poultry inspectors are on the take or which fail to exercise their duties. They know how taxi meters and automobile odometers are rigged by design or manipulated to cheat the rider or driver. They know of violations of work safety laws. Indeed, many of the main consumer and environmental problems are rooted in secrets known to hundreds if not thousands of workers. The value of such information can be seen by occasional acts of courage when an assembly line worker discloses evidence of deffectively designed products.

Beginning in 1966 Edward Gregory, a quality control worker in GM's Fisher Body plant in St. Louis, reported to the federal government a welding defect affecting over two million Chevrolets which were subsequently recalled in 1969 after exhaust fume leakage claimed a number of lives. If mechanisms can be developed to convey such information about abuses to people and groups who can do something about them, workers can begin to have an opportunity to exercise broader allegiances to principles of fair play and corporate responsibility. Such mechanisms would permit the humblest worker to relate his sense of values to the deeper significance of what is being produced for thousands or millions of citizens as well as to substitute participation for complicity. Whistle-blowing, or the ethic of employees appealing to higher authorities than a negligent, criminal, or stagnant management permits, would lead to internal organizational reforms that would provide greater participation and respect for employees in their work. It should be clear by now that meaningful work for many laborers includes the right and opportunity to apply their sense of justice to their surroundings and the products or services being produced. The feeling of being an automaton is partly due to being denied a normative role on the job. Other countries have experimented with worker councils with some managerial responsibilities at the plant level, and their experiences deserve study.

3. A great deal of manual or blue-collar labor is fatiguing, grimy, hazardous, and boring. Exposure to unsafe working conditions and toxic gases, chemicals, and dust in mines and factories produces thousands of fatali-

ties and millions of injuries and diseases every year. To its credit, the *Wall St. Journal* devoted two lead articles in July, 1971, to describing selected occupations, such as a foundry worker, that wear the body and dull the mind. Given overtime or moonlighting, or even without those additional laboring hours, a worker comes home too tired to think about ways to make a contribution to society in a nonwork capacity. In a twist of the Marxist dictum, work becomes the opiate of the people, draining them of energy to contemplate their citizenship roles in their hours away from the job. Notice how some of the workers described in this book spend their evenings—in utter exhaustion with eyes heavy-lidded before a TV set. This pointedly suggests the desirability of further concentrating the workweek along the lines of the recently touted four-day forty-hour week.

A new study by two British occupational psychologists reported the case of a military officer who left his career in his forties to become a milkman at much lower earnings. However, his workday ends about 2:00 P.M., which allows him to play golf and engage intensively in village political and administrative activities. New life styles in the after-work hours can be developed through participation in community college activities and other educational opportunities which would increase one's options of employment or chances for promotion. Such personal development would also increase the likelihood of postretirement careers in community and citizenship work which would replace the empty, meaningless existence of so many retired people.

4. Neither unions nor government is paying sufficient attention to erosions of wage and fringe benefit gains by inequitable taxes, business frauds, monopolistic practices, crime, pollution, political corruption, or governmental incompetence. What is obtained through employment is seriously depleted outside of employment by deteriorating conditions which have few institutional watchdogs or safeguards. The compelling challenge is how to focus new remedies on the interrelatedness of blue-collar workers with forces beyond their control and often beyond their awareness—forces that reduce the value of their income, impair their health, safety, inflict psychic stresses on them and their families, and generally reduce the quality of their lives, even as their pay checks increase.

The emergence of black community organizations in the inner cities reflects the dissolution of minimally responsive government. Similarly, the growth of the white urban ethnic movement with its dualism of defense and reform is symptomatic of the obsolescence of the old organizations in and out of government. Some politicians, sensing the potential of rising popular ferment, begin to develop rhetoric that turns the mass of the people against the downtrodden. Other more cautious politicians then begin to drift toward evasion of the issues for fear of alienating a bewildered mass middle class victimized by many of the same forces which bear down so heavily on blacks, Chicanos, and Indians.

Barbara Mikulski of the Southeast Community Organization in Baltimore described the feelings of the urban ethnic portions of the middle class this way:

The ethnic American is overtaxed and underserved at every level of government. He does not have fancy lawyers or expensive lobbyists getting him tax breaks on his income. Being a home owner, he shoulders the rising property taxes—the major revenue source for the municipalities in which he lives. Yet he enjoys very little from these unfair and burdensome levies.

Because of restrictive eligibility requirements linked either to income or "target areas," he gets no help from Federal programs. If he wants to buy in "the old neighborhood," he cannot get an F.H.A. loan. One major illness in his family will wipe him out. When he needs a nursing home for an elderly parent, he finds that there are none that he can afford, nor is he eligible for any financial assistance.

His children tend to go to parochial schools which receive little in the way of government aid and for which he carries an extra burden. There is a general decline of community services for his neighborhood, e.g., zoning, libraries, recreation programs, sanitation, etc.

His income of $5,000 to $10,000 per year makes him "near poor." He is the victim of both inflation and anti-inflationary measures. He is the guy that is hurt by layoffs and by tight money that chokes him with high interest rates for installment buying and home improvements.

Manufacturers, with their price fixing, shoddy merchandise and exorbitant repair bills, are gouging him to death. When he complains about costs, he is told that it is the "high cost of labor" that is to blame. Yet he knows he is the "labor" and that in terms of real dollars he is going backward.

The ethnic American also feels unappreciated for the contribution he makes to society. He resents the way the working class is looked down upon. In many instances he is treated like the machine he operates or the pencil he pushes. He is tired of being treated like an object of production. The public and private institutions have made him frustrated by their lack of response to his needs. At present he feels powerless in his daily dealings with and efforts to change them.

Unfortunately, because of old prejudices and new fears, anger is generated against other minority groups rather than those who have power. What is needed is an alliance of white and black, white collar, blue collar and no collar based on mutual need, interdependence and respect, an alliance to develop the strategy for new kind of community organization and political participation.

Perhaps the most remarkable context of these expressed grievances is that during the 'sixties there was a booming overall economy which in 1970 amounted to a trillion dollars of gross national product. The contrast between this massive aggregate economic growth and serious problems of poverty, health, housing, pollution, transportation, urban rot and conflict seems to be endemically ignored. The country needs a new political economy giving quality to growth and redirecting resources toward the various problems. The growth ethic is wearing very thin in light of the realities: an increasingly unequal distribution of wealth, and a tragic mismatching of public and private wealth with needs that are acknowledged daily in our newspaper headlines. According to recent statistics covering the post World War II period, the redistribution of income through taxes and the welfare state has simply not occurred. Yet the advertisements of aggregate growth and unreal wage gains inspire persistent myths that automatic progress has occurred as a result. Even buying into their future incomes through the credit economy is interpreted as present gains for workers.

The portraits in the preceding pages reveal a pathetic display of the treadmill effect. These hard working people are achieving little beyond providing the basic necessities for their families. To do this, they have forfeited the opportunity to develop and contribute as individuals and citizens. But a modern industrial economy is supposed to give workers a greater chance to accomplish just that. The earth cynicism which some of these workers reveal toward any change for the better indicates the absence of hopes for any alternatives. No system, no ideology, no utopia lights their sense of optimism. Their plea, such as it is, focuses on simple standards of honesty, neighborliness and decency—with hardly any specific ideas of their role in helping to apply such principles beyond themselves.

Here is the crux of the working person's problem. Most cannot or do not wish to recognize that their wholesale delegation of citizenship duties to elected and appointed officials is failing them badly. At a time when citizenship must receive a new definition and commitment of time and energy—as an obligation to be discharged continually on and off the job, individually and collectively—there is little thinking about replacing past abdications with new resolves. The role of the victim has too often been to bewail his victimization, to the exclusion of doing something about it. This attitude generates despair, discouragement and disgust. What is needed is indeed rigorous: a citizenship that engages public problems well beyond sporadic elections and develops into a relevant use of human talents. It must become an important portion of what constitutes the human experience, an obligation rather than a free lance hobby for a few determined mavericks.

In concrete terms, the required dedication means an assertion of citizens over larger social organizations. It means organizing to decide, propose and guide the near and far institutions—corporations, governments, and unions—by the people they are supposed to serve. This kind of initiatory democracy is not an end to itself, but rather a means of placing just values on factual situations through duly constituted channels of power or authority. It is a way of generating a popular demand for skills, resources and laws to be responsive to people's needs. It is also a way of encouraging independence of activity with accountability for performance. To view the plight of the blue-collar worker in anything less than this broader environment is to permit frustrated emotion to be exploited by calculating power brokers.

A first step toward putting the "demos" back into democracy is accepting the need for professional full-time citizen advocates to represent the interests of the unrepresented. Such advocates—lawyers, economists, scientists, engineers, physicians, and others of various talents—should work outside institutionalized frameworks and outside bureaucracies. To imprint the interests of the mass of citizens on institutions that are not working. One of the greatest ideas of the latter twentieth century will be the one that can organize the funding of such advocates from small contributions by large numbers of the people especially affected by the conditions to be changed, and make these supporters want to participate and contribute their own involvement. Once such movements get underway the workers would have recovered their nerve. And with the recovery of nerve will come the virtues and actions that can change the world for the better.